CW01424517

FRAUDULENT CLAIMS

For my family

FRAUDULENT CLAIMS:

DECEIT, INSURANCE AND PRACTICE

Matthew Chapman,
Barrister

xpl

© Matthew Chapman 2007

Published by

xpl publishing
99 Hatfield Road
St Albans AL1 4JL
UK

www.xplpublishing.com

ISBN 978 1 85811 377 7

All rights reserved. No part of this publication may be reproduced, stored in a retrieval system, or transmitted, in any form or by any means, electronic, mechanical, photocopying, recording or otherwise, without the prior permission of the publisher.

Printed and typeset in the UK

CONTENTS

PREFACE

In December 2005 I gave a lecture which formed part of a one day practitioner conference on Dishonest Insurance Claims. At that time fraudulent claims were preoccupying the courts in my core area of practice: personal injury work. Indeed, in one of the leading Court of Appeal authorities the Vice-President had commented, with a note of resignation, that the case management of claims involving an allegation of fraud had, like credit hire agreements, the service of claim forms and withdrawal of admissions before it, spawned a large amount of satellite litigation. In spite of the fact that fraud seemed to be a big topic there were, to my surprise, no textbooks that dealt exclusively with fraud and dishonesty of the sort that the common law practitioner might regularly encounter. The idea for this book was born.

This work is a little longer than I originally envisaged. It has been necessary to add some extra topics during its writing and my own interest in the subject matter has resulted in a fuller treatment than I had planned. It is hoped, however, that this book, while hardly pocket-sized, has not become so bulky that it ceases to be portable and that it will be reasonably easy to navigate when the need arises.

A Preface is the place to acknowledge the assistance that I received while it was being written. I am grateful to Andrew Griffin and XPL Publishing for giving me the opportunity to commit these thoughts to paper. I should also like to thank my clerks for assisting me with finding the time to write and to Alan Saggerson and my other colleagues in the personal injury team at 1 Chancery Lane who, perhaps without realising it, have influenced what follows. Nicholas Mercer deserves particular thanks for volunteering to cast an editorial eye over the first half of the book. I am indebted to him for pointing out a number of errors of citation and other solecisms and hope that he will forgive me for those that remain. It probably goes without saying that all errors in the material which follows are mine alone. Finally, I would like to thank my parents and family for their patience and love. This book is dedicated to them and to the memory of my grandparents. The law is stated to the best of my knowledge as at 16 February 2007.

Matthew Chapman
1 Chancery Lane
London
WC2A 1LF

INTRODUCTION

" *Welcome, thou kind deceiver!*
Thou best of thieves; who, with an easy key,
Dost open life, and, unperceived by us,
Even steal us from ourselves. "

(John Dryden, *Amphitryon*)

"*Fraud is infinite in variety; sometimes it is audacious and*
unblushing; sometimes it pays a sort of homage to virtue, and then it
is modest and retiring; it would be honesty itself if it could only
afford it. But fraud is fraud all the same; and it is the fraud, not the
manner of it, which calls for the interposition of the court."

Lord Macnaghten, *Reddaway* v *Banham* [1896] AC 199, 212
(HL(E)).

Fraudulent claims

Fraud is big business. More specifically, insurance fraud is big business. In July 2005 the Association of British Insurers ("ABI") estimated that commercial insurance claims fraud cost the UK economy £550 million every year. Fraud is also a growth industry. An annual study into the incidence of fraud suggests that commercial fraud more than doubled in the period between 2000 and 2005.[1] A recent ABI publication which presented statistical information polled by a market research organisation contained the following conclusions:

> The majority of fraudulent claims arise from the exaggeration of genuine incidents ...Other ways of committing fraud include inventing a claim or providing false information on an application for insurance. Six per cent of companies are aware of instances of withholding or providing false information on an application. However, this figure rises to 40% of the largest companies. The most costly frauds are those which are either entirely bogus or staged. Invented or staged claims are relatively low in volume, but

---

[1] KPMG Annual Fraud Barometer. This measures fraud cases in the Crown Court where the financial value of the fraud exceeds £100,000.

higher in cost, because the costs of the claims are generally higher. Whatever the type of fraud, the cost ultimately falls on businesses in the form of higher premiums. The better news is that only 8% of businesses believe exaggerating an insurance claim is acceptable. However, people working in smaller firms are five times as likely to see insurance fraud as acceptable. Fifteen per cent of sole traders feel it is acceptable to exaggerate a property insurance claim, compared with 3% for firms employing more than 500 people ... in the last two years: * Nine per cent of businesses received a false personal injury claim from a member of the public; * Two per cent had a false compensation claim made by an employee ... And employees are too often ready to make a fraudulent claim. Nearly a quarter (22%) of employees thought it would be easy to exaggerate a genuine illness suffered in the workplace to gain compensation from the employer. A further 17% thought it would be easy to invent a similar claim against their employer. Other reasons for fraud by employees included: * a wish to 'cover up' negligence in order to avoid punishment; * to make money; * or to get back at their employer because of a previously bad relationship.[2]

There has been significant legislative activity in the criminal regulation of fraud in recent years. The Fraud Act 2006 (which came into force on 15 January 2007) has built on work by the Law Commission in replacing the deception offences contained in the Theft Acts with a new, broadly defined statutory offence of fraud. The Proceeds of Crime Act 2002 regulates and controls, in a robust (some might say draconian) way, the profits of fraud. However, in the civil arena, fraud is dealt with by a complex web of (largely) common law rules. This book attempts to identify what some of these are.

Where to start?

The principal title of this book is *Fraudulent Claims.* Its writing was inspired by a conference at which I spoke in December 2005 on the theme of Dishonest Insurance Claims. There were speakers on topics ranging from insurance fraud and malingering personal injury claimants to the rules for pleading fraud to fraudulent claims for spoilt holidays. At first sight the conference consisted of lectures on a number of disparate subjects which appeared to have only the loosest connection to each other. However, what linked the lectures was a sense that the various topics were related; that there was, within the causes of action, defences and procedural rules discussed, a broad connection located in the presence of dishonesty or what is referred to

---

[2] ABI, *UK Commercial Insurance Fraud Study 2005. A summary of a research report prepared by MORI for the Commercial Insurance Fraud Steering Group* (2005).

in one of the cases discussed below as "*iniquity*".[3] This book might as easily have been entitled, *Dishonest Claims* or some variant of the same, but what connects the subjects which it discusses is deceit in the sense that, by words or conduct, a person has advanced a proposition knowing that it is false or, at least, being reckless as to whether it is true or false. It is in this sense that the wrongdoer has been referred to as having "*a wicked mind*".[4] Deceit of this kind lies at the heart of the cause of action which bears the same name.

A natural starting point for this book seemed, therefore, to be the tort of deceit. *Bullen, Leake & Jacob* properly point out that an action in fraud will usually include one or more of a number of distinct causes of action and they go on to list the torts of deceit, conspiracy (to defraud), unlawful interference/inducing breach of contract, bribery, actions for money had and received and knowing receipt and dishonest assistance in the context of constructive trusts.[5] A longer and more comprehensive work on civil fraud than this would deal separately with each of these causes of action. However, this book is written from a common law perspective. It concentrates on topics which, it is hoped, might be of relevance and practical use to the common lawyer and there is a bias towards personal injury practice. A discussion of the tort of deceit presented an opening for a consideration of topics like disclosure in the context of insurance and of fraudulent insurance claims. Equally, it is difficult to know how to raise fraud as a defence unless there is an understanding of how it works as a cause of action. Limiting my discussion to one tort also prevented me from trying to turn this book into *The Key to all Mythologies*.

The protean quality of fraud

Having identified where to start, other problems presented themselves. Foremost among these was a definitional difficulty. Judges, lawyers and draftsmen can be careless in their use of terminology. The use of shorthand and legalese is hard to avoid and "fraud" is often used in a manner which can confuse the uninformed and offend the pedant. This word is frequently deployed in a context which has little to do with the tort of deceit in the *Derry* v *Peek*[6] sense. Some examples of this include:

---

[3] *Barclays Bank Plc* v *Eustice & Others* [1995] 4 All ER 511, 521g *per* Schiemann LJ (CA).
[4] *Le Lievre* v *Gould* [1893] 1 QB 491, 498 *per* Lord Esher MR (CA), "*A charge of fraud is such a terrible thing to bring against a man that it cannot be maintained in any Court unless it is shewn that he had a wicked mind. That is the effect of Derry v Peek.*"
[5] Lord Brennan QC and W Blair QC, *Bullen, Leake & Jacob's Precedents of Pleadings* (15th ed, 2004), para 48-01.
[6] (1889) 14 App Cas 337 (HL(E)).

- A personal injury case where the Defendant's contention that the Claimant was malingering was referred to, by the trial judge, as "*the defendant's case on fraud*".[7]

- An appeal from the decision of a district judge dismissing the Claimants' claims in a fast track road traffic accident case where it was alleged that the Claimants had sustained personal injury and where, on appeal, the Defendant was criticised by the Claimants for failing to plead "fraud" in the context of a contention that the Claimants had suffered no injury at all. It was held that the Defendant was not, by alleging "fraud", contending that the tort of deceit had been committed.[8]

- Cases where the appellate courts have considered the categories of fraud and/or general dishonesty that might, where disclosure is sought, defeat a claim of legal professional privilege – what seems to be required is general "*iniquity*" and it is not necessary for there to be a reasonable suspicion that the tort of deceit has been committed.[9]

These issues are, perhaps, most sharply focused when it comes to the pleading of statements of case. A great deal of time and costs have been expended in determining whether, where the Civil Procedure Rules and earlier procedural codes refer to fraud, a party is required to plead this in terms where the cause of action or defence relied on involves a specific allegation of general dishonesty, rather than the commission of the tort of deceit. In the personal injury field a partial answer to this question has now been given. The procedural guides for the divisions of the High Court provide some further assistance. However, it remains difficult to pin down a working definition of "fraud" which will have utility for all of the applications which are discussed in this book and which might be relevant to the pleading of a statement of case.[10]

---

[7] *Cooper* v *P & O Stena Line Limited* [1999] 1 Ll Rep 734, 743 *per* Miss Belinda Bucknall (QBD.

[8] *Lawrenson and Lawrenson* v *Lawrenson and Equity Red Star* (2005) June 30, Liverpool County Court *per* HHJ Stewart QC) (unreported).

[9] See, e.g. *Barclays Bank Plc* v *Eustice & Others* [1995] 4 All ER 511 (CA).

[10] Cf. the position in criminal law where, as indicated above, the Fraud Act 2006 introduces a new statutory offence of fraud.

Serious allegations require fair dealing

The reason why so much time and energy is spent arguing about whether fraud has been properly identified as a cause of action or defence, whether in a statement of case or otherwise, is because it is treated by the courts as one of the most serious allegations that can be levelled at a litigant:

> The principles [of procedural fairness] apply with particular force in personal injury litigation when it is to be contended that the claimant is a malingerer, or fabricating evidence, or wildly exaggerating symptoms or their effect. Sometimes claimants do lie, embellish or fantasise, but if that is to be the defendant's case fairness demands that the claimant should have a reasonable opportunity to deal with these allegations.[11]

Anxiety about the need for fairness when confronting a litigant with an allegation of dishonesty finds expression, as the discussion below will reveal, in rules and codes of professional conduct governing (among other matters):

- the pleading of statements of case;
- the instruction of expert witnesses and case management; and,
- the handling of witnesses in court.

The emphasis is upon giving reasonable notice of the alleged dishonesty to the litigant accused of it and affording him an opportunity to comment and respond. While this approach was evident prior to the coming into force of the Civil Procedure Rules the "cards on the table" ethos of the Rules has encouraged judges to be even more robust in requiring fair dealing when it comes to allegations of fraud or dishonesty.

The scope of this book

As I have indicated, this book commences with a discussion on the tort of deceit. It then deals with issues of disclosure and fraud in the context of insurance claims. The next chapter covers fraud as a defence to claims in tort and contract. The front section of the book, which deals with substantive civil law matters, concludes with a consideration of the burden and standard of proof where an allegation of fraud is made in a short chapter which deals with Evidence.

There is then consideration of some criminal law rules where statute has a large part to play: perjury and contempt of court (what might generally be

---

[11] *Ford* v *GKR Construction Limited* [2000] 1 WLR 1397, 1401A-B *per* Judge LJ (CA).

referred to as lying in court) and regulating the profits of fraud by means of the Proceeds of Crime Act 2002.

The book concludes with consideration of some rules of practice: the pleading of statements of case; case management; detecting and proving fraud and costs. The Appendix collects together some of the statutory material that is referred to in the text.

These topics are only broadly connected. As I have indicated, what links them is the presence of dishonesty in the *Derry* v *Peek*[12] sense: the advancement of a proposition knowing that it is false or, at least, a *"conscious indifference"* to the truth (as one writer has referred to it).[13] This book aims to be of assistance to the general practitioner by dealing with a series of specific subject areas that may be encountered in the course of mainstream (common law) practice. It is a miscellany of fraud, iniquity and dishonest conduct and the rules which seek to control and penalise the same.

---

[12] (1889) 14 App Cas 337 (HL(E)).
[13] John G Fleming, *The Law of Torts*, (9th ed, 1998), p 699.

TABLE OF CASES

TABLE OF STATUTES

Chapter 1

AN INTRODUCTION TO FRAUD: THE TORT OF DECEIT

1. GENESIS

1.001 The emergence of fraud or deceit[1] as an independent cause of action happened relatively recently: at around the time that the action on the case developed as a cause of action. A number of early cases are entertainingly collected in Baker & Milsom's *Sources of English Legal History*.[2] The predominant subject matter is unsound horses. In *Ferrers* v *John, Vicar of Dodford* (1307),[3] for example, the Court of King's Bench heard an action brought by John Ferrers against the Vicar of Dodford who had sold him a horse (under guarantee) which Ferrers wished to ride to assist the King's Scottish campaign. The vendor had, under oath, stated that the horse was *"sound in all its members and not maimed."* In fact, the horse's left shoulder was injured and, in the subsequent action on the case for trespass, the Claimant complained that the horse's injury had prevented him from joining the King in Scotland. The vicar denied all misconduct. Unfortunately, the report does not record the Court's decision.

1.002 In a later (1382) case, also involving the sale of a horse (this time alleged to be blind), the following formula was deployed by the Claimant,

> …whereas P had bargained to buy from D a horse, D knowing the horse to be blind, falsely and fraudulently sold it to P by warranting it sound in eye and limb. [4]

---

[1] In the modern cases and in most textbooks deceit and fraud are used interchangeably and I have done the same.
[2] J H Baker & S F C Milsom, *Sources of English Legal History: Private Law to 1750* (1986), Chapter 20.
[3] Select cases in the Court of King's Bench III, Selden Society Volume 18, p 179.
[4] *Aylesbury* v *Wattes* (1382) YB Mich 6 Ric II p 119, p l27.

It has been pointed out that the essence of deceit in this context lay in the allegation that the buyer had been *"persuaded to buy something which he would not have bought had he known the truth."* [5] There was comparatively little focus, during this period in the tort's development, upon the state of mind of the vendor. This approach might relate to the view expressed by Holdsworth that it was thought impossible to base civil liability upon an intention to deceive because, *"it was impossible to try the thought of a man."* [6]

1.003 These early actions on the case for deceit concerned false warranties in the context of what we would now term contracts. Indeed, some writers have described deceit as having, *"played a modest part in developing the incipient law of contract."* [7] During the early history of deceit as a cause of action, trespass, covenant and assumpsit were all being deployed in circumstances which we might now recognise as giving rise to contractual causes of action. However, by the late eighteenth century, the writ of assumpsit came to be used for actions for false warranty [8] which paved the way for the action for deceit to be detached from contract law.

1.004 Most writers regard the 1789 case *Pasley* v *Freeman* [9] as the founding source of the modern law of deceit. This case concerned an enquiry made by the Claimant of the Defendant as to the financial standing of a man with whom the Claimant had entered negotiations for the sale of 16 sacks of cochineal. The Defendant informed the Claimant that he could extend credit to the third party, notwithstanding the fact that the Defendant knew this man to be insolvent. There was no contract between the Claimant and Defendant. This was, however, regarded as irrelevant to the Claimant's action for deceit,

> ...if there be fraud or deceit, the action will lie, and that knowledge of the falsehood of the thing asserted is fraud and deceit. [10]

In other words, knowledge of the falsehood had come to be regarded as lying at the heart of the action (which was available even in circumstances where the Defendant had not himself obtained financial gain). In the later case of *Langridge* v *Levy* Parke B defined the tort of deceit as being dependent upon

---

[5] J H Baker, *An Introduction to English Legal History* (4th ed, 2002), p 331.
[6] Sir William Holdsworth, *A History of English Law* Volume V, p 417.
[7] John G Fleming, *The Law of Torts*, (9th ed, 1998), p 694.
[8] See, *Williamson v Allison* (1802) 2 East 446, 451: cited in H Carty, *An Analysis of the Economic Torts* (OUP).
[9] (1789) 3 TR 51 (KB).
[10] *Pasley v Freeman* (1789) 3 TR 51, *per* Buller J.

"a falsehood told with an intention that it should be acted upon by the party injured." [11]

1.005 The absorption of the action for breach of warranty into, first, assumpsit and, later, contract law, meant that from the late eighteenth/early nineteenth century deceit and false warranty were able to develop independently:

> The tort action for deceit requires proof of fraudulent intent, while breach of contractual warranty became independent of any intention to mislead or other fault. [12]

1.006 While deceit had played a part in the development of contract law and had also, as we have seen, ripened into an independent tortious cause of action, it also acted as a significant brake on the development of actions for misrepresentation that were not based on fraud. In *Derry* v *Peek*, [13] decided towards the end of the nineteenth century, the House of Lords made it clear that mere negligence (unaccompanied by any intention to deceive) was not a basis for liability in misrepresentation. This decision, apparently regarded at the time as wrong by *"all Lincoln's Inn"*, [14] continued to act as a roadblock to developments in the law of misrepresentation until the 1960s when, in quick succession, *Hedley Byrne & Co* v *Heller & Partners Limited* [15] was followed by the Misrepresentation Act 1967. [16]

2. THE MODERN TORT OF DECEIT:
Derry v Peek

1.007 The factual background concerned the development of a new tram system for Plymouth. An Act of Parliament authorised the Plymouth,

---

[11] (1837) 2 M & W 519.

[12] John G Fleming, *The Law of Torts*, (9th ed, 1998), p 695.

[13] (1889) 14 App Cas 337.

[14] As reported by Sir Frederick Pollock: M DeWolfe Howe (ed), *The Pollock-Holmes Letters* Vol I, p 215, "*Haldane asked me last week to a tobacco talk of Derry v Peek and the possibility of minimizing its consequences. The Lords are going to hold that it does not apply to the situation created by a positive fiduciary duty such as a solicitor's, in other words go as near as they dare to saying it was wrong, as all Lincoln's Inn thought at the time.*"

[15] [1964] AC 465 (HL).

[16] See, for an historical overview, C M Reed, "*Derry v Peek and Negligence*" (1987) 8 J Legal History 64 and M Lobban, "*Nineteenth Century Frauds in Company Formation: Derry v Peek in Context*" (1996) 112 LQR 287.

Devonport and District Tramways Company to construct tramways. The
legislation provided that the trams were to be drawn by horses unless the
special consent of the Board of Trade was obtained for trams to be moved by
steam or other mechanical means. The Directors of the Company issued a
prospectus which indicated that the Company had the absolute right to use
steam or mechanical power to drive the trams. Sir Henry Peek saw the
prospectus and, relying on the representation that the Company had the
absolute right to use steam or mechanically powered trams, bought shares in
the Company. The tramways were constructed, but the Board of Trade
refused, in the main, to permit the use of steam or mechanical power. The
Company was wound up and Sir Henry commenced proceedings against the
Directors seeking damages for fraudulent misrepresentation. The action was
dismissed at first instance on the basis of findings that, while the
representation in the prospectus was untrue, it was not made by the
Directors with "*intentional deceit*".[17] This decision was reversed by the
Court of Appeal on the basis that the Directors had no reasonable grounds
for their belief in the truth of the representation (however sincerely this belief
was, in fact, held).[18] The Directors appealed. The essence of the argument for
the Directors on appeal was that,

> However unbusinesslike a man may be he is not fraudulent if he acts
> honestly. The natural consequences of words or acts must be taken to have
> been intended, but not so as to impute fraud to honesty. No honest mistake,
> no mistake not prompted by a dishonest intention, is fraud.

1.008 There were five concurring speeches in the House of Lords. Lord
Herschell gave the leading speech. He commenced by distinguishing a claim
in equity for rescission of a contract on the basis of a material
misrepresentation from an action for deceit,

> Where rescission is claimed it is only necessary to prove that there was
> misrepresentation; then, however honestly it may have been made, however
> free from blame the person who made it, the contract, having been obtained
> by misrepresentation, cannot stand. In an action of deceit, on the contrary,
> it is not enough to establish misrepresentation alone; it is conceded on all
> hands that something more must be proved to cast liability upon the
> defendant ... [19]

---

[17] (1887) 37 Ch D 541.
[18] Sir James Hannen, one of the Court of Appeal Judges in this case, deployed the phrase "*legal fraud*", as distinct from "*actual fraud*", to convey the ingredients of the cause of action which he found proved. When this case reached the House of Lords Lord Bramwell was disparaging about the use of this formula.
[19] (1889) 14 App Cas 337, 359.

1.009 Lord Herschell made it very clear that the absence of reasonable grounds for belief in the truth of a representation was not sufficient to give rise to an action for deceit, "*... to support an action of deceit fraud must be proved, and ... nothing less than fraud will do.*"[20] He went on to conduct a full review of the authorities[21] starting with *Pasley* v *Freeman* before arriving at the formula for the action:

> I think the authorities establish the following propositions: First, in order to sustain an action of deceit, there must be proof of fraud, and nothing short of that will suffice. Secondly, fraud is proved when it is shewn that a false representation has been made (1) knowingly, or (2) without belief in its truth, or (3) recklessly, careless whether it be true or false. Although I have treated the second and third as distinct cases, I think the third is but an instance of the second, for one who makes a statement under such circumstances can have no real belief in the truth of what he states. To prevent a false statement being fraudulent, there must, I think, always be an honest belief in its truth. And this probably covers the whole ground, for one who knowingly alleges that which is false, has obviously no such honest belief. Thirdly, if fraud be proved, the motive of the person guilty of it is immaterial. It matters not that there was no intention to cheat or injure the person to whom the statement was made.[22]

1.010 At first sight Lord Herschell's direction that fraud could be found where the representor was reckless or careless as to the truth of the representation in issue might be thought close to the Court of Appeal's conclusion that an action of deceit could be maintained where the representor lacked reasonable grounds for belief in the truth of his representation. However, this would elide the difference between that which evidences the fraud and that which constitutes the fraud. Lord Herschell, commenting in an earlier passage of his speech on a decision by the House of Lords in a Scottish case,[23] explained the difference in the following terms,

> A consideration of the grounds of belief is no doubt an important aid in ascertaining whether the belief was really entertained. A man's mere assertion that he believed the statement he made to be true is not accepted as conclusive proof that he did so. There may be such an absence of reasonable ground for his belief as, in spite of this assertion, to carry conviction to the mind that he had not really the belief which he alleges. If the learned Lord ... intended to go further ... and to say that though the belief was really

---

[20] At p 367.

[21] Dismissing, along the way, a number of earlier authorities in which notions of "*equitable fraud*" were referred to.

[22] (1889) 14 App Cas 337, 374.

[23] *Western Bank of Scotland* v *Addie* (1867) Law Rep 1 HL Sc 145. The speech on which Lord Herschell was commenting was that of Lord Chelmsford.

entertained, yet if there were no reasonable grounds for it, the person making the statement was guilty of fraud in the same way as if he had known what he stated to be false, I say, with all respect, that the previous authorities afford no warrant for the view that an action of deceit would lie under such circumstances [24]

1.011 In other words, a *"wilful"* fraud was needed, either in the sense that the statement was known by the representor to be untrue or because he was so reckless or careless as to the truth of what he was saying that he could not have entertained any honest belief in the truth of the same (this is described by Professor Fleming as *conscious* indifference to the truth, as distinct from mere negligence).[25] Conversely, if it were found as a fact that – however unreasonable the belief in the truth of the statement – the representor had honestly believed in the veracity of what he had represented then an action for deceit became unsustainable. The Court of Appeal had, therefore, fallen into error in concluding that a false statement, made through carelessness and without reasonable grounds for believing it to be true, amounted to a fraudulent misrepresentation in circumstances where, as a matter of fact, the representors had an honest belief in the truth of what they had represented.

3. REPRESENTATION

1.012 The requirement that there be a representation is something that an action for fraud shares with other actions for misrepresentation. There is, therefore, a good deal of overlap between this ingredient of the cause of action and what is similarly required for negligent misrepresentation and actions brought under the 1967 Act. There are also some important differences, particularly with respect to the categories of statement which will give rise to the tort. These are discussed below.

1.013 The tort of deceit shares with other causes of action based on misrepresentation, the requirement that there be a misrepresentation of present fact or law. The position was ably summarised in the speech of Viscount Maugham in *Bradford Third Equitable Benefit Building Society* v *Borders*:[26]

---

[24] (1889) 14 App Cas 337, 369.
[25] John G Fleming, *The Law of Torts*, (9th ed, 1998), p 699.
[26] [1941] 2 All ER 205 (HL).

> First, there must be a representation of fact made by words, or, it may be, by conduct. The phrase will include a case where the defendant has manifestly approved and adopted a representation made by some third person. On the other hand, mere silence, however morally wrong, will not support an action of deceit ... [27]

1.014 Accordingly, in order to constitute a representation sufficient to give rise to a cause of action:

- words or conduct will suffice, provided that the other ingredients of the tort are satisfied; and

- the adoption, by the representor, of the representation of another can also suffice.

1.015 An intriguing, and relatively recent example of a successful plea of misrepresentation by conduct concerned a pop video and photographs of all five original members of the Spice Girls.[28] The Claimant's case was that it had been induced to enter into a sponsorship deal by a representation, implicit in the conduct of the pop group's promoters in releasing the video and photographs, that the group would remain intact in its original line-up. In fact, as history relates, it was the express intention of Geri Halliwell[29] to leave the band before the end of the Claimant's sponsorship contract. The Claimant's action succeeded; the Defendant company had a duty to correct a misrepresentation by conduct.[30] A Defendant who drafts a document which is wilfully obscure and designed to camouflage the falsehoods which are contained within it may be found to have made a representation sufficient to give rise to an action in deceit.[31]

1.016 Silence, or passive non-disclosure, will not, however, be sufficient to give rise to the tort. It has been rightly observed that the courts have, on occasions, emphasised that, in this area of the law, the misrepresentation should be an active one.[32] By contrast, it is clear that telling half-truths or making a statement which is only true in part and is intended to convey a falsehood can give rise to liability for deceit. *Peek* v *Gurney*[33] concerned the

---

[27] At p 211A-B.
[28] The case concerned a cause of action based on the Misrepresentation Act 1967, rather than the tort of deceit.
[29] Ginger Spice.
[30] *Spice Girls Ltd* v *Aprilia World Service BV* [2000] CLY 887, (2000) *The Times*, April 5 (ChD).
[31] See, e.g. *Whife* v *Cullen* [1993] EGCS 193 (CA).
[32] J Cartwright, *Misrepresentation, Mistake and Non-disclosure* (2nd ed, 2007), para 5.06.
[33] (1873) LR 6 HL 377.

sale and purchase of shares in a company. A share prospectus was published for the consumption of the public at large. The Claimant was not an original allottee of shares in the company; he purchased his shares at a later date and, he argued, was induced to do so by a misrepresentation and concealment of facts in the original prospectus. The Claimant sustained loss when the company was wound up. Lord Chelmsford directed himself in the following terms,

> Assuming that mere concealment will not be sufficient to give a right of action to a person who, if the real facts had been known to him, would never have entered into a contract, but that there must be something actively done to deceive him and draw him in to deal with the person withholding the truth from him, it appears to me that this additional element exists in the present case … It is said that the prospectus is true as far as it goes, but half a truth will sometimes amount to a real falsehood … [34]

1.017 Similarly, Lord Cairns' speech in the same case contains the following,

> There must, in my opinion, be some active misstatement of fact, or, at all events, such a partial and fragmentary statement of fact, as that the withholding of that which is not stated makes that which is stated absolutely false. [35]

More recently, in *Smith New Court Securities Limited* v *Scrimgeour Vickers (Asset Management) Limited*,[36] Lord Steyn pointed out that, "*… a cocktail of truth, falsity and evasion is a more powerful instrument of deception than undiluted falsehood.*" [37]

1.018 If a Defendant takes active steps to conceal a state of affairs then this can give rise to liability for deceit. A Defendant letting premises who, for example, takes active steps to conceal dry rot with the (intended) result that the Claimant does not become aware of the defect in the let premises will be liable for deceit.[38] The position would be different if the Defendant simply remained silent about the deficiencies of the premises.

1.019 In common with the other actions for misrepresentation, deceit shares the proposition that a statement as to future intention will not give rise to the tort. There are, however, some important qualifications to this rule:

---

[34] At pp 391-392.
[35] At p 403.
[36] [1997] AC 254 (HL).
[37] At p 274.
[38] *Gordon* v *Selico Ltd* (1986) HLR 219.

- A representation of present intention can give rise to liability, prompting the oft-cited observation of Bowen LJ in *Edgington* v *Fitzmaurice*,[39]

  > The state of a man's mind is as much a fact as the state of his digestion. It is true that it is very difficult to prove what the state of a man's mind at a particular time is, but if it can be ascertained it is as much a fact as anything else.[40]

- Equally, a person who makes a promise to another can be liable for deceit in those cases where it can be proved that, at the time of making the promise he, in fact, had no intention of fulfilling it.[41] By contrast, a promise which is not (later) fulfilled by the Defendant will not give rise to an action in deceit if, at the time of making the promise, the Defendant had an honest intention of fulfilling it. In these circumstances, if the Claimant has any cause of action then it lies in contract.

1.020 An elegant summary of the rules in this area (and the reasons for them) appears in Professor Fleming's textbook:

> ... every promise contains an implied statement of fact, that is, of a present intent as to the future. What is really meant is that, if I make a promise with every intention of fulfilling it, I cannot be liable for deceit, should I subsequently become unable or unwilling to do so. The reason for this, however, is not that my promise is a statement of fact, but rather that I believed the statement of my present intention to be true when I made it. So, if I never entertained an intention of fulfilling my promise, I commit a fraud by falsifying my present intention, as when I pass a cheque, knowing that it is not covered and not intending to honour it.[42]

1.021 The problems in this area lie not in the conceptual justification for finding that promises and statements of future intent can amount to misrepresentations sufficient to lead to liability, but, instead, in obtaining the evidence needed to satisfy this element of the tort.

1.022 Similar observations can be made with respect to statements of opinion. If, at the time of giving his opinion, the representor does not

[39] (1885) 29 ChD 459 (CA).
[40] At p 483.
[41] Again, as Bowen LJ observed in *Edgington*, the problem in cases of this kind is generally one of evidence. An action in these circumstances will always be vulnerable to the defence from the representor that he has simply changed his mind.
[42] John G Fleming, *The Law of Torts*, (9th ed, 1998), p 697.

honestly hold the opinion and yet intends the dishonest expression of the same to be acted on then he will be guilty of deceit.[43] This might be thought by some to place an unjustified fetter on commercial negotiations by reducing the parties' room for manoeuvre. Why should a party who has made a false representation contained in an expression of opinion be at risk of a finding of deceit when the recipient of his opinion has equal knowledge of the facts on which the opinion is based? The answer is that, in this commercial context, the requirement that there is an intention that the representation be relied on, that the representation be (materially) relied on and that damage results, achieves, by different means, a satisfactory control on the boundaries of the tort.

1.023 The present academic consensus appears to be that statements of law can, given the problems involved in distinguishing a statement of fact from a statement of law, be considered to give rise to an action for deceit.[44] Indeed, it has been suggested that,

> ... as a general rule, the fraud of the representor overrides the policy reasons for distinguishing between a statement of fact and a statement of opinion, law or intention. Although the rule can be kept intact by recharacterising fraudulent statements of opinion, law and intention into statements of fact, it is suggested that the better approach for the tort of deceit would be to discard altogether the rule that the representation be one of fact, and simply to say that the tort applies to any fraudulent statement which was intended to be acted upon by the representee.[45]

1.024 Accordingly, a significant difference between the tort of deceit and the other actions for misrepresentation is the more relaxed approach to the categories of statement or conduct that will be found to constitute the tort. The more liberal approach is justified, on policy grounds, by the dishonesty of the representor.

1.025 Finally, it should be noted that actions for deceit cannot, as a specific exception to the general rules discussed in this section, be maintained on the basis of a misrepresentation by a vendor of the lowest price that he is prepared to accept for an item or by a purchaser of the highest price that he is prepared to pay.[46] There seems to be little justification for this approach,

---

[43] As Clerk and Lindsell rightly observes, the same goes for the facts on which the opinion is based: *Clerk & Lindsell on Torts* (19th ed, 2006), para 18-12.
[44] See, e.g. *Clerk & Lindsell on Torts* (19th ed, 2006), para 18-13; J Cartwright, *Misrepresentation, Mistake and Non-disclosure* (2nd ed, 2007), para 5.08; WVH Rogers, *Winfield & Jolowicz on Tort* (15th ed, 1998), p 356.
[45] J Cartwright, *Misrepresentation, Mistake and Non-disclosure* (2nd ed, 2007), para 5.08.
[46] See, *Vernon* v *Keys* (1810) 12 East 632.

save that the law allows a certain latitude and some exaggeration in the course of straightforward commercial negotiations.

4. STATE OF MIND

1.026 Much of the history of this element of the tort has been considered above. *Derry* v *Peek* remains the primary authority for the proposition that the representor must be fraudulent in the sense that he does not honestly believe in the truth of his statement or, insofar as this is different, is consciously indifferent to the truth of what he has stated. The test is subjective; the unreasonableness of what has been stated, tested objectively, may be evidence of the fraud, but will not give rise to liability unless it is proved that the representor lacked an honest belief in the truth of what he has represented. This forms an obvious point of contrast with the criminal law where the test for offences of dishonesty, formulated in *R* v *Ghosh*[47] combines both objective and subjective elements.

1.027 There is an additional limb to this element of the tort of deceit: the Defendant representor must intend the representee to act upon his statement. It is not sufficient that the Defendant representor merely foresees that there may be reliance on his representation. In *Bradford Third Equitable Benefit Building Society* v *Borders*[48] Viscount Maugham, in the course of his summary of the elements of the cause of action, put the matter in this way,

> [the representation] … must be made with the intention that it should be acted upon by the plaintiff, or by a class of persons which will include the plaintiff, in the manner which resulted in the damage to him.[49]

As this makes clear, it does not matter that the representor does not know the representee and it is not a requirement that the representation be addressed specifically to the individual who relies on it; it is sufficient that the representee form part of a class intended to act on the representation (the relevant class can be as wide as the public at large). Cases in which the Claimants did not form part of the class intended to be induced to act by the relevant representation prove the rule. Thus, in *Peek* v *Gurney*[50] the false

---

[47] [1982] QB 1053. An approach which is intended to be translated to the deception offences contained in the new Fraud Act 2006.
[48] [1941] 2 All ER 205 (HL).
[49] At p 211C.
[50] (1873) LR 6 HL 377.

statements in the prospectus at issue were directed to shareholders and not to the Claimant who purchased on the stock market. In *Gross* v *Lewis Hillman Limited*[51] the Claimants were not the parties to whom the representations hade been made. The representations were made by the vendors of property to the purchasers who then offered to let the Claimant have the benefit of the contract on payment of commission. In fact, it was held that there was no fraud, but, in the course of his judgment, Harman LJ emphasised that some limits should be placed on the class of persons (in a chain of commercial contracts) able to bring an action for deceit,

> The representation is made to A; A buys on the strength of it; and the fact that it goes further down the line ad infinitum does not mean that everybody who comes to know of it can rely on it. [52]

It appears to be the case that, as in the criminal law, a Defendant is likely to be treated as having intended the consequences of his action if he could foresee a result as a natural consequence or (as sometimes now recharacterised) a virtually certain consequence of the same (in a criminal law context, this is sometimes referred to as "*oblique*" intention).[53] This requirement is of less direct relevance than it might otherwise be because the Claimant is entitled to rely on a rebuttable presumption that, where a representation is made fraudulently, it was intended to be acted upon:

> In the general law it is beyond doubt that even a fraudulent misrepresentation must be shown to have induced the contract before the promisor has a right to avoid, although the task of proof may be made more easy by a presumption of inducement.[54]

As we have already seen, the Defendant representor's motive is, in this context, irrelevant; it will not matter that he does not intend to cheat the Claimant provided that he knows that what he has represented is false and provided that the other elements of the tort are satisfied.

1.028 The tort of deceit is completed when the representee acts upon the representor's false statement.[55] It is therefore necessary to test the

---

[51] [1970] Ch 445 (CA).

[52] At p 463G.

[53] See, for example, the discussion of the *mens rea* for murder in *R* v *Moloney* [1985] AC 905 (HL), *R* v *Hancock and Shankland* [1986] AC 455 (HL), *R* v *Nedrick* [1986] 1 WLR 1025 (CA) and *R* v *Woollin* [1999] AC 82 (HL).

[54] *Pan Atlantic Insurance Co Ltd* v *Pine Top Insurance Co Ltd* [1995] 1 AC 501, 542A-B *per* Lord Mustill (HL). The founding authority supportive of this proposition is *Smith* v *Chadwick* (1884) 9 App Cas 187, 196 *per* Lord Blackburn (HL). See also *Barton* v *County Natwest Bank Ltd* [1999] Ll Rep (Banking) 408, 421 *per* Morritt LJ (CA).

[55] *Briess* v *Wolley* [1954] AC 333, 353 (HL).

representor's state of mind, deploying the subjective approach described above, at the time that the representee relies on the statement. This can create problems of timing; the following may arise:

- There is a delay between the making of the false statement and the Claimant's reliance on the same – the Defendant will be liable in deceit because his representation, made with respect to an existing state of affairs, is deemed to continue throughout the period of delay.[56]

- The Defendant knows facts which suggest that his statement is untrue, but has forgotten these by the time that he makes the statement and the Claimant relies on the same – the Defendant has not committed the tort of deceit because it cannot be proved that the Defendant lacks an honest belief in the truth of the statement at the time that it is made and relied upon.

- The Defendant makes a statement which he believes to be true, but which, by the time that it is later relied on, he knows to be false – the Defendant will be liable for deceit if he does not correct the Claimant's false impression (an exception to the general principle, discussed above, that passive silence will not constitute the representation necessary for liability).

- The Defendant makes a statement which is, in fact, true at the time that it is made, but which, before the Claimant has relied on it, becomes untrue as a result of later events – again, the Defendant will be liable in deceit in circumstances where he is aware of those later events and does not correct the misapprehension.

1.029 The third and fourth situations summarised above were considered in *Brownlie* v *Campbell*[57] and in *Bradford Third Equitable Benefit Building Society* v *Borders*.[58] In *Brownlie*, Lord Blackburn stated as follows,

> ... when a statement or representation has been made in the bona fide belief that it is true, and the party who has made it afterwards comes to find out that it is untrue, and discovers what he should have said, he can no longer honestly keep up that silence on the subject after that has come to his knowledge , thereby allowing the other party to go on, and still more,

---

[56] This is referred to in the textbooks as a continuing representation: see, *Slough Estates Plc* v *Welwyn Hatfield DC* [1996] 2 PLR 50.
[57] (1880) 5 App Cas 925.
[58] [1941] 2 All ER 205, 220C-D *per* Lord Wright.

inducing him to go on, upon a statement which was honestly made at the time when it was made, but which he has not now retracted when he has become aware that it can no longer be honestly persevered in.[59]

5. RELIANCE

1.030 In order to be able to establish liability, the Claimant has to establish that he relied on the Defendant's representation. If the Claimant would have acted in the same way, even if the representation had not been made, then his action will fail.[60]

1.031 Deceit is not an inchoate wrong; an attempt to deceive will not suffice. This element of the tort is, perhaps, best treated as one aspect of the requirement that the Claimant bears the burden of proving causation.[61]

1.032 In the nineteenth century case *Horsfall* v *Thomas*[62] the Defendant employed the Claimant to make a gun for him. The gun was delivered to the Defendant with a defect that was, or would have been, patent or obvious to both parties. The Defendant accepted the gun without examining it and delivered a bill of exchange to the Claimant. The Claimant later wrote to the Defendant stating that the gun had no defects of which he was aware. The gun worked well for a time, but then exploded as a result of the patent defect. The Claimant brought an action against the Defendant on the basis of the bill of exchange. The Defendant countered that the bill had been procured by the fraudulent misrepresentation of the Claimant as to the patent defect. The Defendant's defence failed on causation grounds; indeed, it was described as "*mischievous*". Bramwell B stated that while the position would be different if the defect was latent,

> ... if there be a defect [known to the manufacturer] which is patent, and of which the purchaser is as capable of judging as the manufacturer, he is not bound to call the attention of the purchaser to it. It would be mischievous if he were, for in such case he would be bound to point out everything which might by any possibility be considered a defect; and the consequence would be that if the manufacturer, for prudence sake, pointed out some flaw which

---

[59] (1880) 5 App Cas 925, 950.
[60] See, *Smith* v *Chadwick* (1884) 9 App Cas 187 (HL(E)).
[61] See, *Gipps* v *Gipps* [1978] 1 NSWLR 454, 460E *per* Hutley JA, "*To state that a person is induced by a statement is to affirm a causal relation which is a question of fact, not of law.*"
[62] (1862) 1 H& C 90; 158 ER 813.

made no difference whatever in the value of the article, the purchaser would immediately say, 'There is a defect, I must have an abatement of the price.'[63]

1.033 One is struck, as sometimes happens when reading nineteenth century cases, by the overt manner in which an economically liberal, *laissez faire*, approach is used to justify the proposition of law. The rules on causation have been relaxed considerably since this case was decided.

1.034 In common with other torts, the Claimant does not now need to prove that the misrepresentation was the sole cause of his subsequent actions, provided that the same made, in causative terms, a material contribution. It will not matter if part of the reason for the Claimant's actions was a mistake on his part, provided that the Defendant's misrepresentation makes a material contribution.[64] By extension, the Defendant cannot, where a Claimant is able to prove causation in these circumstances, mount a defence on the basis that the Claimant had access to the information that would have led him to discover the Defendant's dishonesty; the test here is, again, a subjective one and, therefore, directed to the Claimant's state of mind.[65] Accordingly, the Defendant cannot argue that causation has not been established on the basis of the excuse that, *"the person to whom he had made ... [the representation] had available the means of correction"*,[66] or on the basis that the Claimant has relied on a representation in circumstances where, judged objectively, no reasonable person would do so.[67] The Claimant might have some awareness of the falsity of the Defendant's representation and yet still establish that he was caused to act on the basis of the same, provided that his knowledge of the falsity does not *"wholly dissipate"* his false belief, such that it cannot be said that he has relied on the misrepresentation.[68] It follows from the discussion above, and for policy reasons that will be obvious, that contributory negligence, whether at

---

[63] At p 817.
[64] See, *Edgington* v *Fitzmaurice* (1885) 29 ChD 459, 481 *per* Cotton LJ; 483 *per* Bowen LJ (CA).
[65] But compare *Downs* v *Chappell* [1997] 1 WLR 426, 433 (CA) where Hobhouse LJ stated as follows, *"A representation is material when its tendency, or its natural and probable result, is to induce the representee to act on the faith of it in the kind of way in which he is proved to have in fact acted. The test is objective."* This sits uneasily alongside other authority, unless it is simply treated as an expression of the rebuttable presumption that the representor intends his misrepresentation to be acted on. See also, *Bristol and West Building Society* v *Mothew* [1998] Ch 1 (CA), a case which concerns negligent misrepresentation, but in which *Downs* v *Chappell* is commented upon.
[66] *Nocton* v *Ashburton* [1914] AC 932, 962 *per* Lord Dunedin (HL(E)).
[67] *White* v *Cullen* [1993] EGCS 193 (CA).
[68] See, *Gipps* v *Gipps* [1978] 1 NSWLR 454, 460 *per* Hutley JA.

common law[69] or under the Law Reform (Contributory Negligence) Act 1945,[70] does not give rise to any defence to an action in deceit.

1.035 The Claimant has to prove that he himself relied on the falsehood;[71] it will not be sufficient for him to prove that he has suffered loss if the reliance on the representation was by a third party.[72] Accordingly, it has been pointed out that, in its classic form, the tort of deceit is a two-party action which is of limited relevance to cases where the Claimant has, by an indirect route, suffered loss as a result of dishonest anti-competitive conduct.[73] Consider, for example, a Defendant who lies about his goods in order to obtain a competitive advantage. Those who act on the lies may be able to maintain an action against the Defendant, but the Claimant (the Defendant's competitor) will be unable to do so.

1.036 It should be noted that the tort of deceit is to be distinguished from the separate, intentional, tort of infliction of harm (sometimes referred to as "the *Wilkinson* v *Downton* tort"). In *Wilkinson* v *Downton*[74] the Defendant, as a practical joke, falsely represented to the Claimant that her husband had been involved in an accident in which both his legs were broken. The Defendant made the statement with the intention that it should be believed to be true. In fact, the Claimant did believe the statement and paid for some people to travel by rail to the scene of the "accident" to ask after her husband. More seriously, the Claimant also developed a nervous shock illness. The Claimant brought an action both for the return of the rail fare and for her own pain, suffering and loss of amenity. She was successful on both counts. In the course of his judgment, Wright J had no doubt that the Claimant was entitled, on what he described as *Pasley* v *Freeman* (i.e. deceit) grounds, to the return of the rail fares. This was because he accepted that this loss was "*a misrepresentation intended to be acted on to the damage of the plaintiff.*"[75] However, he did not believe that the award made by a jury for pain and suffering could be justified on the same basis. The reasons for this remain a little obscure in the judgment itself, but it has been suggested that this is because, "*in such a case there is no reliance but rather harmful*

---

[69] See, *Alliance & Leicester Building Society* v *Edgestop Ltd* [1993] 1 WLR 1462, 1474 *per* Mummery J (ChD).
[70] See, *Standard Chartered Bank* v *Pakistan National Shipping Corporation (No 2)* [2000] 1 Ll LR 218, 226 *per* Evans LJ (CA).
[71] See, for a good example of this, *T J Larkins* v *Chelmer Holdings Pty Ltd* [1965] Qd R 68.
[72] *Clerk & Lindsell* point out that, in these circumstances, the Claimant might have an action in negligence, malicious falsehood, passing off or unlawful interference with trade: *Clerk & Lindsell on Torts* (19th ed, 2006), para 18-32.
[73] H Carty, *An Analysis of the Economic Torts*, p 134.
[74] [1897] 2 QB 57 (QBD).
[75] At p 58.

effects from the lies told."[76] In other words, no causal connection could be drawn between the false representation and the illness which resulted.[77]

6. DAMAGES

1.037 The Claimant who manages to prove the other elements of the tort will not obtain a finding of fraud and, therefore, liability against the Defendant unless he is also able to prove that he has suffered loss (deceit does not fall into the category of torts which are actionable *per se*): "*I think no one will venture to dispute that the plaintiff cannot recover unless he proves damage*"[78] (deceit developed, as we have seen, out of the action on the case). Deceit is a tort and it follows that the defrauded Claimant is entitled to the tortious, rather than contractual measure of damages. Accordingly, the Claimant is placed, by the damages awarded, in the position that he would have been in if the tort had not been committed, rather than the position that he would have been in if the false representation had been true. Professor Treitel has pointed out that the effect of this approach to the assessment of damages in deceit is to protect the Claimant who would have made a bad bargain even if the representation had been true (by contrast, the Claimant who would have made a good bargain if the representation had been true will generally do better if the contractual measure of damages is adopted – putting the Claimant in the position he would have been in if the representation had been true (in which case the Claimant may recover something from the Defendant even if the actual value of his purchase is greater than the price that he paid for it)).[79] The court will examine closely the facts of a case in which the Defendant raises the defence that the Claimant has suffered no loss; there is likely, in circumstances where the Claimant is able to prove all the other elements of the tort, to have been some direct or indirect loss:

---

[76] H Carty, *An Analysis of the Economic Torts*, p 142.

[77] Wright J appears to have justified the decision not to treat the award for pain and suffering as falling within the tort of deceit by explaining that the same did not "*naturally result*" from the Claimant having acted on the misrepresentation: see, [1897] 2 QB 57, 58 (QBD).

[78] *Smith* v *Chadwick* (1884) 9 App Cas 187, 195 *per* Lord Blackburn (HL).

[79] G H Treitel, "*Damages for Deceit*" (1969) 32 MLR 556, 558, quoted by Lord Steyn in the course of his speech in *Smith New Court Ltd* v *Scrimgeour Vickers Ltd* [1997] AC 254, 282A-B (HL).

> I confess that I do not look kindly on a defendant who, having got the plaintiff to buy a machine by knowingly telling him an untruth, afterwards says he suffered no damage. [80]

However hard the damage is to assess, the court will ordinarily look closely to ensure that if there is damage it is compensated.

1.038 The Claimant in an action for deceit will generally be seeking recovery for pecuniary loss; typically, the Claimant will have been induced by the fraud to enter into an unprofitable transaction. However, damages can also be awarded for personal injury, damage to property and for certain intangible losses like distress and inconvenience. To take personal injury first, it was held, in a case decided in the first half of the nineteenth century, that the seller of a gun who had falsely stated that it was in a good, safe condition was liable for the injury sustained when the gun exploded while being used. [81] In *Banks* v *Cox* [82] the Claimant was fraudulently induced to buy a nursing home which failed to make a profit. Compensation was awarded for the depressive illness which the Claimant was held to have developed as a result. As I have indicated, it has long been recognised that damages can be awarded in this context for the distress (falling short of personal injury) and any inconvenience that the Claimant suffers as a result of the Defendant's fraud; actions for deceit can, therefore, like claims for spoilt holidays brought in contract, support a claim for damages for distress. In *Mafo* v *Adams* [83] the Claimant and his heavily pregnant wife were induced, by the deceit of the Defendant and his wife, to relinquish a protected tenancy. In addition to the compensation awarded for other heads of loss the Court of Appeal directed that the Claimant was entitled to be compensated for the physical inconvenience that he and his wife had experienced when, after vacating their Rent Act protected accommodation, they were left without alternative accommodation. A sum of £100 was awarded in general damages by the judge in the county court. This sum was approved by the Court of Appeal (apparently on no more scientific basis than that this seemed to be about right). It appears from more recent authority that damages under this heading will be assessed on principles which will be familiar to those with experience of general damages awards for distress, disappointment and loss of enjoyment in the context of spoilt holidays. In *Archer* v *Brown* [84] Peter Pain J, having first directed himself that there was no reason why general

---

[80] *Hornal* v *Neuberger Products Ltd* [1957] 1 QB 247, 260 *per* Denning LJ (CA).
[81] *Langridge* v *Levy* (1837) 2 M & W 519.
[82] [2002] EWHC 2166 (QBD).
[83] [1970] 1 QB 548 (CA).
[84] [1985] QB 401 (QBD).

damages for distress should be limited to contract cases and could also be awarded where the action was in deceit, went on to direct that,

> I can see no reason why such damages should not be awarded in deceit on the same basis as in contract. The authorities make it plain that the sum awarded should be moderate. [85]

In other words, the rather haphazard approach to the assessment of general damages for distress and inconvenience adopted in contract will also be used for actions in deceit.

1.039 The question whether aggravated or exemplary damages can be awarded in successful actions for deceit has exercised the academic writers in this area. In *Archer* v *Brown* Peter Pain J described the award that he was making for injured feelings or distress as an award of aggravated damages and some of the textbook writers adopt the same *nomenclature*,[86] although it has been observed that the victim of a fraud is entitled to recover compensation for his distress and that it is only if the Defendant's conduct is particularly heinous that aggravated damages should be awarded (on the basis that the Defendant's conduct has increased the Claimant's distress).[87] This appears close to the approach of Widgery LJ in the Court of Appeal in *Mafo* v *Adams*:

> ... where there are aggravating circumstances which aggravate the suffering and injury to the plaintiff, then in compensating him for the wrong which has been done, the damages must be similarly increased.[88]

In the circumstances, and given that it is clear that damages for distress/injury to feelings can be awarded in appropriate cases, it probably does not matter very much whether or not such awards are described as aggravated damages. The position is less settled with respect to exemplary damages. In *Archer* v *Brown* Peter Pain J indicated that the purpose of exemplary damages is punitive.[89] If the Defendant had already been punished by a criminal sanction, then it seemed counter-intuitive that exemplary damages should be awarded with the result that the Defendant would be punished twice for the same offence.[90] The present consensus appears to be that exemplary damages are available where the Claimant has established

---

[85] At p 426.
[86] See eg. *Clerk & Lindsell on Torts* (19th ed, 2006), para 18-44.
[87] See, H McGregor, *McGregor on Damages* (17th ed, 2003), para 41-037.
[88] [1970] 1 QB 548, 558D (CA).
[89] [1985] QB 401, 423H (QBD). See also, *Mafo* v *Adams* [1970] 1 QB 548, 558H *per* Widgery LJ (CA).
[90] At p 423H.

fraud,[91] provided that the case meets the conditions for an award of such damages:[92] namely, (1) where there has been arbitrary or unconstitutional action by a public body; or, (2) where the Defendant has made a profit which exceeds the compensation to which the Claimant is entitled.

1.040 It is a feature of the principle that damages for deceit are assessed by the tortious, rather than contractual, measure that damages for loss of profits are generally irrecoverable in actions for deceit; the Claimant cannot recover the profits that he would have made if the Defendant's representation had been true. In appropriate cases the Claimant can, however, recover the profit that he would have made if the money, time and effort that he invested in the transaction which was fraudulently procured by the Defendant had been properly invested elsewhere. Recovery of profit in this sense does not offend the principle that damages are intended, in this context, to place the Claimant in the position that he would have been in if the fraud had not been committed.[93]

1.041 The Claimant's loss will generally be measured at the time that he relies on the Defendant's false representation. In most cases this means that where the Claimant has, in reliance on the Defendant's misrepresentation, entered into a contract for the purchase of an article, damages will be assessed on the basis of the difference between the price that the Claimant paid and the market value of the goods purchased at the time of the transaction. Accordingly, where the value of the goods later rises or falls this will be left out of account with the result that the purchaser, rather than the vendor, takes the risk if, at a date later than the transaction, the (resale) value of the goods plummets. There are some important advantages to this rule. First, it neatly side steps some potentially difficult questions of causation; whether the loss based on a later valuation of the relevant goods was caused by the original representation, rather than extraneous factors. Second, if the asset purchased can be readily sold on and there is no reason why the Claimant might be constrained to retain it then it is fair that the causative potency of the original representation is treated as having come to an end and the Claimant's loss is measured only by reference to the real value of the goods at the date of the transaction. However, it has long been recognised that a strict and inflexible application of the general rule should

---

[91] See, J Cartwright, *Misrepresentation, Mistake and Non-disclosure* (2nd ed, 2007), para 5.42 and *Clerk & Lindsell on Torts* (19th ed, 2006), para 18-44. The consensus is based on the decision of the House of Lords in *Kuddus* v *Chief Constable of Leicestershire Constabulary* [2002] 2 AC 122 (HL(E)).

[92] Derived from the speech of Lord Devlin in *Rookes* v *Barnard* [1964] AC 1129 (HL).

[93] See, *East* v *Maurer* [1991] 1 WLR 461 (CA) and, more recently, *Clef Aquitaine SarL* v *Laport Minerals (Barrow) Ltd* [2001] QB 488 (CA).

not be adopted where, "*... to do so would prevent ...* [the Claimant] *obtaining full compensation for the wrong suffered.*"[94] The courts have, therefore, developed categories of cases in which it will generally be reckoned appropriate to depart from the general rule that the Claimant's loss is measured by the difference between the price that the Claimant paid and the market value of the goods purchased at the time of the transaction:[95]

- Where the price at the date of acquisition was the result of a false market created by the Defendant's fraudulent misrepresentation to the market at large – in such cases it has long been recognised that it is appropriate, with the benefit of hindsight, to calculate the true market value at the date of the transaction in order to avoid the risk of under-compensating the Claimant.[96]

- Where the misrepresentation has continued to operate after the Claimant purchased the asset and has induced him to retain it – the "*continuing representation*".

- Where the Claimant has, by reason of the fraud, become "*locked into*" the retention of the asset.

1.042 In *Doyle* v *Olby (Ironmongers) Limited*[97] the Claimant, relying on the fraudulent misrepresentation of the Defendant vendor, purchased an unprofitable ironmongers' business. The Court of Appeal treated the Claimant as, effectively, locked into the retention of the business. Lord Denning MR said,

> Mr Doyle ... had to remain in occupation. He had burnt his boats and had to carry on with the business as best he could. He tried to sell it, but there were difficulties. One was that the landlord, Mr Cecil Olby, would not give him a licence to assign, and so forth. After three years he did manage to sell it for a sum of some £3,700. This cleared off the mortgage to Askinex Ltd, but he was left with many outstanding debts to the bank, to suppliers, and the like. His

---

[94] *Smith New Court Ltd* v *Scrimgeour Vickers Ltd* [1997] AC 254, 267B *per* Lord Browne-Wilkinson (HL(E)).
[95] These categories were summarised by Lord Browne-Wilkinson in the *Smith New Court* case, although he also counselled that the circumstances in which it would be appropriate to depart from the general rule could not be comprehensively stated.
[96] *McConnel* v *Wright* [1903] 1 Ch 546 (CA).
[97] [1969] 2 QB 158 (CA).

debts came to £4,000, and he has been sued in the county court by many of his creditors.[98]

1.043 Confronted with such a tale of woe the Court had little hesitation in departing from the general (date of transaction) rule and based Mr Doyle's award on the difference between the sum that he paid to acquire the business and the sum that he was later constrained to sell it for (less the benefits that he had obtained during his time running the business). In other cases, decided more recently, the courts have shown little hesitation in departing from the date of transaction rule where they have been satisfied that the Claimant has, by reason of the Defendant's fraud, become locked into the asset and where only a later valuation date will provide proper compensation.[99]

1.044 In *Smith New Court Limited* v *Scrimgeour Vickers Limited*[100] Lord Steyn treated the categories in which it has been thought appropriate to depart from the general (date of transaction) rule as examples of the overriding compensatory rule:

> ... the date of transaction rule is simply a second order rule applicable only where the valuation method is employed. If that method is inapposite, the court is entitled simply to assess the loss flowing directly from the transaction without any reference to the date of the transaction or indeed any particular date. ... There is in truth only one legal measure of assessing damages in an action for deceit: the plaintiff is entitled to recover as damages a sum representing the financial loss flowing directly from his alteration of position under the inducement of the fraudulent representations of the defendants ... In an action for deceit the price paid less the valuation at the transaction date is simply a method of measuring the loss which will satisfactorily solve many cases. It is not a substitute for the single legal measure: it is an application of it.[101]

1.045 *Smith New Court Limited* was the first occasion on which the House of Lords considered the issue of timing in respect of the measure of damages in deceit. The facts were rather unusual and did not fit easily into any of the existing categories in which departure from the general rule had been thought appropriate. The Defendant represented to the Claimant (at various times) that, in bidding to buy shares in a public company, the Claimant would be competing with two other companies, that the Defendant would

---

[98] At p 165A-B.
[99] See eg. *East* v *Maurer* [1991] 1 WLR 461 (CA) and *Downs* v *Chappell* [1997] 1 WLR 426 (CA).
[100] [1997] AC 254 (HL(E)).
[101] At p 284B-E.

disclose the competing bids after the Claimant made its bid and that two other (named) companies had bid for the purchase of the shares. In reliance on these representations the Claimant decided to pay 82.25 pence per share. The Claimant also relied on the representations in deciding to retain the shares on a long term basis and only to sell them when the appropriate opportunity arose. To this extent the Claimant was, by reason of the Defendant's fraud, "*locked into*" the retention of the asset. If the Claimant had not intended to retain the shares in the longer term (that is, if there had been no misrepresentations) then its evidence was that it would only have offered 78 pence per share and would have looked to make a quick sale of the shares it purchased.[102] In fact, as a result of an earlier wholly unrelated fraud on the company (of which both the Claimant and Defendant were unaware at the time of sale), the shares were only worth 44 pence each as at the date of the sale. The issue in the case was whether damages should be assessed on the basis of the difference between the price actually paid and the, much lower, price later realised on resale or on the basis of the difference between the price that the Claimant would have offered, absent the false representations (i.e. 78 pence per share), and the price that the Claimant actually paid. At first instance, the judge assessed damages on the basis of the difference between the actual market value and the purchase price (i.e. the difference between 82.25 p and 44 p per share). This was reversed on appeal when the Court of Appeal found that the proper measure of loss was the difference between the price that was paid and the price that would, absent the misrepresentations, have been paid (i.e. the less generous difference between 82.25 p and 78 p per share). The Claimant appealed. In the House of Lords it was held that the Claimant would be very significantly under-compensated if required to give credit for the price that it would have paid for the shares if not induced to pay a higher price by reason of the Defendant's misrepresentations. Lord Browne-Wilkinson stated that the Claimant could not have disposed of the shares for 78 pence each as at the date of the transaction. The Claimant was, instead, "*locked into*" retaining the shares in the longer term by reason of the Defendant's misrepresentations and,

> "It … [was] not realistic to treat Smith as having received shares worth 78 p each when in fact, in real life, they could not commercially have sold or realised the shares at that price on that date".[103]

---

[102] Although there was evidence that if 78 pence had been offered for the shares then it would have been rejected.
[103] [1997] AC 254, 268C-D (HL(E))

The House of Lords restored the valuation adopted by the trial judge; the Claimant was entitled to the difference between 82.25 pence and 44 pence per share.

1.046 In the same way that the Defendant's fraudulent conduct justifies departure from the date of transaction rule (in order to ensure that the Claimant is properly compensated) the courts have also relaxed the rules on remoteness of loss in order to achieve the same result. The leading case in this context is *Doyle* v *Olby (Ironmongers) Limited.*[104] The Court of Appeal rejected submissions that damages should be limited by reference to the tests on remoteness of loss found either in contract (the reasonable contemplation of the parties) or in negligence (reasonable foreseeability):

> In contract, the damages are limited to what may reasonably be supposed to have been in the contemplation of the parties. In fraud, they are not so limited. The defendant is bound to make reparation for all the actual damages directly flowing from the fraudulent inducement ... All such damages can be recovered: it does not lie in the mouth of the fraudulent person to say that they could not reasonably have been foreseen.[105]

1.047 Accordingly, the courts are willing to entertain claims for more unusual consequential loss (perhaps of a kind not obviously connected to the original false representation) where the Defendant's conduct is deceitful, rather than simply negligent. There are two justifications for this relaxed approach to remoteness and, indeed, the more stringent approach taken to the assessment of loss in deceit by contrast with, say, the tort of negligence. First, the approach in deceit, "*serves a deterrent purpose in discouraging fraud*" and second,

> ...as between the fraudster and the innocent party, moral considerations militate in favour of requiring the fraudster to bear the risk of misfortunes directly caused by his fraud. [106]

1.048 It will be obvious from the discussion in this section and above that the Claimant has the burden of proving causation; that is, proving that his loss was caused by the Defendant's misrepresentation. In the event that all of the other ingredients of the tort are satisfied, this is unlikely to prove a very heavy burden to discharge. This issue was dealt with in short form in both

---

[104] [1969] 2 QB 158 (CA). This is a celebrated and oft-cited case, although it is interesting to note that it was argued, successfully, by a litigant in person and the judgments were not reserved.

[105] At p 167B-C *per* Lord Denning MR.

[106] *Smith New Court Ltd* v *Scrimgeour Vickers Ltd* [1997] AC 254, 279H – 280C *per* Lord Steyn (HL(E)).

Downs v *Chappell*[107] (described by Hobhouse LJ as simply a *"question of fact"*) and in *Smith New Court Limited.* In the second of these cases Lord Steyn recognised that there is a considerable overlap between causation, remoteness and mitigation in the context of damages for deceit. He went on to say (somewhat apologetically):

> ... it is settled that at any rate in the law of obligations causation is to be categorised as an issue of fact. What has further been established is that the 'but for' test, although it often yields the right answer, does not always do so. That has led judges to apply the pragmatic test whether the condition in question was a substantial factor in producing the result. On other occasions judges assert that the guiding criterion is whether in common sense terms there is a sufficient causal connection. ... There is no material difference between these two approaches. While acknowledging that this hardly amounts to an intellectually satisfying theory of causation, that is how I must approach the question of causation.[108]

1.049 The Claimant remains under a duty to mitigate his loss. However, for obvious reasons, the duty to mitigate only arises once the Claimant becomes aware of the fraud because, by this stage, he is no longer *"locked into"* the fraud.[109] It may be appropriate at this stage for the Claimant to seek to mitigate his loss by, for example, selling the property acquired as a result of the fraud. It should, however, be remembered that the burden of proving that the Claimant has failed to act reasonably in mitigating his loss will fall on the Defendant and, in the context of losses caused by the Defendant's fraud, this may prove a heavy burden to discharge.

7. EMPLOYEES AND AGENTS

1.050 The conceptual difficulty in imposing liability on an employer or principal lies in the requirement that the fraudster should lack an honest belief in the truth of a representation or should, at least, be consciously indifferent to the truth of the same. It is, naturally, more difficult to establish the requisite dishonest state of mind when dealing with an alleged fraud committed by more than one actor (but forming the same legal person). This problem was articulated by Devlin J who stated that the tort would not be committed by,

---

[107] [1997] 1 WLR 426 (CA).
[108] [1997] AC 254, 285A-C.
[109] See, *Smith New Court Ltd* v *Scrimgeour Vickers Ltd* [1997] AC 254, 266G-H *per* Lord Browne-Wilkinson and 285D *per* Lord Steyn (HL(E))

...combining an innocent principal and agent so as to produce dishonesty ... You cannot combine an innocent state of mind to an innocent state of mind and get as a result a dishonest state of mind.[110]

1.051 It is necessary in cases involving more than one actor to distinguish the employer or principal's potential vicarious liability from his potential primary liability and to identify clearly the actor who possesses the requisite dishonest state of mind. First, it is tolerably clear that an innocent employer will be liable for the deceitful conduct of his employee acting in the course of his employment.[111] This will be the position even if the false statement made by the employee reaches the Claimant by means of the employer[112] or through another innocent agent.[113] In order for such vicarious liability to arise, however, the Claimant must prove that the employee's acts, in addition to being dishonest, complete all the elements of the tort. In addition, it is a feature of the requirement that the employee's dishonest actions be committed in the course of employment that the employee has actual or ostensible authority to make the statement. Indeed, it has been suggested in this context that the focus is less on the course of employment test, adopted in respect of vicarious liability for other torts, and more on the actual or ostensible authority of the employee to make the false statement.[114] In *The Ocean Frost*, Lord Keith said this, "*dishonest conduct is of a different character from blundering attempts to promote the employer's business interests*"[115] and, therefore,

... the essential feature for creating liability in the employer is that the party contracting with the fraudulent servant should have altered his position to his detriment in reliance on the belief that the servant's activities were within his authority, or, to put it another way, were part of his job. [116]

1.052 Equally, and unsurprisingly, an innocent principal will be liable for fraud committed by his agent provided that it was within the agent's actual or ostensible authority to make the representation (and provided, of course, that the other elements of the tort are present).[117]

---

[110] *Armstrong* v *Strain* [1951] 1 TLR 856, 872.
[111] See, e.g. *Barings Plc (in liquidation)* v *Coopers & Lybrand (Issues re liability)* [200] PNLR 639 (ChD).
[112] *Pearson* v *Dublin Corporation* [1907] AC 351 (HL(I)) and *Anglo-Scottish Beet Sugar Corporation* v *Spalding UDC* [1937] 2 KB 607 (KBD).
[113] *Armstrong* v *Strain* [1952] 1 KB 232, 243 and 248 (CA).
[114] H Carty, *An Analysis of the Economic Torts*, p 145.
[115] *Armagas Ltd* v *Mundogas SA* [1986] AC 717, 780 (HL(E)).
[116] At p 781.
[117] *Briess* v *Woolley* [1954] AC 333 (HL(E)) and *Direct Line* v *Khan* [2002] Ll Rep IR 364 (CA).

1.053 The situation where the employer or principal acts with a guilty mind and the employee/agent does not is more straightforward. If the employer or principal authorises his employee or agent to make a representation which the former knows to be false then he will bear a primary liability for the tort. If the employee or agent shares knowledge of the falsehood then he will also bear a primary liability (potentially, as a joint tortfeasor).[118] It is also the case that if the employer or principal conceals facts from an employee or agent knowing that the latter will, innocently, make a false statement or pass on false information to a third party then the employer or principal will have committed a fraud.[119]

8. DEFENCES

1.054 In keeping with the policy evident in the discussion above with respect to damages, only limited defences are available to a Defendant who has acted fraudulently. The courts have been keen to limit the circumstances in which a Defendant can insulate himself against the consequences of his deceitful conduct.

1.055 First, as indicated above, contributory negligence is not available as a defence to fraud either at common law[120] or pursuant to the Law Reform (Contributory Negligence) Act 1945.[121]

1.056 Equally, it is not possible for a person to use a notice or contractual term to exclude liability that would otherwise arise as a result of his own fraud,[122] although, subject to the statutory controls on exclusion clauses,[123] it might be possible to exclude liability for losses sustained as a result of a fraud committed by a third party (an agent, for example). In the latter case it should be noted that,

---

[118] *Standard Chartered Bank* v *Pakistan National Shipping Corporation (No 2)* [2003] 1 AC 959 (HL).
[119] *Standard Chartered Bank* v *Pakistan National Shipping Corporation (No 2)* [2000] 1 Ll LR 218, 225 *per* Evans LJ (CA).
[120] See, *Alliance & Leicester Building Society* v *Edgestop Ltd* [1993] 1 WLR 1462, 1474 *per* Mummery J (ChD).
[121] See, *Standard Chartered Bank* v *Pakistan National Shipping Corporation (No 2)* [2000] 1 Ll LR 218, 226 *per* Evans LJ (CA).
[122] *HIH Casualty & General Insurance Ltd* v *Chase Manhattan Bank* [2003] 2 Ll Rep 61 (HL).
[123] See the Unfair Contract Terms Act 1977 and Unfair Terms in Consumer Contracts Regulations 1999 (SI 1999/2083).

> ... if a party to a written contract seeks to exclude the ordinary consequences of fraudulent or dishonest misrepresentation or deceit by his agent, acting as such, inducing the making of the contract, such intention must be expressed in clear and unmistakeable terms on the face of the contract.[124]

1.057 The circumstances in which a defence of illegality will succeed in an action in deceit are tightly confined. *Winfield & Jolowicz* summarise the position as follows,

> The test is whether the plaintiff has to plead or rely on the illegality; he is not defeated simply because the title or claim on which he relies arose in the course of an illegal transaction.[125]

Accordingly, a Claimant succeeded in an action for fraudulent misrepresentation which was based on certain false statements about the condition of a residential property that he was purchasing, notwithstanding the fact that the contract of sale contained a false statement of the value of the property with a view to the evasion of stamp duty.[126] The Claimant had engaged in illegal conduct, but his action was based on the tort of deceit, rather than on the contract and, accordingly, the illegality defence failed. Similarly, in *Standard Chartered Bank* v *Pakistan National Shipping Corporation*[127] Aldous LJ again expressed the proper approach to a defence of illegality in the context of the tort of deceit,

> ... public policy requires that the Courts will not lend their aid to a man who founds his action upon an immoral or illegal act. The action will not be founded upon an immoral or illegal act, if it can be pleaded and proved without reliance on fraud.[128]

The difficulty of establishing the *ex turpi causa* defence is such that *Clerk & Lindsell* observe that the defence has, apparently, never succeeded where the cause of action is deceit.[129]

---

[124] *HIH Casualty & General Insurance Ltd* v *Chase Manhattan Bank* [2003] 2 Ll Rep 61 *per* Lord Bingham (HL).
[125] WVH Rogers, *Winfield & Jolowicz on Tort* (15th ed, 1998), p 871.
[126] *Saunders* v *Edwards* [1987] 1 WLR 1116.
[127] [2000] 1 Ll LR 218 (CA).
[128] At p 232.
[129] *Clerk & Lindsell on Torts* (19th ed, 2006), para 18-47, n 6.

1.058 Finally, there is a rather curious legislative provision: section 6 of the Statute of Frauds Amendment Act 1828 (*"Lord Tenterden's Act"*). This provides:

> No action shall be brought whereby to charge any person upon or by reason of any representation or assurance made or given concerning or relating to the character, conduct, credit, ability, trade, or dealings of any other person, to the intent or purpose that such other person may obtain credit, money, or goods upon, unless such representation or assurance be made in writing, signed by the person to be charged therewith.

1.059 The Statute of Frauds 1677 provides that no action is to be brought on a contract of guarantee unless the contract is in writing and is signed by the Defendant or by his agent. Following the decision in *Pasley* v *Freeman* litigants began to use the tort of deceit to provide them with a cause of action against someone who had fraudulently misrepresented the credit-worthiness of another in circumstances where, given the absence of any written contract, the Statute of Frauds would otherwise have precluded the bringing of a claim. The 1828 provision was intended to prevent this evasion of the Statute of Frauds. It provides a defence to a cause of action in deceit in the circumstances to which section 6 of the 1828 Act refers. Notwithstanding the breadth of the statutory language, section 6 only applies to:

- actions for fraudulent misrepresentation;[130]

- unwritten representations made about the credit-worthiness of a third party which induced a party to make a loan or supply goods to the third party.

9. LIMITATION

1.060 Deceit is a tort and, therefore, has a six-year limitation period, calculated in the conventional way from the date on which the cause of action accrued, pursuant to section 2 of the Limitation Act 1980. However, this provision is qualified by section 32 of the 1980 Act which states (under

---

[130] *Banbury* v *Bank of Montreal* [1918] AC 626 (HL). There is some authority for the proposition that the defence may be available where the cause of action is section 2(1) of the Misrepresentation Act 1967.

the heading, "*Postponement of limitation period in case of fraud, concealment or mistake*"):

> (1) ... where in the case of any action for which a period of limitation is prescribed by this Act, either – (a) the action is based upon the fraud of the defendant; or (b) any fact relevant to the plaintiff's right of action has been deliberately concealed from him by the defendant ... the period of limitation shall not begin to run until the plaintiff has discovered the fraud, concealment ... (as the case may be) or could with reasonable diligence have discovered it. References in this subsection to the defendant include references to the defendant's agent and to any person through whom the defendant claims and his agent.

1.061 The purpose of this provision is to, "*ensure that the Act does not operate to bar the claim of a plaintiff whose ignorance of the relevant law is due to the improper actions of the defendant*".[131] In this area, as in others discussed above, the fraudulent conduct of the Defendant justifies a relaxation of the general law to the benefit of the defrauded Claimant.

1.062 It will be noted that the protection afforded by the Act to the Claimant is located in the provision that time does not start to run until the Claimant has discovered the fraud or concealment or "*could with reasonable diligence have discovered it*".[132] The burden of proof in this regard lies on the Claimant seeking to take advantage of the protection of the Act. Unsurprisingly, there has been a good deal of argument and authority on the meaning of reasonable diligence in this context. In *Paragon Finance Plc* v *DB Thakerar & Company*[133] Millett LJ stated as follows:

> The question is not whether the plaintiffs should have discovered the fraud sooner; but whether they could with reasonable diligence have done so. The burden of proof is on them. They must establish that they could not have discovered the fraud without exceptional measures which they could not reasonably have been expected to take. In this context the length of the applicable period of limitation is irrelevant. In the course of argument May LJ observed that reasonable diligence must be measured against some standard, but that the six year limitation period did not provide the relevant standard. He suggested that the test was how a person carrying on a business of the relevant kind would act if he had adequate but not unlimited

---

[131] *Sheldon* v *RHM Outhwaite (Underwriting Agencies) Ltd* [1996] AC 102, 142F *per* Lord Browne-Wilkinson (HL).
[132] It should be noted that if the fraud can or could be discovered then the Claimant cannot rely on section 32(1)(a), even if he does not know the present location or identity of the fraudster: *R B Motor Policies at Lloyds* v *Butler* [1950] 1 KB 76 (KBD).
[133] [1999] 1 All ER 400 (CA).

staff and resources and was motivated by a reasonable but not excessive sense of urgency. I agree.[134]

1.063 "*Innocent third party purchasers*" of property for valuable consideration and any persons claiming through them are accorded special status by the 1980 Act. When an action is brought for the recovery of property or the value of property or for the enforcement of a charge against property or the setting aside of a transaction with respect to the same, postponement of the ordinary limitation period[135] will not be available against the innocent third party.[136] The Act defines the innocent third party in the following terms,

> ...in the case of fraud or concealment of any fact relevant to the plaintiff's right of action, if he was not a party to the fraud or (as the case may be) to the concealment of that fact and did not at the time of the purchase know or have reason to believe that the fraud or concealment had taken place.[137]

Whether the Defendant to an action constitutes an innocent third party purchaser will be a question, essentially, of fact. It should be noted that the protection afforded to an innocent third party also extends to "*any person claiming through him*". The 1980 Act itself provides that a person is treated as claiming through another if he became entitled [to the property in question] by, through or under the act of the original [innocent] purchaser.[138] Is the purchaser to be regarded as claiming through all of the earlier vendors of the property or does the provision refer only to the person who made the sale to the index purchaser? It has been stated that,

> There is no reported authority on the point since the 1980 Act, but it is submitted that ... the intervention of an innocent third-party purchaser anywhere in the chain deprives the original owner of the benefit of section 32.[139]

1.064 The 1980 Act contains no definition of fraud for the purposes of section 32(1)(a). This issue was considered in *Beaman v ARTS Limited*.[140] This concerned the bailment of goods. Some years before the outbreak of the

---

[134] At p 418. See also, *Biggs* v *Sotnicks (A Firm)* [2002] Ll Rep PN 331 (CA). It has also been observed that Millett LJ's statement of the position pre-supposes that there is some desire to investigate the position by the defrauded party.
[135] Pursuant to s 32(1).
[136] Limitation Act 1980, s 32(3).
[137] Section 32(4)(a).
[138] Section 38(5).
[139] A McGee, *Limitation Periods* (4th ed, 2002), para 20.036 – referring to cases decided under the 1939 Act.
[140] [1949] 1 KB 550 (CA).

Second World War the Claimant, who was due to depart for Turkey, deposited packages with the Defendant, an Italian owned company, for safe-keeping. It was her instruction that the packages were to be sent to her as soon as she gave notice requiring this. The Defendant was unable to send the Claimant most of the packages as a result of regulations in Turkey and then the outbreak of war. On the entry of Italy into the war the Defendant business was taken over by the custodian of enemy property. The Defendant wished to wind the business up and, after examination of the Claimant's property, decided to donate it to the Salvation Army. The Defendant had formed the view that the property was valueless (although it was the Claimant's evidence that the property held considerable sentimental value for her). The Claimant's consent was not sought for the donation and no steps were taken to make her aware of it. The Claimant did not return to England until 1946 and enquired after the whereabouts of her property. When she learnt that it had been donated without her consent she commenced an action for damages in conversion. More than six years had passed since the property was disposed of and the Claimant sought to rely on the fraud of the Defendant to postpone the limitation period. It was her case that the conversion was fraudulent. Denning J, at first instance, held that it was not necessary, in order to rely on the relevant provision, that fraud be an ingredient essential to the cause of action, however, he decided that there was neither fraud[141] nor deliberate concealment. He dismissed the Claimant's action as time-barred. On appeal, Lord Greene MR said this,

> It must be borne in mind that ... [what is now section 32] is a section of general application. It applies to every sort of action which is affected by the Act. Of these many can properly be said to be based upon fraud: for example, an action for damages for deceit and an action claiming rescission of a transaction brought about by fraud. In all such cases fraud is a necessary allegation in order to constitute the cause of action. In other actions covered by the Act fraud is not a necessary allegation at all and the action of conversion is one of them. Indeed, the word 'fraudulent' in connexion with conversion, however important it may be in a criminal matter is, in the civil action of conversion, so far as regards the cause of action, nothing more than an abusive epithet. I am of the opinion, therefore, that the language of para (a) means what it says and that the action was not based on fraud.[142]

Accordingly, it was only if fraud was an essential element of the Claimant's claim that, what is now, section 32(1)(a) could be relied upon. However, by

---

[141] Denning J's view was that there would be no fraud for the purposes of the Act where the Defendant honestly believed that the Claimant consented to the disposal of the goods or, if it honestly believed that, had she been informed, she would have so consented.
[142] [1949] 1 KB 550, 558 (CA).

contrast with the decision of the trial judge, the Court was of the view that there had been a deliberate concealment and, accordingly, the Claimant's appeal was allowed. In *Regent Leisuretime v Natwest Bank Plc*[143] it was (unsurprisingly) held by the Court of Appeal that an action framed in fraudulent misrepresentation was based on fraud for the purposes of section 32 of the 1980 Act.[144]

1.065 Section 32(1)(b) of the 1980 Act refers to deliberate concealment, whereas its forerunner contained the wording, "*where ... (b) the right of action is concealed by the fraud of any other person.*"[145] It has been pointed out that the judicial interpretation of these words in the earlier statute was often so wide that, by the time that the requirement for a fraudulent concealment was dropped (with the enactment of the 1980 Act), the fraud element was, effectively, redundant.[146] Indeed, in *Beaman v ARTS Limited* which is discussed above, the Court of Appeal was quite able to support the trial judge's finding that there was no fraud sufficient to support reliance on what is now section 32(1)(a) while at the same time finding that there had been a fraudulent concealment.

1.066 Some useful observations about the ambit of section 32(1)(b) were provided by the Court of Appeal in *Williams v Fanshaw Porter & Hazelhurst (a firm)*.[147] This case concerned a clinical negligence action conducted, on the Claimant's behalf, by the Defendant firm of solicitors. In August 1994, after the commencement of proceedings, the claim was compromised by the Defendant on the Claimant's behalf, although no instructions had been obtained from the Claimant to do so and the Claimant was unaware that this had been done. Later the same year the Defendant made an application in an unsuccessful attempt to remedy the situation, but again without informing the Claimant or obtaining her instructions. In July 1995 the Defendant informed the Claimant about what had happened, but delayed a further year before advising her to seek independent legal advice (by which time a second action had been commenced and struck out with the striking out order being upheld on appeal). The Claimant did not bring proceedings against the Defendant until December 2000. The Defendant sought to have the proceedings struck out on the basis that more than six years had passed since the original proceedings were compromised. It was held on appeal that the Claimant was entitled to rely on section 32(1)(b). Notwithstanding the fact

---

[143] [2003] EWCA Civ 391.
[144] See also, *GL Baker Ltd v Medway Building and Supplies Ltd* [1958] 1 WLR 1216 (QBD) which involved a fraudulent transfer of money from the Claimant company to the Defendant.
[145] Limitation Act 1939, s 26(1)(b).
[146] A McGee, *Limitation Periods* (4th ed, 2002), para 20.009.
[147] [2004] 1 WLR 3185 (CA).

that the Defendant had concealed the existence of the compromise until 1995 in an effort to spare itself embarrassment (and in the mistaken belief that it could remedy its error) rather than to conceal a cause of action against it, the Claimant was entitled to the protection of section 32(1)(b). The Court of Appeal provided the following précis of the application of the subsection:

- The entire cause of action did not have to be concealed in order for the Claimant to rely on section 32(1)(b), it was sufficient for the Defendant to conceal a fact relevant to the cause of action.

- The Defendant did not have to know that the fact which was concealed was relevant to the case of action, although this would usually be the case.

- It was sufficient for any relevant fact to be concealed, it was not necessary for the Defendant to conceal all of the facts relevant to the cause of action.

- Deliberate concealment required a conscious concealment.[148]

1.067 *Williams* v *Fanshaw Porter & Hazelhurst (a firm)* is also authority for the proposition that the operation of the ordinary six-year limitation period may be postponed by reason of the Defendant's deliberate concealment even if the cause of action accrued before the Defendant deliberately concealed a relevant fact from the Claimant. *Sheldon* v *RHM Outhwaite (Underwriting Agencies) Ltd*,[149] a case decided in the House of Lords, also supports this proposition, although it has been the subject of academic criticism.[150]

1.068 In *Cia de Seguros Imperio* v *Heath (REBX) Limited*,[151] it was held that a fact would be relevant to a Claimant's cause of action for the purposes of section 32(1)(b) if it were capable of constituting or completing a cause of action, not all facts which are or prove to be significant in a merely evidential sense will be "*relevant*" for these purposes.

---

[148] The subsection has been interpreted as requiring an intentional, rather than mistaken concealment: see, *Brocklesby* v *Armitage & Guest* [2001] 1 WLR 598 (CA) and *Phillips-Higgins* v *Harper* [1954] QB 411 – the latter being a case decided, of course, under the 1939 Act.
[149] [1996] AC 102.
[150] A McGee, *Limitation Periods* (4th ed, 2002), para 20.024.
[151] [1999] 1 All ER (Comm) 750 (QBD). See also, *Johnson* v *Chief Constable of Surrey* (1992) *The Times*, November 23 (CA) in which relevance in this context was treated as meaning a fact which, if not proved, would leave the cause of action incomplete.

1.069 There is a partial definition of "*deliberate concealment*" which is provided by section 32(2). This provides as follows,

> For the purposes of subsection (1) above, deliberate commission of a breach of duty in circumstances in which it is unlikely to be discovered for some time amounts to deliberate concealment of the facts involved in that breach of duty.

1.070 In *Cave* v *Robinson Jarvis and Rolf (a firm)*,[152] the House of Lords considered the meaning of section 32(2). Lord Scott made it clear that section 32(2) provided an alternative route by which the Claimant could obtain the protection of section 32(1)(b). For the purposes of section 32(2) the focus was upon the commission of the breach of duty, as opposed to the concealed facts themselves. The Claimant could invoke section 32(2) to bring his case within section 32(1)(b) where (1) he could prove that the Defendant knew he was committing a breach of duty or intended to commit a breach of duty and (2) where the circumstances[153] were such that the breach of duty was unlikely to be discovered for some time.

---

[152] [2003] 1 AC 384.
[153] Judged objectively, rather than by reference to the Defendant's belief: *Brown* v *Bird & Lovibond* [2002] EWHC 719 (QBD).

Chapter 2

INSURANCE: DISCLOSURE AND FRAUDULENT CLAIMS

1. INTRODUCTION

2.001 A number of the themes discussed below will be familiar from the preceding chapter and its discussion of the tort of deceit. However, insurance fraud deserves specific treatment for two reasons. First, because it differs from common law contract in that there is a mutual duty, imposed on both insurer and insured prior to the conclusion of the insurance contract, to disclose every fact which is material to the insured risk.[1] This is generally referred to as a component (the key component) of the duty of utmost good faith.[2] It extends not only to fraudulent non-disclosure, but also to the more common phenomenon of inadvertent or innocent non-disclosure (whether negligent or otherwise).[3] In order to understand the manner in which fraudulent insurance claims are dealt with by the courts it is necessary to map the boundaries of the duty to disclose. The second reason for dealing specifically with insurance fraud is that the context in which the duty of good faith operates – particularly with respect to disclosure – is heavily circumscribed by statute. The Marine Insurance Act 1906 which has been held to apply to non-marine as well as marine insurance claims has been described as "*codifying*" the common law of insurance.[4]

2.002 The present judicial and textbook trend is to treat disclosure and fraudulent claims separately and I propose to follow the same course (although there are a number of areas of overlap). In broad terms, the first section below deals with the duty of utmost good faith in its application to the period before the contract is concluded and the consequences of a breach of the duty. The second section deals with the presentation of a claim which

---

[1] See, D Friedmann, "*Contract Law and the Law of Insurance*" (2004) 120 LQR 407.
[2] The doctrine of *uberimmae fidei*.
[3] The intention of Lord Mansfield CJ who is generally credited, in *Carter v Boehm* (1766) 3 Burr 1905, with the creation of the duty of utmost good faith (although he did not refer to it as such) was to create a duty applicable to all categories of contract. However, this ambition was unrealised: see, Lord Atkin in *Bell v Lever Bros* [1932] AC 161, 227 (HL).
[4] J Birds and N Hird, *Birds' Modern Insurance Law* (6th ed, 2004), p 127.

is fraudulent in the context of a concluded policy and the impact that such conduct has both on the claim and on the policy as a whole.

2. DISCLOSURE

Utmost good faith: section 17 of the Marine Insurance Act

2.003 As I have indicated, the common law has, to a large extent, been codified in this area by the Marine Insurance Act 1906 which has been held to apply, in the context of disclosure and representations, both to marine and non-marine policies.[5] The doctrine of utmost good faith is given statutory recognition by section 17 of the 1906 Act which provides:

> A contract of marine insurance is a contract based upon the utmost good faith and, if the utmost good faith be not observed by either party, the contract may be avoided by the other party.

2.004 The mutual nature of the obligation should be noted. The origins of the duty recognised in section 17 pre-date the statute and are generally regarded as deriving from the judgment of Lord Mansfield CJ in *Carter* v *Boehm*.[6] The facts concerned a policy taken out by the then Governor of Sumatra against the risk of an attack by the French on a defensive fortification. The French attacked and a claim on the policy was rejected on the grounds that the insured had failed to disclose how vulnerable the fort was to a (likely) French assault. Lord Mansfield CJ characterised the duty as requiring an answer to the question,

> ...whether there was, under all the circumstances at the time the policy was underwritten, a fair representation; or a concealment; fraudulent, if designed; or, though not designed, varying materially the object of the policy, and changing the risqué understood to be run?"[7]

The stated reasons for the rule were: (a) (in a general policy sense) that it prevented fraud and encouraged good faith; and, (b) that insurance was a "*contract upon speculation*" in which special knowledge as to facts affecting the insured contingency was held only by the insured; a duty of good faith

---

[5] See, among other cases, *PCW Syndicates* v *PCW Reinsurers* [1996] 1 WLR 1136 (CA) and *Manifest Shipping Co Ltd* v *Uni-Polaris Insurance Co Ltd*, "*The Star Sea*" [2003] 1 AC 469, 493F *per* Lord Hobhouse (HL).
[6] (1766) 3 Burr 1905.
[7] At p 1911.

was needed to protect the trust of the underwriter.[8] The insured succeeded in *Carter* v *Boehm*. It was held that the underwriter was aware that the insurance was for the Governor of Sumatra, was aware that the Governor could not (consistent with his duties) disclose the state of the defences at the Fort and also knew that, by reason of his insuring the risk, the Governor anticipated an attack. In the circumstances, the facts affecting the risk insured against were known to the insurer and were not "*within the private knowledge of the governor only*".

2.005 There has been a good deal of academic and judicial discussion about the source of the duty of good faith and how it is best characterised. This discussion is carefully summarised in *Insurance Law: Doctrines and Principles*[9] in which the authors indicate that discussion has focused on whether the duty of good faith is best characterised as an implied term of the insurance contract itself or whether, alternatively, it should be regarded as arising out of a fiduciary relationship between the parties or, in the further alternative, as a duty in tort. In *March Cabaret Club & Casino Limited* v *London Assurance*[10] May J expressed doubt that the duty of utmost good faith had any contractual foundation given that the Marine Insurance Act 1906 appears to treat the duty to disclose as operating outside the contractual framework. In *Banque Keyser Ullmann SA* v *Skandia (UK) Insurance Limited*[11] Slade LJ, in the course of his judgment, declined the opportunity to create a novel tort based on breach of the duty to disclose. The authors of *Insurance Law: Doctrines and Principles* conclude that,

> The solution may well lie in holding that the respective parties to an insurance contract are so-called 'fact-based' fiduciaries whereby the fiduciary duties arise not by virtue of the particular status of the individual concerned (as with, for example, company directors, and trustees) but out of the factual situation underlying the particular relationship.[12]

---

[8] Lord Mansfield CJ did make it clear, however, that the duty of good faith was mutual: "*Good faith forbids either party, by concealing what he privately knows, to draw the other into a bargain, from his ignorance of that fact, and his believing the contrary.*" At p 1909. Thus, "*not actual fraud as known to the common law but a form of mistake of which the other party was not allowed to take advantage.*" Per Lord Hobhouse in *The Star Sea* [2003] 1 AC 469, 492 (HL).
[9] J Lowry and P Rawlings, *Insurance Law: Doctrines and Principles* (2nd ed, 2005), p 80. The authors comment that this issue is of considerable potential practical importance in that it may, for example, impact on questions of limitation and remedy.
[10] [1975] 1 Ll Rep 169.
[11] [1990] 1 QB 665 (CA).
[12] J Lowry and P Rawlings, *Insurance Law: Doctrines and Principles* (2nd ed, 2005), p 80.

What should be disclosed by the insured? Section 18 of the Marine Insurance Act

2.006 The Act provides, at section 18(1), as follows (under the heading, "*Disclosure by assured*"):

> ... the assured must disclose to the insurer, before the contract is concluded, every material circumstance which is known to the assured, and the assured is deemed to know every circumstance which, in the ordinary course of business, ought to be known by him. If the assured fails to make such disclosure, the insurer may avoid the contract.

2.007 Accordingly, the key to unlocking disclosure is materiality which is separately discussed below. The insured's duty to disclose "*every material circumstance*" extends only to the facts which he knows, although this is subject to the caveat that he will be deemed to know every circumstance which, in the ordinary course of business, he ought to know. Insurance law textbooks tend to cite the well-known proposition that "*you cannot disclose what you do not know*"[13] which has found like expression in a number of the reported cases, although the absolute nature of this proposition is, of course, substantially qualified by the deeming provision/caveat in section 18(1). The wording of the caveat is important: it extends only to that which ought to be known in the "*ordinary course of business*" and, therefore, imposes no duty on the insured to undertake inquiries beyond the call of his ordinary business affairs. For example, if an insured is ignorant of a material circumstance because the same has been concealed by his agent's fraud then the insured will not be deemed to know of it.[14] In circumstances where the insured is not in business and where there is no question of agency, he will not be tainted with constructive knowledge of the value of insured goods if he could only have discovered the value by the instruction of experts.[15] The insured is not, in general, under any positive duty to identify the full and accurate position in order to comply with his duty to disclose.

2.008 Section 18(3) of the Act goes on to list those circumstances which, in the absence of enquiry, need not be disclosed (which is to say that the following facts and matters[16] do not need to be disclosed, unless the insured is expressly questioned about them by the insurer):

---

[13] See, e.g. R Merkin, *Colinvaux's Law of Insurance* (8th ed, 2006), para 6-06 and J Lowry and P Rawlings, *Insurance Law: Doctrines and Principles* (2nd ed, 2005), p 81.

[14] *PCW Syndicates* v *PCW Reinsurers* [1996] 1 WLR 1136 (CA).

[15] See *Economides* v *Commercial Union Assurance Plc* [1998] QB 587 (CA).

[16] Marine Insurance At 1906, s 18(4) defines circumstance to include, "*any communication made to, or information received by, the assured.*"

... (a) any circumstance which diminishes the risk; (b) any circumstance which is known or presumed to be known to the insurer. The insurer is presumed to know matters of common notoriety or knowledge, and matters which an insurer in the ordinary course of his business, as such, ought to know; (c) any circumstance as to which information is waived by the insurer; (d) any circumstance which it is superfluous to disclose by reason of any express or implied warranty.

2.009 The principle to which section 18(3)(a) refers found early expression in the course of Lord Mansfield CJ's judgment in *Carter* v *Boehm* where he stated expressly that,

> The underwriter needs not be told what lessens the risqué agreed and understood to be run by the express terms of the policy.[17]

Notwithstanding the likely materiality of such facts, the insurer's interests are not adversely affected by the non-disclosure and, therefore, the relevant circumstances need not be disclosed. Thus, for example, the fitting of additional and enhanced security systems at the premises where the insured item is to be stored or its storage at an alternative, more secure, site need not be disclosed to the insurer.

2.010 Section 18(3)(b) deals with "*any circumstance which is known or presumed to be known to the insurer.*" There are a number of matters which the courts, guided (insofar as the modern authorities are concerned) by section 18(3)(b), have held that an insurer ought to know about, even if there was no actual knowledge:

- "*matters of common notoriety or knowledge*" – *Carter* v *Boehm* provides an example of this where it was held that the conduct of the war, the movements and likely movements of the French navy and the general state of affairs in the East Indies were either within the general public domain or were matters within the particular knowledge of the underwriter;

- the circumstances of the insurer's previous dealings with the insured – for example, claims previously made by the insured;[18]

- usages and business practices in the relevant trade.[19]

2.011 Waiver of the right to know is dealt with by section 18(3)(c) of the 1906 Act. It can arise in a number of different ways. First, it seems clear that an insurer can expressly waive his right to know, although there are some limits to this proposition. In *HIH Casualty and General Insurance Limited* v

---

[17] (1766) 3 Burr 1905, 1911.
[18] *Coronation Insurance* v *Taku Air Transport* (1992) 85 DLR (4th) 609.
[19] *Glencore International AG* v *Alpina Insurance Co Ltd* [2004] 1 Ll Rep 111.

Chase Manhattan Bank[20] the insured sought to rely on clauses in the contract of insurance which, it argued, disentitled the insurer to avoid the policy on grounds of their agent (the broker's) fraudulent non-disclosure; the argument was, essentially, that the insurer had, by reason of the clauses, expressly waived its right to disclosure. The question whether this was a tenable argument reached the House of Lords. The wording of the specific clauses appears in the speeches. Lord Bingham regarded the phrasing of the index clauses as, potentially, apt to cover a fraudulent non-disclosure. However, in common with both the judge at first instance and Rix LJ in the Court of Appeal he was not prepared to conclude that, insofar as the principal to the policy was concerned, an exclusion clause could override the necessity to disclose in circumstances where the failure to disclose was fraudulent. The reasons for this will be familiar from the discussion above with respect to the tort of deceit. "*Fraud*", stated Lord Bingham, "*unravels all*" and public policy did not permit a contracting party to exclude liability for his own fraud in the making of the contract. Lord Bingham did not express a concluded view as to whether the insured could, if not able to exclude his own fraudulent non-disclosure, do so with respect to his agent.[21] However, he stated that, if this were possible, then it had to be done in clear and unambiguous terms and he did not believe that the wording of the index clauses achieved this result in any event.[22]

2.012 While there is a presumption in favour of the insurer that the questions on a proposal form relate to material circumstances,[23] the insurer may be taken to have waived his right to disclosure by the manner in which the questions posed in the proposal form are drafted. In *Hair* v *Prudential Assurance Company*[24] Woolf J formulated the test as follows,

> ... if questions are asked on particular subjects and the answers to them are warranted, it may be inferred that the insurer has waived his right to information either on the same matters but outside the scope of the questions or on kindred matters to the subject-matter of the question.

It was emphasised that, in assessing whether there had been such waiver, it was necessary to arrive at a true construction of the proposal form and to ask,

---

[20] [2003] 2 Ll Rep 61 (HL).
[21] The tenor of his speech is such that he is clearly sceptical about whether this could be done.
[22] A number of different views were expressed by their Lordships about whether it was possible to exclude liability for the agent's fraudulent non-disclosure. The majority shared Lord Bingham's view that while this may be theoretically possible, the relevant clauses had not managed to do it. See, for commentary, K R Handley, "*Exclusion Clauses for Fraud*" (2003) 119 LQR 537.
[23] See, *Glicksman* v *Lancashire & General* [1927] AC 139, 144 *per* Lord Dunedin (HL).
[24] [1983] 2 Ll Rep 667.

> Would a reasonable man reading a proposal form be justified in thinking that the insurer had restricted his right to receive all material information and consented to the omission of the particular information in issue.

A *contra proferentum* approach to construction is appropriate.[25] Thus, in *Revell v London General Insurance Company Limited*,[26] the insurer's proposal form contained a number of questions about an insured's convictions for motoring offences. It was held that the narrow focus on these convictions meant that the insurer had waived any requirement for the insured to disclose convictions for non-motoring offences. This decision can be contrasted with *Schoolman v Hall*[27] in which the insured had a criminal record. The criminal record, which was not disclosed on the insurance proposal form, related to a period which pre-dated the completion of the proposal form by more than five years. The significance of this was that the form asked a series of what were described as trade questions and then, in respect of losses, asked,

> Have you ever sustained a loss or losses? If so, give a statement covering past five years with particulars, amounts claimed, and whether paid in full or otherwise.

It was argued for the insured that the fact, first, that the proposal form was confined to trade questions and, second, that the form contained a *"cut-off"* period of five years back from the date of its completion meant that the insurer had waived any right to disclosure of a criminal record in respect of activity more than five years prior to the completion date. The waiver argument was comprehensively rejected by the Court of Appeal. Cohen LJ stated,

> ... the questions in the proposal form are, in substance, confined to trade matters, and, like the learned Judge, I cannot spell out of it any waiver of the ordinary right of the intending insurer to the disclosure of material facts dealing with other matters which might influence the mind of the insurer in deciding whether or not to issue a policy.[28]

2.013 In addition to losing his rights by waiver an insurer can also be denied the right to avoid the contract by reason of its conduct after loss has been sustained: this is generally referred to as affirmation or estoppel. An affirmation of the insured's breach needs to be communicated by the insurer to the insured, but, by contrast with promissory estoppel, it is unnecessary to establish that the insured has relied, to his detriment, on the insurer's

---

[25] See, R Merkin, *Colinvaux's Law of Insurance* (8th ed, 2006), para 6-71.
[26] (1934) 50 Ll LR 114.
[27] [1951] 1 Ll Rep 139 (CA).
[28] At p 142. See also, in respect of waiver, the more recent case of *WISE Underwriting Agency Ltd v Grupo Nacional Provincial SA* [2004] Ll Rep IR 764 (CA).

representation. Affirmation and estoppel were both considered in detail in *Insurance Corporation of the Channel Islands* v *The Royal Hotel Limited*.[29] Mance J held that, in order for there to be an effective affirmation, the insurer had to have knowledge prior to an unequivocal election to affirm. In respect of the knowledge component of the test, the insurer had to have:

- actual knowledge of the facts giving rise to the right to avoid the contract; and,

- knowledge of the legal right to avoid the contract on the basis of those facts.

The requisite knowledge has to be coupled with an unequivocal communication to the insured of both the decision to affirm and an indication of its awareness of the facts upon which the decision to affirm is based.

2.014 Finally, there is a section 18(3)(d) of the 1906 Act which provides that the duty to disclose a circumstance that would otherwise be material does not arise where such disclosure would be "*superfluous ... by reason of any express or implied warranty*". The thinking behind this provision is, perhaps, obvious. If the insurer has seen fit to protect its position by the insertion of a warranty into the contract itself then the additional protection provided by the right to disclosure would be superfluous. It should be remembered that the provisions of section 18(3)(a)-(d), defining the circumstances which need not be disclosed, only arise "*in the absence of inquiry*". In the event that the insurer asks specific questions about a particular circumstance then the insured, bound by his duty to disclose with utmost good faith, is required to provide an honest answer.

Materiality and inducement

2.015 The duty to disclose does not exist in a vacuum. While section 18(3) of the Act provides, as we have seen, some specific guidance on what need not be disclosed (whether it is material or not), the insured is, in a more general sense, only required to disclose material circumstances. Again, the 1906 Act provides a steer on what is material at section 18(2):

> Every circumstance is material which would influence the judgment of a prudent insurer in fixing the premium, or determining whether he will take the risk.

Section 18(4) of the Act goes on to provide that:

---

[29] [1998] Ll Rep IR 151 (QB (Comm Ct)).

> Whether any particular circumstance, which is not disclosed, be material or not is, in each case, a question of fact.

Accordingly, it appears that:

> the test is an objective one based on the judgment of the prudent or reasonable insurer, rather than the judgment of a particular insurer;

the determination, against this objective marker, of whether an undisclosed circumstance is material is a question of fact.

2.016 In determining what is material the court may well receive the evidence of other underwriters as to their judgment about the materiality or otherwise of particular circumstances. Such evidence – tending to assist the court in its application of the prudent insurer test – is, of course, opinion evidence. It is, therefore, admissible only as expert evidence.[30]

2.017 After a long period of uncertainty the law in respect of materiality and inducement was clarified to a large extent by definitive (or, at least, near definitive) House of Lords authority: *Pan Atlantic Insurance Company Limited* v *Pine Top Insurance Company Limited*.[31] The issues before the House in this case concerned, first, whether, in order to satisfy the test of materiality, it had to be shown that full and accurate disclosure would have led the prudent insurer either to reject the risk altogether or to accept it on less onerous terms. Second, whether materiality was enough or whether, in addition, it had to be established that the non-disclosure had also induced the making of the policy on the relevant terms. The first of these tests was referred to in the course of the speeches delivered in the House as the "*decisive influence test* [of materiality]", the second was referred to as the "*actual inducement test.*" The arguments raised for decisive influence and actual inducement in the House of Lords were an attempt to whittle away the strong position that insurers had earned as a result of earlier authority like *Container Transport International Incorporated* v *Oceanus Mutual Underwriting Association (Bermuda) Limited*[32] and *Highlands Insurance Company* v *Continental Insurance Company*[33] in which it had been held: (1) that the insured was bound to disclose those facts that might have influenced the judgment of the insurer in deciding whether to accept the risk; and, (2) that it did not need to be proved that the influence which non-disclosure had on the judgment of the insurer was decisive in the sense that it induced the making of the policy. In *CTI* v *Oceanus* Kerr LJ held that the proper construction of "*judgment*", as used in section 18(2) of the Act, was

---

[30] See, *Reynolds* v *Phoenix Assurance Company Limited* [1978] 2 Ll Rep 440 (QBD).
[31] [1995] 1 AC 501 (HL).
[32] [1984] 1 Ll Rep 476 (CA).
[33] [1987] 1 Ll Rep 109 (QB (Comm Ct)).

synonymous with "*the formation of an opinion*" (a definition which he took from the Oxford English Dictionary). It was the insurer's judgment, in this sense, which required to have been influenced as Kerr LJ went on to state,

> The word 'influenced' means that the disclosure is one which would have had an impact on the formation of his opinion and on his decision-making process in relation to the matters covered by section 18(2).[34]

2.018 As I have indicated, this ground was fairly comprehensively covered again in *Pan Atlantic* when it reached the House of Lords. Their Lordships were divided on the decisive influence test of materiality; the leading speech for the majority was delivered by Lord Mustill (supported by Lords Slynn and Goff). Lord Mustill's speech commences, with respect to decisive influence, with some observations on the wording of section 18(2) itself. He noted that there had been concentration in argument on the use of the word "*would* [influence]", rather than a more contingent alternative like "*might* [influence]". However, his Lordship went on to state that it was a mistake to concentrate on this part of the statutory formula to the exclusion of what followed. The legislature had, Lord Mustill pointed out, declined to embellish the phrase "*influence the judgment of a prudent insurer*" with additions like "*decisively* [influence]" or "*conclusively* [influence]". It was his view that the expression used in section 18(2) of the Act connoted an influence on the thought processes of the insurer and this was inconsistent with a construction in which it would be necessary to establish that the insurer would have been influenced, in fact, to accept the risk. In rejecting the decisive influence test, Lord Mustill added the following,

> ... it is not the court after the event, but the prospective assured and his broker before the event, at whom the test is aimed; it is they who have to decide, before the underwriter has agreed to write the risk, what material they must disclose. I am bound to say that in all but the most obvious cases the 'decisive influence' test faces them with an almost impossible task. How can they tell whether the proper disclosure would turn the scale? By contrast, if all that they have to consider is whether the materials are such that a prudent underwriter would take them into account, the test is perfectly workable.[35]

Accordingly, a combination of statutory construction and pragmatism led the majority, like the Court of Appeal in *CTI* v *Oceanus*, to reject the decisive influence test.[36]

---

[34] [1984] 1 Ll Rep 476, 492 (CA).

[35] [1995] 1 AC 501, 531-532 (HL).

[36] Lord Lloyd dissented, at p 557, in respect of decisive influence. It was his view that the decisive influence test had, among other virtues, that of simplicity, "*The test should ... be clear and simple. A test which depends on what a prudent insurer would have done satisfies this requirement. But a test which depends, not on what a prudent insurer would have done, but on*

2.019 Lord Mustill went on to deal with the issue of actual inducement. If the insurance industry argument had prevailed on this issue as well then insurers would have retained the very strong position that they achieved after *CTI* v *Oceanus* and *Highlands Insurance Company*. The House of Lords was unanimous in rejecting the insurer's argument on this issue. Lord Mustill made it clear that he took the view that rejecting a need for actual inducement might, in the context of rules which were already "*stern enough*", be unjust and would enable the underwriter to escape liability even where he had suffered no harm.[37] The problem that their Lordships faced was the statutory language itself. The logic of the majority's position in respect of the decisive influence question was that there should be no unnecessary gloss on the statutory language. How could they justify, at the same time, adding a gloss to section 18(2) with a view to ensuring that there was an actual inducement criterion?[38] Lord Mustill started with causation. He appears to have regarded the actual inducement test as a variant of the "*but for*" test of causation familiar to tort lawyers. He moved on to state that in the general law it was beyond doubt that, even where fraudulent misrepresentation was concerned, it was necessary, as we have seen in the preceding chapter, for the representation to have induced the promisee to enter into the contract (although, he accepted that an evidential presumption of inducement made the promisee's task easier in this respect). Lord Mustill referred to the fact that the general law and the 1906 Act clearly treated contracts of insurance as falling into a special category for the reasons which are summarised above; however, he also took the view that these special considerations did not "*in logic or justice*" justify entitling the underwriter to avoid the contract when he had suffered no injustice as a result of the failure to disclose. The unanimous view of the Law Lords was that there should be an additional causative requirement inserted in section 18(2) of the Marine Insurance Act 1906 so that the material non-disclosure should actually have induced the insurer to enter into the contract or to fix the premiums or conditions before the same could justify avoidance of the contract. This requirement, while not justified by the strict wording of the relevant provisions of the 1906 Act, was needed in order to bring the position in line with the general law. Thus, Lord Mustill stated that an inducement was needed, "*using 'induced' in the sense in which it is used in the general law of contract.*"

---

what he wanted to know, or taken into account, in deciding what to do, involves an unnecessary step. It introduces a complication which is not only undesirable in itself but is also, in the case of inadvertent non-disclosure, capable of producing great injustice."

[37] Given that non-disclosure was, in a sizeable proportion of cases, the result of an inadvertent or innocent mistake.

[38] Lord Mustill conceded that there was no mention of the need for any connection between the wrongful dealing and the writing of the risk in sections 17, 18 and 20 of the Marine Insurance Act.

2.020 Following *Pan Atlantic* the position can be summarised as follows (adopting Lord Mustill's own description of what had been decided):

- a circumstance was capable of being material, in the sense used in section 18(2) of the Marine Insurance Act 1906, even though a full and accurate disclosure of it would not have affected the underwriter's decision whether to write the risk at the relevant premium; but,

- if the material non-disclosure did not in fact induce the entering of the contract then the underwriter was not entitled to rely on the same as a basis for avoiding the contract.

2.021 The incidence of the burden of proof with respect to materiality and inducement has been the subject of some academic comment and it has been suggested by one writer of authority that the evidential position may be such that it can be doubted whether *Pan Atlantic* has made any significant changes to the law in this area.[39] The argument runs like this. Lord Mustill clearly regarded there to be a presumption of inducement at work in the general law which had application to the actual inducement test with respect to insurance contracts.[40] If the burden is on the insurer to establish that the undisclosed circumstance is material then, at this point, it will be presumed that the failure to disclose induced the insurer to enter into the contract, unless the insured is able to discharge a burden on him to rebut the presumption. If this is the case then it may be doubted whether the harshness of the position before *Pan Atlantic*, to which Lord Mustill expressly referred, has been mitigated significantly or at all by the decision of the House of Lords. Subsequent case law suggests that the presumption is not available in circumstances where the underwriter is available to attend court, to give oral evidence and to be cross-examined; in these circumstances, the court has its own opportunity to assess whether the underwriter was actually induced by the material non-disclosure. Lord Mustill's presumption of inducement has been further called into question by the decision in *Assicurazioni Generali SpA v Arab Insurance Group (BSC)*[41] in which Clarke LJ indicated that it was his view that the presumption of inducement amounted to no more than the proposition that the evidence before the court might entitle it to infer that the insurer was, as a matter of fact, induced to enter into the contract. Beyond this, Clarke LJ stated,

> There is no presumption of law that an insurer or reinsurer is induced to enter in the contract by a material non-disclosure or misrepresentation...

---

[39] R Merkin, *Colinvaux's Law of Insurance* (8th ed, 2006), para 6-28.
[40] See the discussion in Chapter 1 dealing with the tort of deceit above.
[41] [2003] Ll Rep IR 131 (CA).

and the persuasive burden remained on the insurer's shoulders.[42] This case was decided at Court of Appeal level and seems some distance from what Lord Mustill had in mind in *Pan Atlantic* with respect to the presumption of inducement.

2.022 It was held by the Court of Appeal in *St Paul Fire & Mutual Insurance Company (UK) Limited* v *McConnell Dowell Contractors Limited*[43] that, in common with the position with respect to fraudulent misrepresentation (on which, see *Edgington* v *Fitzmaurice*[44] discussed above), it need not be shown that the material non-disclosure was the sole inducement to the underwriter in entering into the contract as long as it was an inducement. This proposition was affirmed in *Assicurazioni Generali SpA* to which I have already referred.

Moral hazard

2.023 As Lord Mustill indicated in *Pan Atlantic*, the prospective insured faces a daunting task in identifying what he does and does not have to disclose. Section 18(3) of the Marine Insurance Act 1906 provides, as we have already seen, at least some specific guidance. Equally, the test of materiality – albeit that this concentrates on the effect of non-disclosure on the thought process of a hypothetical prudent insurer – provides a further steer. However, the courts have, in a series of decisions, provided more specific guidance with respect to a number of specific categories of information. It is conventional to divide these categories by means of the following criteria:

- the criminal record, integrity and claims history of the prospective insured – collectively referred to as moral hazard;[45] and,

- "*circumstances involving ...* [the insured] *or his business or his property which reasonably suggest that the magnitude of the*

---

[42] At p 149.

[43] [1995] 2 Ll Rep 116 (CA).

[44] (1885) 29 ChD 459.

[45] This is elegantly summarised in R Merkin, *Colinvaux's Law of Insurance* (8th ed, 2006), para 6-44, citing *Locker & Wolf Limited* v *Western Australian Insurance Company* [1936] 1 KB 408, "*... a matter relates to the moral hazard if it affects the desirability of the assured as a person with whom the insurers would want to deal.*" *Colinvaux* provides other examples of moral hazard e.g. changes of name/concealment of identity, over-insurance with respect to the value of goods (where deliberate and intentional), existence of other insurance policies and "*tricky conduct*" on the part of the insured. The author also includes under-insurance (at para 6-56), although cites *Economides* v *Commercial Union Insurance Plc* [1998] QB 587 (CA) as authority against his proposition.

proposed risk may be greater than it would otherwise have been without such circumstances" – referred to as physical hazard.[46]

2.024 It should be remembered however that, as the Marine Insurance Act 1906 itself makes clear,[47] materiality is a question of fact to be determined (perhaps with the assistance of expert evidence) in each case; it is not possible to identify a set of closed categories in which a failure to disclose will lead to the avoidance of the contract.

2.025 Physical hazard is considered separately below. This section deals with moral hazard. A failure to disclose a past criminal record, even a fairly stale one, when applying for or renewing an insurance policy has been regarded by the courts as grounds for the insurer to avoid the contract.[48] However, there have been occasions when a court has been prepared to draw distinctions between criminal records that relate to different kinds of offending. In *Roselodge Limited* v *Castle*,[49] for example, the insured, a diamond merchant, took out an all risks policy. The insured did not disclose[50] that he had a criminal record, from the distant past, for bribing a police officer and, further, did not disclose that one of his employees had a conviction for an offence of diamond smuggling for which offence he had been released from prison only one year prior to his employment by the insured. The insured was aware of his employee's record at the time that he completed the proposal form; it was his evidence that he had employed him as a philanthropic gesture to assist in his rehabilitation. McNair J held that there was no duty to disclose the insured's past record for bribing a policeman. The judge rejected what he described as the "*extreme views*" expressed in cross-examination by the expert witnesses called by the insurer and found that the insured's conviction of an offence with no direct relation to diamond trading was not a material circumstance that would have influenced a prudent underwriter. After "*anxious consideration*" he found that the failure to disclose the employee's past record for diamond smuggling was a different matter. The reasonable man, the judge held, might well regard the employee as a potential security risk in the context of a diamond trading business (however impressed he might be by the insured's philanthropy) and there ought to be disclosure in order to afford the insurer the opportunity to take a view himself. The plea of non-disclosure was found proved.

---

[46] See, *Strive Shipping Corporation* v *Hellenic Mutual War Risks Association (Bermuda) Limited (The Grecia Express)* [2002] 2 Ll Rep 88, 131.

[47] Marine Insurance Act 1906, s 18(4).

[48] See, e.g. *Lambert* v *Co-operative Insurance Society Ltd* [1975] 2 Ll Rep 485 (CA) and *Schoolman* v *Hall* [1951] 1 Ll Rep 139 (CA).

[49] [1966] 2 Ll Rep 113 (QB (Comm Ct)).

[50] It is right to point out that the proposal form contained no questions about past convictions.

2.026 Some other examples of the disclosure of moral hazard in cases concerning past criminal activity are as follows:

- It has been held that a failure to disclose an arrest, charge and committal for a criminal offence prior to the renewal of a policy might justify avoidance of the same.[51]

- In the case of motor insurance, previous convictions for motoring offences should, of course, be disclosed.[52]

2.027 What is the position with respect to previous acquittals? In *The Grecia Express*[53] it was held by Colman J that where an insurer sought to avoid a contract on grounds of non-disclosure of moral hazard, the insured could rely on his acquittal as some, albeit not conclusive, evidence of his innocence. In the earlier case of *March Cabaret Club & Casino Ltd* v *London Assurance*[54] May J had held that previous acquittals need not be disclosed unless the insurer's evidence was that the acquittal, as well as being a material circumstance, was also wrong and could be proved (by the insurer) to be wrong. The safest approach may well be to disclose the acquittal. Colman J went on in *The Grecia Express* to state that the prospective insured need not disclose to the insurer,

> ...circumstances involving the proposer or his property or affairs which may to all outward appearances raise a suspicion that he has been involved in criminal activity or misconduct going to moral hazard but which he [the prospective insured] knows not to be the case.

The law draws a distinction, so Colman J held, between cases where a third party (generally, of course, the Crown) has made a specific allegation of criminal misconduct against a prospective insured and cases where there is suspicion which the insured knows to be unfounded. This distinction holds even though a person informed of the facts giving rise to the suspicion might take the view that they had a bearing on the honesty or integrity of the proposed insured. In *Brotherton* v *Aseguradoa Colseguros SA*[55] it was held that there was a further distinction to be drawn between "*mere 'loose' or 'idle' rumours*" concerning the honesty and/or integrity of the proposed insured which need not be disclosed and "*intelligence*" about the same which should be disclosed, even though it might later prove to be unfounded. This

---

[51] *March Cabaret Club & Casino Ltd* v *London Assurance* [1975] 1 Ll Rep 169 (QBD). See also, *Strive Shipping Corporation* v *Hellenic Mutual War Risks Association (Bermuda) Limited (The Grecia Express)* [2002] 2 Ll Rep 88 (QB (Comm Ct)).
[52] *Dunn* v *Ocean* (1933) 47 Ll LR 129 (CA).
[53] *Strive Shipping Corporation* v *Hellenic Mutual War Risks Association (Bermuda) Limited (The Grecia Express)* [2002] 2 Ll Rep 88 (QB (Comm Ct)).
[54] [1975] 1 Ll Rep 169 (QBD).
[55] [2003] EWCA Civ 705.

may be a difficult distinction for a proposed insured, exercising his judgment on the matter, to draw. Again, the sense of the judgment seems to militate in favour of disclosure. In *Brotherton* itself the information in question concerned reports in the media about the wrongdoing of an employee, in a senior position, of the insured bank. It was held that these reports should have been disclosed to the insurer. It should be noted that convictions which are "*spent*" within the meaning of the Rehabilitation of Offenders Act 1974 need not be disclosed.[56]

2.028 The second principal area of moral hazard comprises, as I have indicated, the previous claims history of the prospective insured. It is tolerably clear that a failure to disclose a previous refusal of insurance cover, particularly in the context of an inaccurate or evasive answer to a question about the same on the proposal form, may well be regarded as a material non-disclosure sufficient to justify avoidance of the contract:

- In *Glicksman* v *Lancashire and General Assurance Company Limited*[57] the prospective insured was asked, "*Has any company declined to accept or refused to renew your burglary insurance?*" The insured "*answered*" this by stating, "*Yorkshire* [an insurance company] *accepted, but proposers refused on account of fire proposal*". This answer was, treated generously, evasive because the insured had, in fact, previously proposed burglary insurance to a different insurer and had been turned down. The insured did not disclose this fact to the index insurer. It was held that this was a material non-disclosure[58] and that the insured's failure to disclose it meant that the policy was void.

- In *Locker and Woolf Limited* v *Western Australian Insurance Company Limited*[59] the insured gave a negative answer to the proposal form question: "*Has this or any other insurance of yours been declined by any other company?*" In fact, some two years prior to the index policy being taken out the insured had been refused motor insurance on grounds of non-disclosure and misrepresentation. Unsurprisingly, the insured's non-disclosure was

---

[56] See Rehabilitation of Offenders Act 1974, s 4(2) and 4(3). There is a residual and exceptional discretion, contained in s 7(3), to admit spent convictions. See *Reynolds* v *Phoenix* [1978] 2 Ll Rep 440 (QBD).

[57] [1927] AC 139 (HL).

[58] Or, at least, stated Viscount Dunedin, at p 144, "*the insurance company thought it was material*".

[59] [1936] 1 KB 408 (CA).

sufficient to justify avoidance of the contract, given that it was, "*…
a fact very material for the insurance company to know*".[60]

2.029 In addition to the claims history of the insured the insurer will,
obviously, want to know about the financial circumstances of the insured
(particularly, in circumstances where the insurance cover sought relates to
property).

Physical hazard

2.030 This can be dealt with more succinctly. The matters which may
increase "*the magnitude of the proposed risk*" whether by reference to the
insured himself, his business or the insured goods may be regarded as
reasonably obvious. Most proposal forms will contain a fairly comprehensive
list of what the insurer will wish to know; therefore:

- in the context of life insurance, the insurer will generally wish to
  know about the medical history of the proposed insured, his age and
  any potentially dangerous activities or past-times in which he
  participates (parasailing, bungee jumping, scaling Himalayan
  mountains and so forth);

- in respect of personal property insurance, the insurer will want to
  know where the property is stored and the security systems with
  respect to the same (if a car is insured, for example, is it parked on
  the street or in a garage).

2.031 There will, of course, be limits to what needs to be disclosed. It
would, for example, be absurd for the prospective insured seeking health or
life insurance to disclose the existence of every ordinary headache from
which he has ever suffered.[61] In *Cook* v *Financial Insurance Company
Limited*[62] the insured, an enthusiastic runner, collapsed while out running.
He attended his General Practitioner who found nothing sinister. The insured
later returned to see his GP complaining of breathlessness while he was
running. This time the GP referred him to a consultant in order that a
diagnosis of angina could be excluded. The day after this referral the insured
took out a disability insurance policy. He was later diagnosed with angina
and was constrained to give up work. The insured made a claim on the
policy and the insurer sought to decline cover. The insurer's refusal was
framed by reference to a clause in the contract which read as follows,

---

[60] *Per* Slesser LJ at p 414.
[61] An example used by Fletcher Moulton LJ in *Joel* v *Law Union & Crown Insurance Co* [1908]
2 KB 863.
[62] [1998] 1 WLR 1765 (HL).

No benefit will be payable for disability resulting from (a) any sickness, disease, condition or injury for which an insured person received advice, treatment or counselling from any registered medical practitioner during the 12 months preceding the commencement date.

It was held that there were two issues. First, did the insured in fact receive "*advice*" within the meaning of the exclusion clause prior to the commencement date of the policy (which was the day after the GP referral to a specialist to exclude a diagnosis for angina)? Second, was it sufficient for the exclusion clause that the Claimant received, in a general sense, "*advice, treatment or counselling*" for symptoms which subsequently were found to result from angina? In respect of the first question it was held that "*advice*" could not be given in circumstances where the registered medical practitioner had no knowledge about the disease for which the advice was given. As Lord Lloyd succinctly pointed out,

> A doctor does not give advice ... by saying, 'I do not know what is wrong with you; go and see another doctor'.[63]

In respect of the second question, it was held that the key word in the exclusion clause was "*condition*" which was construed as requiring, in most cases, something more than just, "*symptoms of a generalised kind which might indicate any number of different diseases, or none*". The index insured's position was analogous to that of the man who attended his GP while suffering from headaches and was prescribed a painkiller in circumstances where, some time later, he was found to have a brain tumour. Lord Lloyd believed that it could not be said that the brain tumour sufferer had received "*advice*" for that "*condition*" when he first visited his GP. In the circumstances the index insured was entitled to cover notwithstanding the exclusion clause.

Continuing duty to disclose

2.032 It is beyond doubt that the duty of disclosure, consistent with the duty of utmost good faith, continues until a binding contract of insurance is concluded between the parties:[64]

- where a material change of circumstances occurs between the proposal by the insured and its acceptance by the insurer then the same should be disclosed;

---

[63] At p 1770.
[64] See, among other cases, *Looker* v *Law Union and Rock Insurance Co Ltd* [1928] 1 KB 554 (KBD).

- in non-life insurance policies (for example, home contents or motor policies) the duty of disclosure will arise on each (annual) renewal; but;

- unless an express term of the insurance contract requires it, the insured is, in general, under no obligation to disclose any changes of circumstance, however material which occur during the currency of the insurance contract; and,

- a contractual right to cancellation by the insurer, contained in the written terms of cover, will not generally be regarded as imposing an implied continuing duty of disclosure on the insured.[65]

2.033 The extent to which the courts are resistant to the notion that there is a continuing duty to disclose during the currency of the agreement is illustrated by *Kausar* v *Eagle Star Insurance Company Limited.*[66] In this case the index policy contained a clause which read as follows, " *You must tell us of any change of circumstances after the start of the insurance which increases the risk of injury or damage*". Saville LJ took the view that this clause simply expressed the general common law position; namely, that the policy would not continue to provide cover where the change of circumstances was such that the new situation was "*something which, on the true construction of the policy...* [the insurers] *had not agreed to cover*".[67] Absent this rather unusual situation, a failure to disclose less significant changes of circumstances during the life of the policy did not amount to a failure to comply with the index clause.

2.034 There is a lively debate about whether the duty of utmost good faith continues, in a more general sense (for example, with respect to the making of claims) during the currency of the contract. It seems appropriate to leave the discussion about this topic to the section on fraudulent claims which follows below.

Consequences of non-disclosure

2.035 As we have seen, section 17 of the Marine Insurance Act 1906 provides that,

> ... if the utmost good faith be not observed by either party, the contract may be avoided by the other party.

---

[65] *New Hampshire Insurance Co* v *MGN Ltd* [1997] LRLR 24 (CA).
[66] [2000] Ll Rep 154 (CA).
[67] At p 159.

2.036 In the event of non-disclosure, whether on taking cover for the first time or on renewal of the same, the effect is that the contract of insurance is voidable at the instance of the party to whom disclosure is owed. The insurer is entitled, in the event of non-disclosure, to avoid the contract as section 17 makes clear. In general, on avoidance of the contract for non-disclosure, the premium is returned to the insured. However, section 84(3)(a) of the Marine Insurance Act 1906 contains special provision in this regard in cases of fraud or illegality. It provides:

> Where the policy is void, or is avoided by the insurer as from the commencement of the risk, the premium is returnable, provided that there has been no fraud or illegality on the part of the assured.

2.037 The insurer must seek to avoid the policy within a reasonable period of time after he has knowledge of the failure to disclose by the insured. It has been held that avoidance of the contract on grounds of non-disclosure is a self-help remedy which does not need the sanction of a court and is not qualified by any requirement of good faith; it should be treated as equivalent to rescission for misrepresentation and, therefore,

> The mere fact that a right to rescind has an equitable origin does not mean that its exercise is only possible if that is consistent with good faith or with a court's view of what is 'conscionable'.[68]

2.038 If the insurer seeks, without justification, to avoid the policy on grounds of material non-disclosure then that will generally amount to a repudiatory breach of contract which the insured can choose either to accept or to reject.

Agents: section 19 of the Marine Insurance Act

2.039 It is common for insurance contracts to be brokered by intermediaries (brokers, underwriting agents and so forth). A large gap would be left in the duty of utmost good faith if the insured were required to disclose material circumstances where the agent had no similar duty (especially in the light of the fact that there may well be facts known to the agent, for example the refusal of a previous proposal, that may not be known by the insured). Section 19 of the Act is aimed at this mischief and provides as follows:

> …[subject to matters which need not be disclosed, as set out in section 18(3) of the 1906 Act, considered above] … where insurance is effected for the assured by an agent, the agent must disclose to the insurer – (a) Every material circumstance which is known to himself, and an agent to insure is deemed to know every circumstance which in the ordinary course of business ought to be known by, or to have been communicated to, him; and

---

[68] *Per* Mance LJ in *Brotherton v Aseguradoa Colseguros SA* [2003] EWCA Civ 705.

(b) Every material circumstance which the assured is bound to disclose, unless it come to his knowledge too late to communicate it to the agent.

2.040 The first limb of section 19, in paragraph (a), requires the *"agent to insure"* to disclose material circumstances to the insurer, regardless of whether the prospective insured had knowledge of the material facts. Again, as with section 18(1), the duty to disclose extends not only to those facts which are known, but also to every circumstance, *"...which in the ordinary course of business ought to be known by, or to have been communicated to"* the agent.

2.041 There are some important limitations on the agent's paragraph (a) duty to disclose which were the subject of discussion in *PCW Syndicates* v *PCW Reinsurers.*[69] This case makes it clear that it is only the *"agent to insure"* who has a duty to disclose. If a prospective insured uses a number of different intermediaries to place a proposal for insurance then it is only the final link in the chain (the broker who places the order) who, as *"agent to insure"*, has the duty of disclosure. The duty does not extend to information as to material circumstances held by agents or intermediaries further up the chain, provided that this is not information of which the insured or agent to insure is aware. In addition, the duty to disclose only arises in the context of material circumstances which are, or ought to be, known by the agent in his capacity as agent. Accordingly, an agent's failure to disclose to the insured a fraud on his principal will not lead to the avoidance of the policy on grounds of non-disclosure (there is no relationship of agency where fraud is concerned and, as was observed in *PCW Syndicates* v *PCW Reinsurers*, it would be fanciful to expect an agent to disclose the fact of his own fraud on his principal).

Misrepresentation: fraud and section 20 of the Marine Insurance Act

2.042 Much of what follows involves concepts familiar from Chapter 1 above dealing with the tort of deceit and it is unnecessary to repeat the material in this section. There is, however, a good deal of statutory prescription with respect to misrepresentation in the context of insurance contracts. This appears in section 20 of the 1906 Act and it is necessary to set this out in full:

(1) Every material representation made by the assured or his agent to the insurer during the negotiations for the contract, and before the contract is concluded, must be true. If it be untrue the insurer may avoid the contract. (2) A representation is material which would influence the judgment of a prudent insurer in fixing the premium or determining whether he will take

---

[69] [1996] 1 Ll Rep 241 (CA).

the risk. (3) A representation may be either a representation as to a matter of fact, or as to a matter of expectation or belief. (4) A representation as to a matter of fact is true, if it be substantially correct, that is to say, if the difference between what is represented and what is actually correct would not be considered material by a prudent insurer. (5) A representation as to a matter of expectation or belief is true if made in good faith. (6) A representation may be withdrawn or corrected before the contract is concluded. (7) Whether a particular representation be material or not is, in each case, a question of fact.

2.043 The following observations can be made about section 20:

- It appears to apply regardless of whether the misrepresentation is innocent, negligent or fraudulent (although cf. *Economides* v *Commercial Union Assurance Company Plc*[70]).

- It applies during the period before the contract is concluded – once the contract is concluded then any subsequent misrepresentation will be ineffective.

- The test of materiality is taken from section 18 and is a question of fact in each case.

- A distinction is drawn by section 18(3) between representations of fact and representations of expectation or belief – both kinds of representation can justify avoidance of the contract.

- The remedy for misrepresentation is, in common with the remedy for non-disclosure, avoidance of the contract (cf. section 2(2) of the Misrepresentation Act 1967 which contains a power for the court to award damages as an alternative to rescission).

2.044 It has been observed by academic commentators that misrepresentation has a relatively narrow scope in the context of insurance contracts for the following reasons:

> ...because, first, insureds are under a positive duty to disclose material facts and so misrepresentation frequently becomes a question of non-disclosure; and, secondly, because of the 'basis of the contract clause', the insured's answers to questions in the proposal form are converted into contractual terms (warranties), thereby pre-empting the issue of misrepresentation arising.[71]

---

[70] [1998] QB 587 (CA).
[71] J Lowry and P Rawlings, *Insurance Law: Doctrines and Principles* (2nd ed, 2005), p 111.

2.045 Despite its necessarily narrow reach misrepresentation and section 20 of the 1906 Act were considered by the Court of Appeal in *Economides* v *Commercial Union Assurance Company Plc.*[72] The facts were as follows. The insured was an 18-year old student whose household contents were insured with the Defendant insurer. £12,000 worth of goods were insured and it was a term of the policy that the amount that could be recovered in respect of any valuables could not exceed one third of the total sum insured. The insured signed a declaration on the proposal form to the effect that the answers he gave to the questions asked were true to the best of his knowledge and belief. At that time the answers given with respect to the value of the items insured were true. A couple of years later the insured's parents moved in with him. His mother had a number of items of expensive jewellery. The insured was aware that his mother had the jewellery and had seen her wearing it from time to time, but had given it little thought. His father advised him that the sum insured on the household contents policy with the Defendant should be increased by around £3,000. In fact, the insured increased the amount of cover to £16,000. On the next renewal he again signed a declaration that the answers he gave to the questions asked were true to the best of his knowledge and belief. There was a burglary and property worth in excess of £30,000 was taken. Most of this was made up of the mother's jewellery and the value of the jewellery exceeded one third of the total value insured. The insurer sought to avoid the contract on grounds of non-disclosure and misrepresentation. Argument at first instance and in the Court of Appeal turned on whether, in order to satisfy the test in section 20(5) and so disentitle the insurer from avoiding the contract, the representation made by the insured simply needed to be made honestly or whether there needed also to be reasonable grounds for that honest belief (it had been held at first instance, as a matter of fact, that the insured had been honest). The Court of Appeal held that the insurer was not entitled to avoid the contract (Peter Gibson LJ and Sir Ian Glidewell appear to have taken the view that the insured had a reasonable basis for his honest belief and, therefore, on the facts there was no breach of duty). However, Simon Brown LJ considered whether it was necessary, in order to satisfy section 20(5), for the insured to have a reasonable basis for his belief. He concluded that this was not necessary and that, provided that the insured was not making a blind guess at valuation (a sort of wilful ignorance), the sole requirement was one of honesty. He summarised and approved the submissions made to him by counsel for the insured:

---

[72] [1998] QB 587 (CA).

> He [i.e. counsel for the insured] accepts, as inevitably he must, that the plaintiff had to have some basis for his statement of belief in this valuation; he could not simply make a blind guess: one cannot believe to be true that which one has not the least idea about. But, he submits, and this is the heart of the argument, the basis of belief does not have to be an objectively reasonable one. What the plaintiff's father told him here was a sufficient basis for his representation: he was under a duty of honesty, not a duty of care. In my judgment these submissions are well founded ...[73]

Insurer's duty

2.046 As indicated at the start of this chapter, the duty of utmost good faith is mutual. It is owed by both insurer and by insured. In *Carter v Boehm*[74] Lord Mansfield CJ stated that,

> Good faith forbids either party, by concealing what he privately knows, to draw the other into a bargain, from his ignorance of that fact, and his believing the contrary.

The reciprocal basis of the duty of utmost good faith and its corollary, the duty to disclose, is also recognised by section 17 of the Marine Insurance Act 1906.

2.047 In spite of this element of mutuality and the breadth of the insured's duty to disclose, the courts have, at least for the time being, confined the insurer's duty within narrow bounds. In *Banque Keyser Ullmann SA v Skandia (UK) Insurance Co Ltd*[75] Slade LJ directed, when the case was decided by the Court of Appeal,[76] that the remit of the insurer's duty,

> ...must at least extend to disclosing all facts known to him which are material either to the nature of the risk sought to be covered or the recoverability of a claim under the policy which a prudent assured would take into account in deciding whether or not to place the risk for which he seeks cover.[77]

When the case reached the House of Lords there was some support for this view (although the appeal was disposed of on other grounds).[78] In the course of his speech Lord Jauncey indicated that the test was whether the factual information held by the insurer materially increased or decreased the risk

---

[73] At p 598. See also, *Eagle Star Insurance Co Ltd v Games Video Co* [2004] Ll Rep IR 867, 885 *per* Simon J (QB (Comm Ct)).
[74] (1766) 3 Burr 1905.
[75] [1990] 1 QB 665 (CA).
[76] A decision described by one Court of Appeal Judge, albeit extra-judicially, as "*timorous*": Sir Andrew Longmore, "*Good Faith and Breach of Warranty: Are we Moving Forwards or Backwards?*" [2004] LMCLQ 158, 165.
[77] [1990] 1 QB 665, 772 (CA).
[78] [1991] 2 AC 249 (HL).

which was insured; the suggestion was that if the information did neither then there was no duty to disclose. It was made clear that the insured's remedy for non-disclosure by the insurer was rescission; that is, to the return of the premium paid, rather than the more generous remedy of damages.

2.048 The narrow scope of the insurer's duty to disclose and the limited range of remedies available in the event of breach of duty have since been confirmed by the Court of Appeal.[79]

3. FRAUDULENT CLAIMS

What is insurance fraud?

2.049 There is, in one sense, an easy answer to this question. Chapter 1 dealt with the tort of deceit and its proper boundaries and, "*... as regards insurance claims, fraud appears to be common law fraud*".[80] In other words,

> A claim can only be fraudulent if the assured is dishonest or at the very least culpably reckless. Mere negligence on the part of the assured will not suffice...[81]

(the description of fraud which is set out above is not repeated here). Unsurprisingly, however, the case law would suggest that it is more complicated than that. First, it is common to find a clause in the insurance policy itself which provides for certain prescribed results (generally that the policy is rendered void and all benefits are forfeit) in the event that a fraudulent claim is pursued. The policy condition, often referred to as a forfeiture clause, may contain a definition of fraud. Alternatively, an implied definition of what constitutes fraud in this context may be discernible from the construction of the policy as a whole. In addition, the common law has evolved rules by which fraudulent claims are identified (often by category) and then dealt with. As Mance LJ indicated in *The Aegeon* these common law rules might or, might not, coincide with the definition of fraud in a forfeiture clause of the policy.[82] It is, therefore, often necessary to specify what is meant by the rather loose term, "*insurance fraud*". Does this mean,

---

[79] See, *Aldrich* v *Norwich Union Life Assurance Co Ltd* [2000] Ll Rep IR 1.
[80] M Clarke, "*Lies, Damned Lies, and Insurance Claims: the Elements and Effects of Fraud*" (2000) NZLR 233, 237.
[81] R Merkin, *Colinvaux's Law of Insurance* (8th ed, 2006), para 9-20.
[82] [2002] Ll Rep IR 573, 579 (CA), his Lordship indicates that fraud in the policy condition might, for example, be limited to a fraud in the formal presentation of the claim.

for example, that the insured has simply submitted a claim when he has suffered no loss at all or is it capable of embracing also the situation where the insured has exaggerated the extent of his loss or where he has deployed fraudulent means to gild a genuine claim? These and other issues were the subject of consideration by the Court of Appeal in *Agapitos* v *Agnew, "The Aegeon"*[83] which is discussed separately below.

2.050 *The Aegeon* was decided relatively recently. There is, however, nothing novel about the common law's anxiety about what constitutes a fraudulent claim. In the course of his judgment in *The Aegeon*,[84] Mance LJ set out a large passage from the summing up to the jury of Willes J in the mid-nineteenth century case: *Britton* v *The Royal Insurance Company* (a case heard in the Maidstone Civil Court during the Kent Summer Assizes).[85] *Britton* concerned a fire insurance policy taken out by a Chatham clothier. He made a claim for indemnity under the policy in respect of losses suffered after a fire at the house where his stock was stored. The insurer became aware that the insured had changed his name prior to the taking out of the index policy and had also made two previous claims in respect of losses allegedly sustained after fires. On the basis of the suspicions raised by this information the insurer refused indemnity on grounds of fraud. There was an issue about whether the index fire was started by the insured himself: arson in these circumstances would clearly amount to fraud and would prevent recovery. A more interesting conceptual issue was whether an exaggerated claim might also justify avoidance of the policy on the ground of fraud.

In respect of this Willes J directed the jury in the following terms (in the course of his summing-up which was cited in *The Aegeon*. It is worth setting it out in full because it touches on a number of issues which are the subject of discussion in this section):

> ... suppose the insured made a claim for twice the amount insured and lost, thus seeking to put the office off its guard, and in the result to recover more than he is entitled to, that would be a wilful fraud, and the consequence is that he could not recover anything. This is a defence quite different from that of wilful arson. It gives the go-bye to the origin of the fire, and it amounts to this – that the assured took advantage of the fire to make a fraudulent claim. The law upon such a case is in accordance with justice, and also with sound policy. The law is, that a person who has made such a fraudulent claim could not be permitted to recover at all. The contract of insurance is one of perfect good faith on both sides, and it is most important that such good faith should be maintained. It is the common practice to insert in fire policies conditions that they shall be void in the event of a

---

[83] [2003] QB 556 (CA).
[84] At p 563D–G.
[85] (1866) 4 F & F 905; 176 ER 843.

fraudulent claim; and there was such a policy in the present case. Such a condition is only in accordance with legal principle and sound policy. It would be most dangerous to permit parties to practise such frauds, and then, notwithstanding their falsehood and fraud, to recover the real value of the goods consumed. And if there is wilful falsehood and fraud in the claim, the insured forfeits all claim whatever upon the policy.[86]

2.051 Following this direction the jury found for the insurer on the plea of fraud. Fraud was established on the basis that the insured had been guilty of wilful fraud in the exaggeration of his claim; the "*use*" of the fire to make a fraudulent claim. As will be clear, in 1866 Willes J took the view that insurance fraud was a relatively straightforward matter. It clearly embraced exaggerated claims and the reason it did so was because the duty of utmost good faith survived the conclusion of the contract and equally applied to the making of a claim. In addition, and by contrast with the more qualified views expressed by Mance LJ in *The Aegeon*, the policy conditions dealing with fraud were simply an expression of the common law position (treated as though they were synonymous with it).

2.052 For these and other reasons it is necessary to deal discretely with fraudulent insurance claims. Notwithstanding the views of Willes J in *Britton*, it remains a little unclear, and certainly controversial, whether there is a continuing duty of utmost good faith and, more importantly (if there is), where and how it applies. What is the position with respect to the submission of claims by the insured, are these considered within the duty of utmost good faith and section 17 of the Marine Insurance Act 1906? The treatment which follows picks up on the discussion of the duty of utmost good faith which is set out above. In addition, the different categories of fraudulent, or potentially fraudulent, insurance claims justify dealing with this topic separately.

A continuing duty of utmost good faith?

2.053 As we have seen, section 17 of the Marine Insurance Act 1906 is a little opaque in relation to this issue.[87] The duty does not appear to be limited to the period before the contract itself is concluded and is certainly not expressly limited in this way (section 17: "*A contract of marine insurance is a contract based upon the utmost good faith and, if the utmost good faith be not observed by either party, the contract may be avoided by the other party*"). In some respects it may not matter very much, except in an academic sense, what the position is with respect to the post-contractual

---

[86] At p 909.
[87] See *The Star Sea* [2003] 1 AC 469, 481F *per* Lord Clyde, "*What has caused me greater difficulty is the broad provision in section 17 which appears to be unlimited in scope.*"

period. Longmore LJ has argued, in an extra-judicial capacity, that the room within which a continuing duty of utmost good faith can operate is necessarily limited because variations to the risk, renewals of the risk and additions to the risk are accurately characterised as examples of new contracts to which pre-contractual duties of good faith will, in any event, apply.[88] He went on to observe that,

> The only post-inception situations where it is easy to see that either party to the contract may owe good faith obligations to the other are those in which information is exchanged or money is spent dealing with a claim made by or against the insured.[89]

Notwithstanding the confined scope of the post-contractual duty of good faith, it has exercised a powerful grip on the thinking of both academics and judges in cases decided at the highest level. It has remained unclear, until relatively recently, whether it applies to fraudulent claims which were discussed and defined in *The Aegeon* (a Court of Appeal case which is the subject of discussion below).[90]

2.054 A convenient entry point for the recent run of appellate decisions is *Orakpo v Barclays Insurance Services*.[91] In this case no less an authority than Hoffmann LJ had no doubt that the duty of utmost good faith endured beyond the conclusion of the contract. He put it like this:

> In principle insurance is a contract of good faith. I do not see why the duty of good faith on the part of the assured should expire when the contract has been made. The reasons for requiring good faith continue to exist. Just as the nature of the risk will usually be within the peculiar knowledge of the insured, so will the circumstances of the casualty; it will rarely be within the knowledge of the insurance company. I think that the insurance company should be able to trust the assured to put forward a claim in good faith. Any fraud in making the claim goes to the root of the contract and entitles the insurer to be discharged.[92]

2.055 In recent years, courts of authority have been far less confident about the potentially expansive reach of a continuing duty of good faith of the kind clearly contemplated by Hoffmann LJ. *Manifest Shipping Company Limited*

---

[88] Sir Andrew Longmore, "*Good Faith and Breach of Warranty: Are We Moving Forwards or Backwards?*" [2004] LMCLQ 158.
[89] At p 169.
[90] In a case decided just prior to *The Aegeon*, *Direct Line v Khan* [2002] Ll Rep IR 364, the Court of Appeal held, at p 371, that it was unnecessary to decide whether the index fraud was characterised as a breach of a continuing duty of utmost good faith which would justify avoidance of the contract *ab initio* or, alternatively, whether it should be dealt with under the fraudulent claims rule which might result in the less drastic remedy of forfeiture of the claim.
[91] [1995] LRLR 443 (CA).
[92] At p 451.

v *Uni-Polaris Shipping Company Limited, "The Star Sea"*[93] concerned a cargo ship which caught fire and, upon being towed to safe harbour, was discovered to be beyond economic repair. A claim was made on the insurance policy. The insurers resisted the claim on the basis that the ship had, with the knowledge of the insured, been put to sea in an unseaworthy condition. An additional argument was deployed by the insurer in seeking to avoid the contract; namely, that there had been a breach of a duty to give disclosure in accordance with a continuing requirement of utmost good faith which endured beyond the conclusion of the contract. The insurers based their argument on, among other sources of authority, section 17 of the 1906 Act. The insurers argued that the insured had failed to disclose with their claim expert reports concerning maintenance which suggested a fault with the vessel. The reports post-dated the entering into of the contract of insurance, but pre-dated the voyage during which the vessel caught fire and was damaged. When this issue reached the House of Lords there were some subtle differences between the three substantive speeches (of Lord Clyde, Lord Hobhouse and Lord Scott).

2.056 Lord Clyde made it clear that his sympathy lay with the view that the duty of utmost good faith did not survive beyond the pre-contractual stage; it was his view that a clue to the reach of section 17 could be obtained from the fact that the section appeared in a division of the Act which contained a group of statutory provisions dealing with pre-contractual disclosure and representation. However, in the light of authority, Lord Clyde expressed the view that limiting the scope of section 17 to the period ending with the conclusion of the contract was a solution which *"now appears to be past praying for."*[94] However, he did not go on to state that the continuing duty of utmost good faith mimicked in all or, indeed, in many, respects the pre-contractual duty. Lord Clyde's preferred approach was a *"flexible construction"* of the duty which did not, in contrast with the pre-contractual duty, require *"the highest degree of openness ... at the stage of a disputed claim."* Lord Clyde characterised the duty, at the stage of presenting the claim, as one of good faith and openness which could embrace a duty of disclosure and which would vary in content and substance *"according to the circumstances."*

2.057 Lord Hobhouse referred to the fact that Counsel had conceded in argument that the duty continued beyond the pre-contractual phase and that there was a weight of judicial and academic authority which supported the same proposition. However, he went on to express a number of doubts about the scope of a post-contractual duty of utmost good faith, particularly

---

[93] [2003] 1 AC 469 (HL).
[94] At p 482B.

in the context of the requirement of disclosure. First, the criterion for disclosure (a test of materiality) was much more problematic in the post-contractual than in the pre-contractual period. Second, a post-contractual right to disclosure by insured to insurer might provide the insurer with a mechanism for bad faith on its part which the law should, if at all possible, seek to avoid. Third, the only remedy for non-disclosure in breach of the duty of utmost good faith was avoidance of the policy. As we have seen, this is not an even-handed remedy because it would almost always be of more value to the insurer than to the insured in the event of a breach of duty (an insured would ordinarily be better served by a remedy in damages). Accordingly, Lord Hobhouse agreed with Lord Clyde that there were important differences in the duty of utmost good faith between its application to the pre- and post-contractual periods.

2.058 Lord Scott also agreed with this proposition. Having established, by reference to the authorities, that there was a difference in the content of the duty as it applied to the periods before and after the contract was concluded, he went on to consider what the content of the post-contractual duty was. Lord Scott concluded that the duty was one of honesty.[95] He made it clear that,

> The presentation of a dishonest or fraudulent claim constitutes a breach of duty that entitles the insurer to repudiate any liability for the claim and, prospectively at least, to avoid any liability under the policy.[96]

Lord Scott left open the question whether such dishonest conduct should have retrospective effect. He rejected the submission, for the insurers, that "*culpable non-disclosure*", short of dishonesty or fraud, should give rise to avoidance of the contract under section 17 of the 1906 Act.

2.059 Accordingly, it appears clear that there is a continuing duty of utmost good faith, although there was clearly some reluctance on the part of the Law Lords in *The Star Sea* to acknowledge its existence. However, it is equally clear from that case that the duty in its post-contractual setting has some significant differences from its sibling: the pre-contractual duty. It will not operate with the same vigour as the pre-contractual duty and, it appears tolerably clear, will require fraud on the part of the insured (ordinary negligence or inadvertence will not suffice to justify avoidance of the policy). It is also apparent from the majority decision in *The Star Sea* that, once the process of litigation has commenced, the ambit of the duty to disclose, as consistent with the duty of utmost good faith, is subsumed within and governed by the procedural rules on disclosure which are set out in the Civil

---

[95] At p 515C.
[96] At p 514H.

Procedure Rules; by this stage the duty of utmost good faith has, in the disclosure sense, no further part to play (a proposition approved, after commentary, by Mance LJ in *Agapitos* v *Agnew, The Aegeon*[97] – on which see below).

2.060 The continuing duty of utmost good faith is, in this context, a creature of the common law justified on policy grounds. What is the position with respect to forfeiture clauses contained within the insurance policy itself? Insurance contracts commonly contain a clause which imposes on the insured a duty not to make false/fraudulent claims and which also prescribes the consequences of breach: typically, avoidance of the contract and forfeiture of all benefits. In the light of the fact that such clauses are commonly found in insurance contracts it has been held that it is unnecessary to bring them to the specific notice of the prospective insured at the time that the contract is made in order for them to take effect (a general reference to terms and conditions in a proposal form will be sufficient to incorporate a forfeiture clause).[98] A typical forfeiture clause is that which was found in the insurance contract in *K/S Merc-scandia XXXXII* v *Certain Lloyd's Underwriters & Others, The Mercandian Continent.*[99] This clause, derived from the first page of the *pro forma* Lloyds J Form, read as follows,

> If the assured shall make any claim knowing the same to be false and fraudulent, as regards amount or otherwise, the policy shall become void and all claims hereunder shall be forfeited.[100]

Are such clauses necessary? Is it not, in any event, the position at common law that a fraudulent claim will result in the avoidance of the contract?

2.061 In *The Star Sea* Lord Hobhouse dealt with the status of the post-contractual duty of utmost good faith. He said this:

> This result [viz. the refusal of indemnity with respect to the fraudulently presented claim] is not dependant upon the inclusion in the contract of a term having that effect or the type of insurance; it is the consequence of a rule of law. Just as the law will not allow an insured to commit a crime and then use it as a basis for recovering an indemnity ... so it will not allow an

---

[97] [2003] QB 556 (CA).
[98] *Nsubuga* v *Commercial Union Assurance Co Plc* [1998] 2 Ll Rep 682, 685 (QB (Comm Ct)) *per* Thomas J, " *The* [forfeiture] *clause in question is a very common type of clause to be found in fire insurance policies. Indeed that has been so for over 100 years ... As such it is a common term in a policy, there was no need for it to be brought specifically to the Plaintiff's attention.*"
[99] [2001] Ll Rep IR 802 (CA).
[100] The clause had no effect in *The Mercandian Continent* because a claim under the policy was pursued not by the insured, but by the victim of the insured's negligence pursuant to The Third Parties (Rights Against Insurers) Act 1930. The remedy under the Act could not be pursued until a judgment had been obtained against the insured and judgment post-dated the index fraudulent act of the insured by several years.

insured who has made a fraudulent claim to recover. The logic is simple.
The fraudulent insured must not be allowed to think: if the fraud is
successful, then I will gain; if it is unsuccessful, I will lose nothing.[101]

2.062 The proposition that forfeiture clauses are simply declaratory of the
general position at common law was confirmed by Longmore LJ in *The
Mercandian Continent.*[102] This case, decided by the Court of Appeal in 2001
(hot on the heels of *The Star Sea*), subjected the House of Lords decision and
the continuing duty of utmost good faith to further analysis. It continued a
trend, already evident in *The Star Sea*, of narrowing the space within which
the post-contractual duty of utmost good faith operates and the motivation
for this was to avoid the consequences of breach; namely, the blunt
instrument of rendering the contract void *ab initio* (as section 17 directs). In
The Mercandian Continent the insured company were ship repairers based in
Trinidad. There was a negligent repair of a ship and its owners commenced
proceedings in England against the insured company who, in turn, gave
notice of the claim to their insurers. The proceedings were commenced in
England as a result of a jurisdictional clause in an agreement between the
assistant general manager of the ship repair company insured and the owners
of the vessel. The insured company's directors forged a document which
purported to direct that the ship owners had agreed with the directors of the
insured that only the managing director of the insured, rather than the
assistant general manager, had any authority to deal with the claim (the
forged document was a misguided attempt to be helpful to the insurance
company – the forged document was not material because it had been
produced on the mistaken assumption that the liability position in the
Trinidadian jurisdiction would be more favourable to the insurer than the
position in England). The forgery was discovered and an application to
challenge English jurisdiction was abandoned; the case proceeded to trial in
England. However, the insurance company sought, prior to the trial, to avoid
the policy. There were clauses in the insurance policy contract which
required the provision of information and which directed that the making of
a false and fraudulent claim would result in the policy being void. The trial
was not defended and, on obtaining judgment, the ship owners (the insured
ship repairers having been wound up), stepped into the shoes of the insured
under the Third Parties (Rights Against Insurers) Act 1930. The issue was
whether the insurer was, by reason of the (immaterial) forgery, entitled to
avoid the policy and, therefore, defeat the third party claim on the grounds
of the insured's want of good faith.

---

[101] [2003] 1 AC 469, 499C-D.
[102] [2001] Ll Rep IR 802 (CA). See also, *Galloway* v *Guardian Royal Exchange (UK) Ltd* [1999]
Ll Rep IR 209, 211 *per* Lord Woolf MR (CA).

2.063 At first instance (before Aikens J) it was held that the duty of good faith did not apply post-contract unless (a) the insurer was being invited to renew his risk;[103] or (b) the insured was prosecuting or pursuing a claim on the policy. Given that neither of these situations was present, section 17 of the 1906 Act could not be relied on to justify avoidance of the contract. It was further held that the insured's fraud was not, in any event, material. In the Court of Appeal it was held that there was a continuing duty of utmost good faith, but that, as in *The Star Sea*, its operation was heavily circumscribed. Longmore LJ criticised the argument presented by the insurers which commenced with reliance on an extra-contractual duty of utmost good faith and only then went on to deal with the contractual position between the parties. Longmore LJ thought that the correct approach was the reverse of this. He went on to suggest that a strictly confined approach to the post-contractual duty of utmost good faith could be used as the means by which to align the contractual and extra-contractual position (insofar as both dealt with duties of disclosure or, as in *The Mercandian Continent* itself, an express contractual duty on the part of the insured to keep the insurer "*fully advised*"). Longmore LJ went on to observe that, while section 17 of the 1906 Act provided that the remedy for breach of the duty was avoidance of the contract, it did not identify the situations in which avoidance was appropriate. He went on to state as follows:

> It is, in my judgment, only appropriate to invoke the remedy of avoidance in a post-contractual context in situations analogous to situations where the insurer has a right to terminate for breach. For this purpose (A) the fraud must be material in the sense that the fraud would have an effect on underwriters' ultimate liability … and (B) the gravity of the fraud or its consequences must be such as would enable the underwriters, if they wished to do so, to terminate for breach of contract. Often these considerations will amount to the same thing; a materially fraudulent breach of good faith, once the contract has been made, will usually entitle the insurers to terminate the contract. Conversely, fraudulent conduct entitling insurers to bring the contract to an end could only be material fraud. It is in this way that the law of post-contract good faith can be aligned with the insurers' contractual remedies. The right to avoid the contract with retrospective effect is, therefore, only exercisable in circumstances where the innocent party would, in any event, be entitled to terminate the contract for breach.[104]

Longmore LJ supplemented this by giving an example of when the severely curtailed post-contractual duty of utmost good faith would operate: "*the*

---

[103] See the extra-judicial comments of Sir Andrew Longmore, set out above, about the limited area in which a post-contractual duty of utmost good faith can operate.

[104] [2001] Ll Rep IR 802, 818.

giving of information, pursuant to an express or implied obligation to do so in the contract of insurance." [105]

2.064 The position is, therefore, that the forfeiture clauses found in insurance contracts are simply declaratory of the position at common law. Within the context of the continuing duty of good faith there are, however, limits on the right to avoid the contract on grounds of fraud and the boundaries are set by *The Mercandian Continent* and a further case in the Court of Appeal, this time decided the following year (2002): *Agapitos* v *Agnew, The Aegeon.*[106] In *The Aegeon* it was again recognised that there was a post-contractual duty of utmost good faith, although, in common with the Law Lords in *The Star Sea*, Mance LJ was unenthusiastic about the application of section 17 of the Marine Insurance Act 1906 to a post-contractual setting. He felt that the manner in which the scope of the duty had been confined by Longmore LJ in *The Mercandian Continent* meant that it would only be in rare cases that the section 17 duty would have any relevance after the contract had been concluded. It was Mance LJ's view that the making of fraudulent claims (as defined and discussed below) should be governed by the common law or contractual stipulation and treated quite separately from section 17 and the duty of utmost good faith.[107] This would have the salutary effect of ensuring that no question of avoidance of the contract *ab initio* would arise. It has been commented that the further tightening of the scope of the duty of utmost good faith in a post-contractual setting which *The Aegeon* represents has "*reduced the possible range of application to a pale shadow*".[108] It may now apply only where the conditions described by Longmore LJ in *The Mercandian Continent* are satisfied and in respect of the giving of information pursuant to a contractual obligation to do so.[109] Given that section 17 will not now apply in the context of a fraudulent claim on the policy it is necessary to look to the common law to identify both what a fraudulent insurance claim is in this context and what the consequences of a fraudulent claim will be.

---

[105] At p 819.
[106] [2003] QB 556 (CA).
[107] At p 575B-C.
[108] H Yeo, "*Post-contractual Good Faith – Change in Judicial Attitude?*" (2003) 66 MLR 425, 438.
[109] Mance LJ's severing of any link between section 17 and fraudulent claims was "*warmly ... welcomed*" by Sir Andrew Longmore: "*Good Faith and Breach of Warranty: Are we Moving Forwards or Backwards?*" [2004] LMCLQ 158, 167.

Categories of fraudulent claim: The Aegeon

2.065 The facts of *The Aegeon* were as follows. A ferry, *The Aegeon*, was insured under a hull and machinery port risks policy. The policy contained a warranty against the carrying out of "*hot works*" on board the vessel unless the same were covered by certification from the London Salvage Association ("*LSA*"). On 19 February 1996 the vessel caught fire while undergoing hot works in a Greek harbour. *The Aegeon* sank. A claim was made by the insured on the policy and was, initially at least, rejected on grounds of breach of warranty; this related to certain minor repair matters (it had been understood by the insurer that the vessel had LSA cover at the time of the hot works). It subsequently transpired that significant hot work had been carried out in the period before LSA cover had been arranged. The insurer sought to capitalise on this discovery and to avoid the policy on grounds of fraud. They applied to amend their Defence in order to do so. This application was refused at first instance by Toulson J. The matter came before the Court of Appeal and Mance LJ delivered the leading judgment. A large part of the judgment is concerned with the task of identifying what a fraudulent insurance claim actually is. A number of different categories of fraudulent claim emerge from the judgment (I have used a shorthand to identify each category of fraudulent claim):

- a claim where the insured knows that he has not, in fact, suffered any loss ("**the no loss claim**");

- a claim where the insured knows that he has suffered a "*lesser loss*" than that which he has claimed or where he is reckless as to whether that is the case ("**the exaggerated claim**");

- a claim where a fraudulent device is used – where the insured believes that he has suffered the loss claimed, but seeks, by lying, to improve or to embellish the facts surrounding the claim ("**the fraudulent device claim**");

- a claim which is, when presented, honestly believed in, but which the insured discovers is exaggerated and yet decides to maintain ("**the late dishonesty claim**");

- a claim to which the insurer has a valid defence, which defence the insured deliberately suppresses ("**the suppressed defence claim**").

2.066 Notwithstanding the fact that the Court of Appeal in *The Aegeon* was, as we have already seen, keen to distinguish fraudulent claims from the duty of utmost good faith and section 17, there are some areas of overlap.

First, the fraudulent claims rule will, it seems, only apply until the commencement of litigation.[110] Second, the fraudulent claims rule expresses the established common law position and is not dependent for its application on an express term of the insurance policy.[111] In *Direct Line Insurance* v *Khan*[112] Arden LJ unsurprisingly rejected the (doomed) submission that the fraudulent claims rule was, in the context of consumer contracts, subject to the Unfair Terms in Consumer Contracts Regulations.[113]

2.067 It was held in *The Aegeon* that, in circumstances where the claim was fraudulent within one of the categories set out above, there was no need to establish that the insurer was actually misled or that he was induced to rely detrimentally on the same,

> The application of the [fraudulent claims] rule [and the consequences of the same] flows from the fact that a fraudulent claim of this nature has been made. Whether insurers are misled or not is ... beside the point.[114]

In the context of lies told as part of a fraudulent device claim, however, the lie should be relevant in the sense that, judged objectively, it tended to improve the insured's prospects of gaining a settlement or of winning at trial (on which, see the discussion below). While this seems tolerably clear, in *Interpart Comerciao E Gestoa SA* v *Lexington Insurance Company*[115] Judge Chambers QC declined to grant summary judgment in the context of a fraudulent devices claim on the basis (at least in part) that there remained questions as to the law about

> ...the degree of nexus that there has to be between the fraudulent conduct and promotion of the claim against insurers.[116]

2.068 One wonders whether similar doubts about the position in law would have been expressed if the issue had arisen at trial, rather than in the context of a summary judgment application. In a yet more recent case, it has been held, in the context of the fraudulent claims rule, that,

---

[110] See *Eagle Star Insurance Co Ltd* v *Games Video Co* [2004] Ll Rep IR 867, 889, para 150 *per* Simon J (QB (Comm Ct)).

[111] See, *Axa General Insurance Ltd* v *Gottlieb* [2005] Ll Rep IR 369, 377, para 27 *per* Mance LJ (CA). See also, the earlier case of *Galloway* v *Guardian Royal Exchange (UK) Ltd* [1999] Ll Rep IR 209, 211 *per* Lord Woolf MR (CA), although, in *Galloway*, the Court of Appeal took the view that the fraudulent claims rule emanated from the duty of utmost good faith.

[112] [2002] Ll Rep IR 364, 371-2 (CA).

[113] Unfair Terms in Consumer Contracts Regulations 1999 (SI 1999/2083). Arden LJ held that the fraudulent claims rule was a rule of law and, therefore, not subject to the 1999 Regulations.

[114] [2003] QB 556, 572 – a proposition which Mance LJ extended as much to fraudulent device claims as to no loss and exaggerated claims. Cf. *Pan Atlantic* [1995] 1 AC 501 (HL) which is considered above.

[115] [2004] Ll Rep IR 690 (QB (Comm Ct)).

[116] At p 695.

> The fraud must be material in that it must have a decisive effect on the readiness of the insurer to pay.[117]

The judge in this case appears, however, to have regarded this proposition as consistent with what Mance LJ stated in *The Aegeon* (which he cited in full, with approval).

Fraud and exaggeration

2.069 The exaggerated claim is, perhaps, the most common species of fraud in an insurance context. There has long been recognition that insureds find it difficult to resist the temptation to "*gild the lilly*" or "*stretch the truth a little*" when submitting a claim. I have deliberately used euphemisms in this context because the judiciary seem to find it extremely difficult to brand such conduct as dishonest or to recognise it as fraud. *Orakpo v Barclays Insurance Services*[118] concerned buildings insurance and, among other areas of alleged fraud, gross exaggeration of a claim based on dry rot, damage to furniture and the loss of rental income from certain let premises. In the course of his (partially dissenting) judgment Staughton LJ observed:

> Of course, some people put forward inflated claims for the purpose of negotiation, knowing that they will be cut down by an adjuster. If one examined a sample of insurance claims on household contents, I doubt if one would find many which stated the loss with absolute truth. From time to time claims are patently exaggerated; for example, by claiming the replacement cost of chattels, when only the depreciated value is insured. In such a case, it may perhaps be said that there is in truth no false representation, since the falsity of what is stated is readily apparent. I would not condone falsehood of any kind in an insurance claim. But in any event I consider that the gross exaggeration in this case went beyond what can be condoned or overlooked.[119]

2.070 It appears that exaggeration, provided that it is not substantial, will not be condoned, but may be overlooked, in the sense that it will not necessarily be branded as fraud (with all the consequences which flow from that). In this approach to exaggerated claims there is an echo of the latitude which is given to parties negotiating about the price of goods and the sums which they may be prepared to accept or reject in sale/purchase (considered in the discussion of the tort of deceit in the preceding chapter). The policy behind this rule is clear enough and was articulated in *Orakpo* itself; namely, that it is to be expected that there will be some exaggeration in the

---

[117] *Danepoint Ltd* v *Underwriting Insurance Ltd* [2006] Ll Rep IR 429, 437 *per* Judge Peter Coulson QC (QB (TCC)).
[118] [1995] LRLR 443 (CA).
[119] At p 450. See also, at p 451 *per* Hoffmann LJ.

submission of a claim because this will reflect a negotiating stance, rather than a true valuation, and such common conduct should not be labelled as fraudulent.[120] There may, however, be objections to this relaxed approach:

- On a pragmatic level, if the boundary between fraudulent and innocent conduct is the extent of a party's exaggeration – how gross must the exaggeration be before it crosses the line? The answer to this is that it is treated as a jury question to be assessed by reference to all of the factual evidence on a case by case basis.[121]

- On a more conceptual level, part of the reason for labelling conduct as fraudulent and for visiting harsh consequences on the fraudster is to provide an incentive to tell the truth (given that, as Hoffmann LJ observed in *Orakpo*, the circumstances of the casualty will be as much within the peculiar knowledge of the insured as the nature of the risk). If this is right then should there not be as great a deterrent to fraud (and encouragement to honesty) where the exaggeration is small and, therefore, more difficult for the underwriter to discover, as where it is gross and/or patent and, therefore, easier to unearth. Shouldn't both types of exaggeration be labelled as dishonest and fraudulent?[122]

2.071 *Nsubuga* v *Commercial Union Assurance Company*[123] also involved exaggeration; this time about the value of retail stock damaged in a fire at shop premises in Tottenham. The insurers accepted as genuine the submission of one claim for stock damaged or partly damaged by the fire in the sum of £10,000. There was a second and third claim with an aggregate value of £10,000. The insurers argued that these claims were fraudulent or, at least, fraudulently exaggerated. The judge, Thomas J, found that it was beyond any doubt that there was fraud in respect of the second and third

---

[120] Professor Clarke has suggested that if the "*mores of the times*" would not regard the insured's conduct (in consciously exaggerating the claim) as fraudulent then it "*may be undesirable to enforce law that is so far out of line with the mores of the times.*" M Clarke, *Policies and Perceptions of Insurance Law in the Twenty-first Century* (1st ed, 2005).

[121] Although there is some guidance from the judgment of Millett LJ in *Galloway* v *Guardian Royal Exchange (UK) Ltd* [1999] Ll Rep 209, 214 (CA) (which is referred to by Mance LJ in *The Aegeon* [2003] QB 556, 570D (CA)).

[122] Millett LJ had some sympathy with a more robust stance: see *Galloway* v *Guardian Royal Exchange (UK) Ltd* [1999] Ll Rep 209, 214 (CA): "*The making of dishonest insurance claims has become all too common. There seems to be a widespread belief that insurance companies are fair game, and that defrauding them is not morally reprehensible. The rule which we are asked to enforce today may appear to some to be harsh, but it is in my opinion a necessary and salutary rule which deserves to be better known by the public.*" This passage was cited with approval by Arden LJ, delivering the leading judgment, in *Direct Line Insurance* v *Khan* [2002] Ll Rep IR 364, 372 (CA).

[123] [1998] 2 Ll Rep 682 (QB (Comm Ct)).

claims. He directed himself, by reference to *Orakpo*, that it had to be recognised that very clear evidence of fraud was needed before the court would find that a claim was fraudulent because, as a matter of commercial reality, it was known that insureds inflated the value of their loss as a negotiating tactic with the insurer. Thomas J went on to direct himself that the insured,

> ...would have to put forward a claim that was so far exaggerated that he knew that in respect of a material part of it, there was no basis whatsoever for the claim. [124]

A very high burden for the insurer to discharge (especially by reference to the enhanced, *Hornal* v *Neuberger Products Limited*, [125] standard of proof – on which, see Chapter 4 on Evidence below).

2.072 In *Galloway* v *Guardian Royal Exchange (UK) Limited*, [126] the insured made a claim for approximately £16,000 in respect of items stolen during a burglary. This was the probable true value of his loss. Unfortunately (for him) he added a further £2,000 claim for the loss of a computer. In fact, no computer had been lost and a receipt for the purchase of the computer had been forged. One could either treat the *Galloway* claim as exaggerated (an extra £2,000 had been added to the claim overall) or as a claim where there had been no loss at all (in respect of the computer). It was submitted for the insured on appeal, by reference to *Orakpo*, that the fraud must be to a "*substantial extent*" and that £2,000 in the context of a claim in excess of £18,000 overall was not substantial. The Court of Appeal accepted the principle, but rejected the submission that £2,000 was not substantial. The approach of the Court to the question of what is substantial exaggeration sufficient to justify branding the same as fraudulent is considerably more robust than in *Orakpo* and *Nsubuga*. In the course of a persuasive concurring judgment, Millett LJ said this about the manner in which it should be assessed whether an exaggerated claim is fraudulent:

> I reject the submission that this is to be tested by reference to the proportion of the entire claim which is represented by the fraudulent claim. That would lead to the absurd conclusion that the greater the genuine loss, the larger the fraudulent claim which may be made at the same time without penalty. In my judgment, the size of the genuine claim is irrelevant. ... In my view, the right approach in such a case is to consider the fraudulent claim as if it were the only claim and then to consider whether, taken in isolation, the making

---

[124] At p 686.
[125] [1957] 1 QB 247 (CA).
[126] [1999] Ll Rep IR 209 (CA).

of that claim by the insured is sufficiently serious to justify stigmatising it as a breach of his duty of good faith so as to avoid the policy.[127]

2.073 It will be apparent that in *Galloway* the discussion of when fraud would be sufficiently substantial to justify being labelled as such was caught up with the Court's consideration of a continuing duty of good faith and the remedy of avoidance of the policy. However, there seems no reason in principle why Millett LJ's approach should not be detached from considerations of good faith and avoidance and applied to exaggerated claims within the context of the common law fraudulent claims rule. The passage set out above was cited in this way in *The Aegeon*. As Professor Birds has observed it now seems very unlikely indeed that a claim which is described as "*preposterously extravagant*" would now be found not to be fraudulent on the basis that it simply reflected a bargaining position.[128]

2.074 Further guidance on when an exaggeration will lead to the claim being treated as fraudulent was given by Judge Peter Coulson QC in the recent case of *Danepoint Limited* v *Underwriting Insurance Limited*.[129] The judge said this:

> It seems to me that mere exaggeration of an insurance claim will not of itself be fraud. On the other hand, exaggeration which is wilful, or which is allied to misrepresentation or concealment will, in all probability, be fraudulent. In addition, I consider that exaggeration is more likely and more excusable where the value of the particular claim or head of loss in question is unclear or a matter of opinion ... Conversely, where the value of the claim is or should be clear-cut, and the information on which it is based is wholly within the control of the insured, exaggeration is much less easy to excuse and thus much more likely to be fraudulent.[130]

2.075 In *The Aegeon* Mance LJ, delivering the leading judgment, referred, without dissent, to the approach taken to exaggerated claims in previous authority;[131] namely, (a) that exaggerated claims fell within what he referred to as the fraudulent claims rule (with the consequences which are separately considered below); and, (b) that it was necessary for there to have been substantial fraud in the extent of exaggeration.[132] However, in *The Aegeon* Mance LJ was more concerned with whether the use of a fraudulent device fell within the fraudulent claims rule and, in the context of his consideration

---

[127] At p 214.
[128] Birds and N Hird, *Birds' Modern Insurance Law* (6th ed, 2004), p 266 commenting on *Ewer v National Employers' Mutual General Insurance Association Ltd* [1937] 2 All ER 193 (KBD).
[129] [2006] Ll Rep IR 429 (QB (TCC)).
[130] At p 438.
[131] I.e. *Orakpo* and *Galloway*.
[132] [2003] QB 556, 571E-F (CA).

of section 17 of the 1906 Act, whether a fraudulent claim would or should lead to avoidance of the contract.

Fraudulent devices

2.076 These were identified and defined by Mance LJ in *The Aegeon* where he said this:

> A fraudulent claim exists where the insured claims, knowing that he has suffered no loss, or only a lesser loss than that which he claims (or is reckless as to whether this is the case). A fraudulent device is used if the insured believes that he has suffered the loss claimed, but seeks to improve or embellish the facts surrounding the claim, by some lie. There may however be intermediate factual situations, where the lies become so significant, that they may be viewed as changing the nature of the claim being advanced.[133]

2.077 Later in the judgment there was a more nuanced (or, at least, more wordy) definition of what was meant by a "*lie*" for these purposes,

> ... any lie, directly related to the claim to which the fraudulent device relates, which is intended to improve the insured's prospects of obtaining a settlement or winning the case, and which would, if believed, tend, objectively, prior to any final determination at trial of the parties' rights, to yield a not insignificant improvement in the insured's prospects – whether they be prospects of obtaining a settlement, or a better settlement, or of winning at trial.[134]

2.078 In *The Aegeon* the clearly expressed view of the Court of Appeal was that the use of fraudulent devices brought a claim within the ambit of the fraudulent claims rule with the result that the consequences of the same would follow. Mance LJ's conclusions were as follows:

- The use of a fraudulent device was a "*sub-species*" of making a fraudulent claim and the same consequences would follow.

- The fraudulent claims rule also applied to late dishonesty and suppressed defence claims.

- In order for the lie in respect of a fraudulent device to bring the claim within the fraudulent claims rule, it had to be relevant in the manner described in the passage from Mance LJ's judgment set out above. He clearly regarded the relevance of the lie as distinct from

---

[133] [2003] QB 556, 569G (CA).
[134] At p 575B-C.

any proposition that it should have induced the insurer to act to his detriment in reliance on the same.[135]

Effects of the fraudulent claims rule

2.079 As we have seen one of the factors which prompted the courts to sever the connection between the duty of utmost good faith in a post-contractual setting and the fraudulent claims rule was the "*one-size-fits-all*" consequence of a breach of the duty of good faith; namely, as section 17 prescribes, avoidance of the contract. However, anxieties about finding that the contract was void *ab initio* did not always inhibit judges from finding that a claim was fraudulent (as cases like *Black King Shipping Corporation* v *Massie, The Litsion Pride*[136] and *Galloway* v *Guardian Royal Exchange (UK) Limited*[137] make clear).

2.080 *The Aegeon*,[138] making it clear that the post-contractual duty of utmost good faith and the fraudulent claims rule were to be considered separately, ushered in a new approach. In his commentary on *Orakpo, Galloway* and *The Star Sea,* Mance LJ indicated reservations about whether the remedy of avoidance was or should be available in the context of a fraudulent claim.[139] He concluded that it should not be available:

> ...my tentative view of an acceptable solution would be ... to treat the common law rules governing the making of a fraudulent claim (including the use of fraudulent device) as falling outside the scope of section 17 ... On this basis no question of avoidance ab initio would arise.[140]

2.081 This has been welcomed by most commentators as "*striking a healthy compromise*".[141] On the one hand, the ambit of the fraudulent claims rule is widened to embrace fraudulent devices, while on the other hand the penalty for fraud is not disproportionate in that section 17 of the Marine Insurance Act 1906 is not to be applied (and the fraudulent claims rule is superseded by the Civil Procedure Rules once litigation has commenced).

---

[135] For a recent application of *The Aegeon* in the context of a New Zealand appeal to the Privy Council: *Stemson* v *AMP General Insurance (NZ) Ltd* [2006] UKPC 30.
[136] [1985] 1 Ll Rep 437, 515 *per* Hirst J (QB (Comm Ct)): "*In my judgment, 'avoidance' in s 17 means avoidance ab initio. Certainly this is the case in relation to pre-contract avoidance ..., and I see no reason for putting a different meaning on the word in relation to post-contractual events.*"
[137] [1999] Ll Rep IR 209, 214 *per* Millett LJ (CA): "*The policy is avoided by breach of the duty of good faith which rests upon the insured in all his dealings with the insurer.*"
[138] [2003] QB 556 (CA).
[139] At p 574.
[140] At p 574H.
[141] H Yeo "*Post-contractual Good Faith – Change in Judicial Attitude?*" (2003) 66 MLR 425, 439.

2.082 Accordingly, the common law rule – forfeiture of the index claim – is the appropriate remedy in respect of fraudulent claims, rather than avoidance of the contract *ab initio*. Forfeiture works in the following way in the context of a fraudulent claim (whether the fraud is present in the context of a no loss claim, an exaggerated claim, a fraudulent device claim, a late dishonesty or a suppressed defence claim):

- The fraud will lead to the forfeiture of the whole of the claim to which the fraud relates (as Mance LJ made clear in *The Aegeon*, confirming the approach taken in earlier cases).[142]

- The fraud will, as a matter of public policy, be regarded as "*tainting*" the claim as a whole and, therefore, it is not only the fraudulent part of the claim that will be forfeit, but the whole of the claim (including any part of the same which is genuine). Accordingly, in *Galloway* v *Guardian Royal Exchange (UK) Limited*,[143] as a result of his fraud in respect of the alleged loss of a computer (valued at £2,000), the insured also forfeited the genuine portion of his claim (valued at approximately £16,000).

2.083 Accordingly the insurer can:

- bring proceedings against the fraudulent insured for recovery of any sums paid out to the same;[144] and,

- withhold payment in respect of a genuine claim which pre-dates the fraud, but which has not yet been paid out to the insured.[145]

2.084 It is worth pointing out that in *The Aegeon*, as part of his "*tentative*" summary of the law, Mance LJ observed, albeit *obiter*,

> ...the fraudulent claim rule may have a prospective aspect in respect of future, and perhaps current, claims, but it is unnecessary to consider that aspect or its application to cases of use of fraudulent devices.

It may be that a fraudulent claims rule which gave the insurer the right to refuse (on grounds of past fraud) future, unrelated and genuine claims would constitute recognition of a remedy closely related to avoidance of the contract *ab initio*. Mance LJ's suggestion has not yet been developed in the

---

[142] [2003] QB 556, 575C (CA).

[143] [1999] Ll Rep IR 209 (CA).

[144] *Direct Line Insurance* v *Khan* [2002] Ll Rep IR 364 (CA). The fact that the insureds in *Khan* might have had a genuine claim in respect of the sums which they recovered by fraud made no difference: "*If the Defendants wished to advance a* [genuine] *claim ... they should have done so honestly.*"

[145] *Galloway* v *Guardian Royal Exchange (UK) Ltd* [1999] Ll Rep IR 209 (CA).

case law,[146] although he stated *obiter*, in the later case of *Axa General Insurance Limited* v *Gottlieb*,[147]

> It is unnecessary to reach any conclusion in this case on the common law position relating to separate claims which are still unpaid at the time of the fraud, though there seems to me some force in the argument that the common law rule relating to fraudulent claims should be confined to the particular claim to which any fraud relates.[148]

2.085 Mance LJ went on in *Axa General Insurance Limited* v *Gottlieb* to decide that:

- Application of the fraudulent claims rule did not require the repayment of prior, separate claims settled under the same policy before the occurrence of any fraud[149] – a contrary finding would have taken the consequence of a fraudulent claim close to avoidance of the contract *ab initio.*

- However, the insureds would be required to repay, "*interim payments made prior to any fraud in respect of genuine losses incurred on the claim to which subsequent fraud related.*"[150] The reason for this was set out by Mance LJ in the course of his judgment,

> If a later fraud forfeits a genuine claim which has already accrued but not been paid, the obvious conceptual basis is that the whole claim is forfeit. ... If the whole claim is forfeit, then the fact that sums have been advanced towards it is of itself no answer to their recovery. The sums previously paid on that claim will have been paid on a consideration which has now wholly failed.[151]

Innocent co-insured

2.086 What is the position where a number of persons are covered by one insurance policy and where one of the co-insured is fraudulent and the others innocent? The answer depends on whether the policy is, as a matter of construction of the index contract, regarded as a joint or composite policy. In a joint policy – commonly taken out by persons jointly interested in property – the insurer's obligation is owed jointly to all of the insureds. By

---

[146] Although the various remedies available are identified and described in an article written by Professor Clarke before *The Aegeon* was decided: M Clarke, "*Lies, Damned Lies, and Insurance Claims: the Elements and Effects of Fraud*" (2000) NZLR 233, 246ff.
[147] [2005] Ll Rep IR 369 (CA).
[148] At p 375.
[149] At p 375.
[150] At p 375.
[151] At p 377.

contrast, in a composite policy the obligation is owed severally to each of the insureds (for example, landlord and tenant or mortgagor and mortgagee).

2.087 It has been held that if the policy is a joint one then the fraud of the co-insured taints the whole policy with the result that the innocent insured also forfeits benefits in relation to the index claim.[152] If, however, as a matter of construction, the contract concerns composite insurance then a claim can be maintained by the innocent co-insured.[153] These issues were discussed, by reference to the well established case law on joint and composite insurance policies, in *Direct Line Insurance* v *Khan*[154] (a case which involved a fraudulent claim by a husband of which his wife was unaware). However, it was held in that case that the husband had acted as agent for his wife within the scope of his authority. Accordingly, she was bound by his fraudulent acts and the consequences of the same.

---

[152] *Samuel & Co Ltd* v *Dumas* [1924] AC 431 (HL).
[153] *General Accident, Fire & Life Insurance Assurance Corporation* v *Midland Bank Ltd* [1940] 2 KB 388 (CA). Commentary on this case and the issues raised in this section can be found in N Campbell, " *Wilful Misconduct, Fraud, and the Innocent Co-insured*" [2000] NZLR 263.
[154] [2002] Ll Rep IR 364 (CA).

Chapter 3

FRAUD AS A DEFENCE TO CLAIMS IN TORT AND CONTRACT

1. INTRODUCTION

3.001 Some judges are less shy than others in seeking to make connections between legal rules and moral conduct. In *Smith New Court Limited* v *Scrimgeour Vickers*[1] Lord Steyn said this:

> ... as between the fraudster and the innocent party, moral considerations militate in favour of requiring the fraudster to bear the risk of misfortune directly caused by his fraud. I make no apology for referring to moral considerations. The law and morality are inextricably interwoven. To a large extent the law is simply formulated and declared morality. And, as Oliver Wendell Holmes ... observed, the very notion of deceit with its overtones of wickedness is drawn from the moral world.[2]

3.002 Drawing moral distinctions between the conduct of the parties to a dispute is easy enough where one is innocent and the other is a fraudster. The real world, however, is often more complicated than this. There may be morally reprehensible conduct by both parties. The Defendant might, for example, have injured a Claimant through his fault in circumstances where the Claimant's own conduct could be labelled as immoral or even illegal.

3.003 It has long been recognised that illegal or obviously immoral actions can provide a defence to a cause of action. This defence is customarily known by the rather cumbersome Latin tag, *ex turpi causa non oritur actio.*[3]

---

[1] [1997] AC 254 (HL(E)).

[2] At p 280B-C.

[3] This has been translated to mean that, "...*no cause of action may be founded on an immoral or illegal act*": see Neill LJ in *Revill* v *Newbery* [1996] QB 567, 576 (CA). This case concerned a burglar who was injured when a shotgun was fired in his direction. The use of the Latin maxim has been criticised: see Balcombe LJ in *Pitts* v *Hunt* [1991] 1 QB 24, 49F (CA), "*I find the ritual incantation of the maxim ex turpi causa non oritur actio more likely to confuse than to illuminate.*"

This chapter seeks to consider the use of an allegation that the Claimant's conduct is fraudulent or dishonest as a defence to claims in tort and contract.

2. EX TURPI CAUSA NON ORITUR ACTION

3.004 The rule was stated by Lord Mansfield CJ in *Holman v Johnson*,[4] *"No court will lend its aid to a man who founds his cause of action upon an immoral or an illegal act."* While this seems a straightforward enough proposition, the scope of the *ex turpi causa* maxim has never been wholly clear. There is controversy about what it means, about whether it accurately expresses the law and, until recently, about whether it is available as a plea in claims founded in tort as well as in contract.[5] The conceptual justification for this maxim remains murky. There has, for example, been academic and judicial discussion on whether the maxim amounts to the proposition that the Defendant owes no duty of care to the Claimant in circumstances where the claim arises out of illegal or immoral conduct or whether it is more properly characterised as a defence to a claim that might otherwise be pursued. In *Vellino v Chief Constable of the Greater Manchester Police*,[6] a case involving a Claimant who was catastrophically injured while trying to escape from police custody, the majority in the Court of Appeal held that the application of the maxim meant that no duty of care was owed. Sir Murray Stuart-Smith was untroubled by the jurisprudential underpinning of this decision,

> ...it does not matter whether the correct legal analysis is that the defendants owed no duty of care, because the third limb of the test in Caparo Industries plc v Dickman ..., namely that it is just, fair and reasonable to impose a duty of care, is not satisfied, or that the maxim affords a freestanding reason for holding that the cause of action does not arise or cannot be pursued.[7]

---

[4] (1775) 1 Cowp 341, 343.
[5] In *Berg v Sadler and Moore* [1937] 2 KB 158 (CA), a case involving an attempt to defraud a trade association, Lord Wright MR said this (at p 162) about *ex turpi causa*, "... *though veiled in the dignity of learned language,* [it] *is a statement of a principle of great importance; but like most maxims it is much too vague and much too general to admit of application without a careful consideration of the circumstances and of the various definite rules which have been laid down by the authorities.*"
[6] [2002] 1 WLR 218 (CA).
[7] At p 234A-B.

Clerk & Lindsell observes that there are (at least) four conceptual justifications for a plea of *ex turpi causa*.[8] First, that it is impossible to identify the appropriate standard of care where illegality or immorality is involved and that, in these circumstances, the courts are justified in denying relief to the Claimant.[9] Second and third, that the maxim should be applied where it would be an affront to the public conscience to grant relief or where the grant of the same would damage the integrity of the legal system. This justification for the rule has been the subject of judicial criticism at the highest level. In *Tinsley* v *Milligan*[10] both Lord Browne-Wilkinson and Lord Goff (who delivered a dissenting judgment) cast doubt on the use of such an "*imponderable factor*" as the public conscience as the justification for the rule. In the more recent Court of Appeal decision in *Vellino*[11] Sedley LJ (dissenting) pointed out that the use of public conscience as a justification for a particular decision begs the question: whose public conscience is being used,

> The public conscience, an elusive thing, as often as not turns out to be an echo-chamber inhabited by journalists and public moralists.[12]

The fourth conceptual justification for the maxim, identified by *Clerk & Lindsell*, is that the Claimant should be denied relief in circumstances where it is necessary for him to rely on the illegality in order to prosecute the claim.[13]

3.005 In addition to disagreements about the conceptual justification for *ex turpi causa*, there has been uncertainty about the categories of illegal and immoral conduct to which the maxim applies. In its consultation paper on illegal transactions the Law Commission declined to answer what it described as a "*surprisingly difficult question*": what is meant by an illegal transaction.[14] The reason for this was that,

---

[8] *Clerk & Lindsell on Torts* (19th ed, 2006), para 3-04ff.
[9] See, the judgment of Mason J in the decision of the Australian High Court in *Jackson* v *Harrison* (1978) 138 CLR 438, 455-456, "...*the plaintiff must fail when the character of the enterprise in which the parties are engaged is such that it is impossible for the court to determine the standard of care which is appropriate to be observed.*"
[10] [1994] 1 AC 340 (HL(E)).
[11] [2002] 1 WLR 218 (CA).
[12] At p 233D.
[13] An approach which found favour with the majority in *Tinsley* v *Milligan* [1994] 1 AC 340 (HL(E)).
[14] Law Commission, *Illegal Transactions: The effect of Illegality on Contracts and Trusts* CP 154 (1999), para 1.4. The Law Commission investigation of this area was prompted by the dissenting speech of Lord Goff in *Tinsley* v *Milligan* [1994] 1 AC 340, 364E (HL(E)).

> Any attempt to set out in legislation all transactions which are contrary to public policy would be extremely difficult, and require frequent modification.[15]

The Commission preferred to leave this task to the courts, allowing Parliament to intervene when the courts fell into error. The shifting boundaries of *ex turpi causa non oritur actio* necessarily reflect its haphazard common law development. There are, however, some aspects of the maxim about which it is possible to be reasonably certain.

3.006 First, it is now clear that:

- a defence of illegality can be raised in tort, as well as in contract (on which, see, *Clunis* v *Camden and Islington Health Authority*);[16]

- the defence has, essentially, the same meaning whether it is deployed in a tortious or contractual setting (see, *Standard Chartered Bank* v *Pakistan National Shipping Corporation & Others (No 2)*),[17] although, where successfully used, its effect will, naturally enough, differ; and,

- the concentration is upon the whether the Claimant's illegal conduct is such that he should be precluded from recovering against the Defendant (on which see, Lord Mansfield CJ in *Holman* v *Johnson*[18] and, more recently, *Cross* v *Kirkby*).[19]

3.007 Second, notwithstanding the Law Commission's original opinion that it is not possible to identify all of the circumstances in which *ex turpi causa* will apply, a number of categories of case have emerged in which the maxim has been successfully raised:

- where the Claimant has been injured whilst participating with the Defendant in a joint enterprise which is illegal;

- where the Defendant's tortious act injures the Claimant whilst the

---

[15] At para 1.14.
[16] [1998] QB 978, 987A-B *per* Beldam LJ (CA) (rejecting the submission that *ex turpi causa* was only available where the cause of action was contractual), " *We do not consider that the public policy that the court will not lend its aid to a litigant who relies on his own criminal or immoral act is confined to particular causes of action.*"
[17] [2000] 1 Ll Rep 218 (CA).
[18] (1775) 1 Cowp 341.
[19] [2000] *The Times*, 5 April (CA).

latter is engaged in an illegal activity;

- where the Claimant has been convicted of an offence and detained and alleges that the offence would not have been committed but for the Defendant's tortious act (a sub-category of this type of claim is where the Claimant seeks indemnity from the Defendant for liability arising from the commission of the offence).

3.008 I interpose at this point that, insofar as *ex turpi causa* is relevant to tortious claims, the Law Commission takes the view that it applies under three broad headings. First,

> ...where the claimant seeks, or is forced, to found the claim on his or her own illegal act.[20]

Second,

> ...where the grant of relief to the claimant would enable him or her to benefit from his or her criminal conduct (or where what is sought is compensation for loss of liberty or an indemnity for the consequences of criminal behaviour).

Third, where the Claimant's claim is so closely or inextricably bound up with his own criminality that the court cannot permit the Claimant to recover without appearing to condone the conduct.[21]

3.009 The remaining general category of cases concerns decisions in contract where there is illegality as to the formation and/or performance of a contract and such illegality is known to one or both parties.

Some examples of the categories outlined above by reference to the authorities are as follows.

---

[20] Law Commission, *The Illegality Defence in Tort* CP 160 (2001), para 2.11.

[21] At paras 2.11 and 2.43. The Law Commission illustrates its third proposition by reference to the decision in *Cross v Kirkby* [2000] *The Times*, 5 April (CA). However, the anxiety which justifies the third category can be found in many of the cases in this area and was criticised by Sedley LJ in *Vellino v Chief Constable of the Greater Manchester Police* [2002] 1 WLR 218 (CA).

Illegal joint enterprise

3.010 *Pitts* v *Hunt*[22] concerned a road traffic accident involving a car and a motor cycle. The Claimant was the pillion passenger on the motor cycle. The Claimant and the rider of the motor cycle had both been drinking prior to the accident (the rider had twice the permitted level of alcohol) and the Claimant knew that the rider of the motor cycle had neither insurance nor a driving licence. At the time of the accident the Claimant was encouraging the motorcyclist to ride in a dangerous and reckless manner. As a result of the accident the rider of the motor cycle died and the Claimant commenced proceedings against his personal representatives and against the driver of the car. The judge dismissed the claim against the personal representatives on application of the *ex turpi causa* maxim. The claim against the driver of the car was also dismissed. The Claimant appealed in respect of the dismissal of his claim against the personal representatives. His appeal was dismissed. It was held by the Court of Appeal that the Claimant had, at the time of the accident, been playing a full and active part in the encouragement of criminal offences which, if a death of a third party had resulted, would have amounted to manslaughter. In the circumstances, his willing participation in an illegal joint enterprise justified the application of the maxim and the dismissal of his claim. Beldam LJ was content to justify the Court of Appeal's decision on public policy grounds.

Claimant's illegal activity

3.011 In *Revill* v *Newbery*[23] the Defendant was the owner of a shed on an allotment and he slept in the shed at night in order to keep watch over his property. The Defendant kept a 12-bore shotgun in the shed. The Claimant and another man attempted to break into the shed one night; it was their intention to steal from the shed. The noise woke the Defendant and, intending only to frighten the intruders, he loaded the shotgun and fired it through a hole in the shed door. The Claimant was standing only five feet away from the door at the time and was injured. Criminal proceedings were brought against the Claimant who pleaded guilty to a charge of attempted burglary. The Claimant subsequently commenced proceedings against the Defendant relying on causes of action in negligence and breach of section 1 of the Occupiers' Liability Act 1984. The Defendant raised a defence of *ex turpi causa non oritur actio*. This defence was rejected by the trial judge who found that the Defendant had been negligent. The damages awarded to the

---

[22] [1991] 1 QB 24 (CA).
[23] [1996] QB 567 (CA).

Claimant were reduced by reason of contributory negligence. The Defendant appealed. His appeal was dismissed. Neill LJ was not helped by the *ex turpi causa* cases like *Pitts* v *Hunt* concerning illegal joint enterprise. Evans LJ articulated the reason for this,

> ... it is one thing to deny to a plaintiff any fruits from his illegal conduct, but different and more far-reaching to deprive him even of compensation for injury which he suffers and which otherwise he is entitled to recover at law.[24]

Neill LJ considered that it was unnecessary for him to stray further than section 1 of the Occupiers' Liability Act 1984 by which Parliament had made it clear that, in defined circumstances, an occupier could not treat a burglar as an outlaw and react accordingly in what Millet LJ described (in the same case) as a "*dangerous and ... [borderline] reckless*" manner.[25]

3.012 In *Cross* v *Kirkby*[26] it was held by the Court of Appeal that the wrongdoing was unilateral and precluded the Claimant from recovering against the Defendant. In this case the Claimant was a hunt saboteur. His partner was being escorted off the Defendant's land by the Defendant when she bit him. The Claimant saw this and raced over to assist his partner. His assistance took the form of brandishing a baseball bat at the Defendant and threatening to kill him (while jabbing the Defendant in the throat and chest with the bat). In the meantime the Claimant's partner had armed herself with an iron bar. The Defendant tried to walk away, but the Claimant struck him with the bat on two further occasions. The Defendant, in an effort to avoid any further blows, grappled with the Claimant and took hold of the baseball bat. He struck the Claimant on the side of the head with a single blow and the Claimant sustained a fractured skull as a result. The Claimant commenced proceedings against the Defendant and, at first instance, was successful on the basis that the Defendant's disproportionate and unlawful use of force prevented him from relying on the *ex turpi causa* defence. The appeal was successful. The Court of Appeal concluded that the Defendant had been acting in self-defence at the relevant time. The Claimant's injury arose from his own serious criminal conduct in assaulting the Defendant and the maxim applied to prevent him from recovering damages. The Court of Appeal observed that the first instance judge's decision that the Defendant was precluded from relying on the *ex turpi causa* defence indicated that he had overlooked the requirement that consideration be given to whether the Claimant's illegal conduct prevented recovery.

---

[24] At p 579E.
[25] At p 580E.
[26] [2000] *The Times*, April 5 (CA).

Claimant's allegation that, but for the Defendant's tort, he would not have acted illegally

3.013 *Meah* v *McCreamer*,[27] decided in the Queen's Bench Division in 1984, provides a curious example of this category of case. The Claimant was a passenger in a vehicle driven by the Defendant who was, at the time, intoxicated. There was an accident caused by the Defendant's negligence and the Claimant sustained brain damage. The brain damage caused a dramatic personality change. The Claimant had a criminal record for offences like theft and burglary, as well as a poor employment record. However, he had no history of violence towards women and had had relationships with women in the past. After the accident the Claimant embarked on a number of violent sexual offences against women and this resulted in convictions and a sentence of life imprisonment. The Claimant brought a claim against the Defendant on the basis that if it had not been for the brain damage sustained in the road traffic accident then he would not have committed the offences which resulted in his imprisonment. The Claimant's claim was successful. The trial Judge (Woolf J) approached the matter on a straightforward causation basis. He reduced the damages awarded to the Claimant in recognition of the fact that he would, as evidenced by his past criminal record, have likely spent time in custody in any event. There was also a reduction in the award to recognise the Claimant's contributory negligence in allowing himself to be carried in a vehicle driven by someone he knew to be drunk. The curious aspect of the case is that the Defendant's counsel did not argue that the Claimant was prevented from recovering against their client by reason of the illegal nature of his actions. This was expressly recorded by Woolf J in the course of his judgment.[28] It has been suggested since that *Meah* v *McCreamer* is questionable authority in the light of the fact that this argument was not raised.[29] There was an interesting footnote to this case. In a separate claim the Claimant's victims brought claims against the Claimant and were awarded £10,250 and £6,750 respectively. The Claimant brought an action against the driver and his insurers seeking indemnity in respect of the sums which had been awarded to his victims. It was held, again by Woolf J, that the damages awarded to the Claimant's victims were too remote to be recoverable. In addition, Woolf J held that it would be contrary to public policy to permit the Claimant to recover an indemnity. In respect of this issue

---

[27] [1985] 1 All ER 367 (QBD).

[28] At p 371j.

[29] See, *Clunis* v *Camden and Islington Health Authority* [1998] QB 978, 990B-C *per* Beldam LJ (CA), "*Whilst any decision of that Judge must be given the greatest weight, we do not consider that, in the absence of argument on the issue of public policy, his decision in Meah v McCreamer ... can be regarded as authoritative on this issue.*"

he held that it would be "*distasteful*" to permit the Claimant to recover in respect of the consequences of his crime.[30]

3.014 *Clunis* v *Camden and Islington Health Authority*[31] concerned a Claimant with a history of schizophrenia who had previously been detained under the Mental Health Act. The Claimant was discharged from in-patient psychiatric care (following his detention under the Act) on 24 September 1992. The Claimant failed to attend any follow up appointments and, on 17 December 1992, Hackney Social Services informed his treating psychiatrist that the police had called them to say that the Claimant was waving around knives and screwdrivers and talking in a disordered manner. Later the same day, while the Claimant's psychiatrist was checking to see which local authority social services team was responsible for him, he killed a commuter at Finsbury Park tube station. The Claimant pleaded guilty to manslaughter on grounds of diminished responsibility. He commenced proceedings against the Defendant health authority in respect of the alleged negligent acts and omissions of his treating psychiatrist in failing in her responsibility as his key worker to liaise effectively and competently with police, social services and other agencies to ensure that the Claimant was assessed and monitored in the period preceding his commission of manslaughter. An application was made to strike out the claim and this was refused at first instance. The Defendant appealed and the appeal was allowed. Beldam LJ gave the judgment of the Court:

> In the present case the plaintiff has been convicted of a serious criminal offence. In such a case public policy would in our judgment preclude the court from entertaining the plaintiff's claim unless it could be said that he did not know the nature and quality of his act or that what he was doing was wrong. The offence of murder was reduced to one of manslaughter by reason of the plaintiff's mental disorder but his mental state did not justify a verdict of not guilty by reason of insanity. Consequently, though his responsibility for killing ...[the victim] is diminished, he must be taken to have known what he was doing and that it was wrong. A plea of diminished responsibility accepts that the accused's mental responsibility is substantially impaired but it does not remove liability for his criminal act.[32]

---

[30] It is of interest that the judge's distaste did not extend to prevent the Claimant from recovering against the driver of the vehicle at the time of the road traffic accident.
[31] [1998] QB 978 (CA).
[32] At p 989E-F.

Illegality as to the formation and/or performance of a contract

3.015 Illegal contracts can be categorised under a bewildering variety of headings. As I have indicated above, the Law Commission, in its 1999 Consultation Paper on this subject, deliberately declined to answer the question, "*What is meant by an 'illegal transaction'?*"[33] Chitty does attempt to classify the objects which may invalidate contracts and proposes five loose categories,

> ... first, objects which are illegal by common law or by legislation; secondly, objects injurious to good government either in the field of domestic or foreign affairs; thirdly, objects which interfere with the proper working of the machinery of justice; fourthly, objects injurious to marriage and morality; and, fifthly, objects economically against the public interest.[34]

3.016 There is not space in this book to consider the examples given under each category and readers interested in pursuing this subject further are directed to the relevant chapter of *Chitty on Contracts.*[35]

3.017 It suffices at this stage to point out that the cases in contract, like those in tort which are considered above, draw a distinction between those situations in which both parties have knowledge of the illegality and those where one party has such knowledge and the other is ignorant. *Ashmore Benson Pease & Company Limited* v *A V Dawson Limited*[36] concerned a contract between a haulage company and another corporate entity for the transportation of items by road using articulated lorries. The lorries were of a type that fell within conditions imposed under road traffic legislation. One of the regulatory conditions was that the load transported should not exceed 30 tonnes. In fact, to the knowledge of both parties to the contract the lorries were loaded to a maximum weight of 35 tonnes. While on the road one of the lorries toppled over and the load was damaged. The Claimant company commenced proceedings against the hauliers alleging negligence in loading an unsuitable lorry and for negligent driving. The Defendant raised a defence of illegality. At first instance it was held that the Claimant company had relied on the hauliers to perform lawfully a contract which was lawful when it was made. The claim succeeded. The Defendant haulier appealed and was successful. The judge's decision at first instance to the effect that the contract

---

[33] Law Commission, *Illegal Transactions: The effect of Illegality on Contracts and Trusts* CP 154 (1999), para 1.4.
[34] *Chitty on Contracts* (29th ed, 2004), para 16-005.
[35] Chapter 16 in the present edition.
[36] [1973] 1 WLR 828 (CA).

was lawful when formed was not disturbed. However, the Court of Appeal was satisfied that the contract was, to the knowledge of both parties, performed illegally and the knowing "*participation*" of the Claimant company in the illegal performance of the contract was sufficient to "*debar*" the Claimant from suing on the contract.[37]

3.018 *Mason* v *Clarke*[38] provides an example of a case where one of the parties to an illegal transaction is innocent. In this case a landowner let land to a farmer, but reserved the right for himself and those he authorised to have game rights on the land. The landowner agreed to allow a rabbit catcher to have rabbiting rights on the land in consideration of an annual sum of £100. The rabbit catcher paid the sum of £100 and was provided with a receipt by the landowner which indicated that the sum paid was a contribution towards the wages of a bailiff. The rabbit catcher laid snares on the land, but the farmer to whom the land was let interfered with the snares and took other steps to disrupt the rabbit catcher's activity on the land. The rabbit catcher and landowner brought proceedings for damages and an injunction against the farmer. The claim was defended on the ground, among other things, that the receipt could not be relied upon because its terms had the object of defrauding the Inland Revenue. It was held that a fraudulent intention had not been established with respect to the receipt, but that, in any event, the rabbit catcher was wholly innocent of any fraudulent intent or knowledge of any actual or intended fraud. In the circumstances, it could not be suggested that,

> ... an innocent party is debarred by the other party's fraudulent intention from enforcing an agreement which is not itself illegal.[39]

3. FRAUD AS A DEFENCE IN TORT

Basic principles

3.019 The simple case concerns the situation where the Claimant relies on his own fraud in the prosecution of his claim. This was the position in

---

[37] See judgment of Lord Denning MR at p 833F-G.
[38] [1955] AC 778 (HL(E)).
[39] At p 794 *per* Viscount Simonds.

Thackwell v *Barclay's Bank Plc*[40] where the Claimant brought an action in negligence and conversion against the Defendant bank in respect of a cheque. The cheque represented the proceeds of the Claimant's own participation in a fraud. On the basis of the judge's findings that the Claimant was a party to a fraudulent refinancing transaction, knew from the outset that it was a fraud and willingly participated in the same, it was conceded that the action for conversion could not be maintained against the bank. In the course of judgment Hutchison J approved the test which was suggested to him by counsel for the Defendant and which,

> ... involved the court looking at the quality of the illegality relied on by the defendant and all the surrounding circumstances without fine distinctions, and seeking to answer two questions: first, whether there had been illegality of which the court should take notice and, second, whether in all the circumstances it would be an affront to the public conscience if by affording him the relief sought the court was seen to be indirectly assisting or encouraging the plaintiff in his criminal act.[41]

3.020 The position is more complicated, as we have already seen in the discussion above, where there is wrongdoing by both parties. In *Saunders* v *Edwards*[42] the Defendant to the action was the vendor of a flat. There was a flat roof which was overlooked by the Defendant's flat and, around the time that he moved in, he decided to make use of the same. Accordingly, the Defendant replaced a sash window with French windows and had a metal staircase installed to provide access to the flat roof. He fenced this off and used the flat roof as an outdoor space. The freeholder objected strongly to the Defendant's use of the roof in this way and voiced his objection in correspondence. The plan of the demised premises was unclear, but it was beyond doubt that the flat roof was not part of the demise. The Defendant was well aware of this fact. The sale particulars for the flat represented that the demise included the roof garden. The Claimants purchased the flat from the Defendant. The roof garden was a principal attraction to them in making the purchase and their evidence was that they would not have proceeded with the purchase if they had known that the roof garden was not part of the demise. The purchase price of the property and certain chattels included within it was £45,000. The Claimants and Defendant agreed that, of this purchase price, £5,000 would be apportioned as representing the value of the chattels. In fact, the chattels were nowhere near this in value. The reason for over-valuing the chattels and, correspondingly, reducing the price attributable to the property itself was that the Claimants wished to evade the

---

[40] [1986] 1 All ER 676 (QBD).
[41] At p 687d-e.
[42] [1987] 1 WLR 1116 (CA).

payment of stamp duty. Soon after completion of the sale the Claimants discovered that they had no right to use the roof garden. They commenced proceedings claiming damages for fraudulent misrepresentation and were successful at first instance. On appeal the Defendant raised *ex turpi causa* as a defence. He relied on the Claimants' defrauding the Inland Revenue by the evasion of stamp duty. Kerr and Nicholls LJJ first considered whether the Claimants' action for fraudulent misrepresentation required reliance on the contract of sale which, by virtue of the apportionment of the price of the property, had an illegal object; namely, the fraudulent evasion of stamp duty. Kerr LJ dealt with this issue in the following terms,

> The possible illegality involved in the apportionment of the price in the contract is wholly unconnected with their cause of action. The plaintiffs' loss caused by the defendant's fraudulent misrepresentation would have been the same, even if the contract had not contained this illegal element. Their claim for damages is in no way seeking to enforce the contract or any relief in connection with it.[43]

3.021 Kerr LJ then went on to suggest that what was required was a balancing of the Defendant's morally and legally dubious conduct against that of the Claimants. He concluded that,

> The moral culpability of the defendant greatly outweighs any on the part of the plaintiffs. He cannot be allowed to keep the fruits of his fraud.[44]

Nicholls LJ approved the test suggested by counsel for the Defendant in the *Thackwell* case.[45] He also felt that, without minimising the seriousness of the Claimants' attempt to defraud of the Inland Revenue, the scales fell in their favour (quite apart from any consideration that they were not relying on the illegal contract in prosecuting their claim) and that it would not, therefore, be an affront to the public conscience to permit them to recover.

3.022 The decision in *Saunders* turned on whether the Claimant's own fraudulent conduct was central to their claim (whether because they relied on a contract with a fraudulent object or otherwise) or whether, as Bingham LJ described it in the same case, the fraud could properly be characterised as *"incidental"* to the claim. This thread runs through a number of the other decisions in this area.

---

[43] At p 1127H.
[44] At p 1127H.
[45] As set out above.

Claims for loss of earnings

3.023 The cases considered under this category generally concern actions in which the Claimant or those claiming as dependents claim loss of earnings/dependency in circumstances where there has been a past record of dishonesty (a) in failing to declare earnings to the Inland Revenue or Benefits Agency; or, (b) in obtaining work in the past or in failing to disclose to the Defendant that, since injury, alternative work has been obtained.

3.024 *Burns* v *Edman*[46] was a fatal accident claim involving a claim for loss of dependency by the widow of the deceased. The deceased had lived a life of crime. There was no evidence before the Court that he had ever had any honest employment and he had no capital assets. It followed that such sums as he gave the Claimant during his lifetime were the proceeds of crime and the Claimant was aware of this. It was held that her claim under the Fatal Accidents Act on behalf of herself and her four children should be dismissed. This decision was based in large part on the fact that their loss of financial dependency represented a deprivation of support flowing directly from criminal offences. The Defendant's defence of *ex turpi causa* succeeded.

3.025 *Hunter* v *Butler*[47] was also a fatal accident case. Again, the widow claimed as a dependent of her deceased husband under the Fatal Accidents Act. The claim for loss of financial dependency was largely based on two unattractive grounds. First, the supplementary benefit which the deceased had obtained by fraudulently concealing the money that he earned from employment. Second, the undeclared earnings which the deceased obtained from moonlighting. The Claimant was herself privy to what her husband was doing and received sums from him in this regard. It was held that the criminal conduct in which the Claimant and her deceased husband had engaged would have continued in the event that he had survived. The Court rejected the submission that the calculation of the Claimant's loss of dependency could include the deceased's undeclared earnings or the fraudulently obtained social security benefit. Hobhouse LJ expressed his conclusions on this issue in the following terms,

> He could only obtain these benefits by making false statements to the benefits office that he was not earning. He obtained the payments by fraud. This amounted to an offence under section 15 of the Theft Act 1968, as well as under the benefits legislation, and since the plaintiff was, on her own evidence, privy to what he was doing and in receipt of the money so obtained, she too was committing offences under the Theft Act 1968. The

[46] [1970] 2 QB 541 (QBD).
[47] [1996] RTR 396 (CA).

present is not a case where the activities of both of them did not involve criminal acts, nor is it one where the criminality was confined to the deceased. If a plaintiff comes to court and asserts as part of her case that she would have committed criminal acts and bases her claim upon such an assertion, she cannot recover in a court of law on that basis.[48]

3.026 *Burns* and *Hunter* were both cases in which it was held that the fraud lay at the heart of the claim. A less robust approach is evident in some of the more recent decisions in this area. A finding that the claim, or at least part of it, can be maintained is often justified on the basis that the fraud is incidental to the claim. The difficulty involved in determining whether the fraud is central or incidental lies, as Clarke LJ observed in *Hewison* v *Meridian Shipping & Others*,[49] in deciding "*on which side of the line*" the index case falls.[50]

3.027 *Newman* v *Folkes*[51] concerned a claim for loss of earnings which the Court of Appeal described as "*little short of scandalous*" founded on "*a concoction of lies and deceit.*" The Claimant sustained some very serious injuries in a road traffic accident. Most seriously, he had suffered a brain injury of sufficient severity to cause temporal lobe damage. The Claimant had undergone a significant change of personality and there was no psychological treatment that might assist him. The medical evidence was to the effect that there would be no spontaneous improvement and it was accepted that the Claimant was incapable of returning to his pre-accident employment as a motor trader. The Claimant's claim for loss of earnings amounted to nearly £285,000 for past loss and over £1,000,000 for future loss. The problem that the Claimant had in respect of his claim was that there was very little, if any, credible evidence on which the judge could rely in determining what, if any loss, the Claimant had and would sustain. First, the Claimant had never paid a penny of income tax or national insurance since the time that he had commenced work.[52] Second, the Claimant in *Newman* had kept no books or accounts and the only documentation on which he could rely were a few invoices and accounts prepared without supporting documents for the purposes of the claim (and these had not been

---

[48] At p 404L-405A-B.
[49] [2002] EWCA Civ 1821.
[50] At para 44.
[51] [2002] EWCA Civ 591.
[52] In an earlier case, *Duller* v *South East Lincolnshire Engineers* [1981] CLY 585 (QBD *per* Mr Jowett QC), a distinction had been drawn between earnings representing the proceeds of crime and earnings which had reached the Claimant honestly and lawfully and which he had then treated fraudulently in his dealings with the Inland Revenue (in respect of the latter category, it was held that the Claimant was entitled to be compensated for loss of earnings, less a deduction to represent the income tax and national insurance that he ought to have paid).

disclosed to the Inland Revenue). Third, the Claimant called no credible evidence from any employer as to his pre-accident earnings. Fourth, such evidence as the Claimant had adduced in documentary form lacked credibility and was contradictory to the written record of employment which the Claimant had produced. This evidence had been collated by a book keeper whom the Claimant did not call to give evidence and whose part in the claim was described by the Court of Appeal as "*sinister*". For all of these reasons the Claimant's main claim failed. However, he had an alternative and secondary case. This related to earnings as a commission agent for other motor traders. In this regard the trial judge permitted the Claimant, at a relatively late stage, to call oral evidence from three witnesses with whom the Claimant had worked. The trial judge made an award to the Claimant in respect of the past and future losses presented under his secondary case. He based the award on the oral evidence of the witnesses and on certain invoices that were produced. The Defendant appealed on the basis that that Claimant's case was,

> ...so egregiously unsatisfactory that the learned judge should not have believed a word of it, should have held that the claimant had simply not proved his loss of earnings claim and should, therefore, have awarded him only a Smith v Manchester Corporation sum to compensate him for the loss of earning capacity caused by the injuries.

3.028 The Defendant's argument on appeal did not rely on the Claimant's defrauding of the Inland Revenue over many years; there was no appeal against the trial judge's decision to award the Claimant loss of earnings less the income tax and national insurance he should have paid. *Ex turpi causa* is not relied on in the course of the Court of Appeal's judgment. Instead, the Defendant's case at first instance and on appeal was that the entire claim for loss of earnings was so tainted by the unsatisfactory nature of the Claimant's evidence and his apparent dishonesty (the "*lies and deceit*") that the entire claim should be rejected. One could analyse this, in a manner consistent with the cases discussed above, as an argument based on the submission that the dishonesty – the fraud – was central, rather than incidental, to the entirety of the claim for loss of earnings and so justified the dismissal of the same. The Defendant's appeal failed. The Court of Appeal was sympathetic to the trial judge's plight in attempting to identify what he described as "*any scrap of information that might assist me in coming to a just conclusion.*" It was for this reason that he permitted late evidence to be adduced from the three witnesses called by the Claimant and whose evidence appears to have made all the difference. One wonders whether the trial judge and/or the Court of Appeal would have found a submission by the Defendant that the Claimant should not, on *ex turpi causa* grounds, be permitted to recover where a fraud lay at the heart of his claim for loss of earnings; as I have indicated, there is no reference in the Court of Appeal judgment to the cases referred to above and it appears that his secondary claim for loss of earnings was as tainted by non-disclosure to the Inland Revenue as his principal claim. However, Ward LJ referred expressly[53] to the fact that the judge had held that the Claimant's failure to disclose his earnings to the Inland Revenue in no way debarred him from recovering lost past and future earnings[54] and observed that, "*Quite correctly, in my view, there has been no appeal against that ruling.*"

3.029 The question whether the Claimant's fraud is central or incidental was considered in detail in *Hewison* v *Meridian Shipping & Others.*[55] In this case the Claimant sustained serious personal injury in the course of his employment by the Defendant as a seaman on a cable-laying vessel. The Claimant brought proceedings in negligence and breach of statutory duty and liability was admitted. The Claimant had ceased working as a seaman (on his account, this was by reason of the accident) and his claim for loss of earnings was based on the proposition that if the accident had not happened, at a time when the Claimant was 35 years of age, he would have continued to work until he was around 62 years of age. The Claimant experienced two epileptic fits after the accident, but he had a history of significant epileptic seizures prior to his employment with the Defendant. He controlled this with medication and the medico-legal evidence was that, but for the index accident, there was only a 20% prospect that he would experience another epileptic fit during his lifetime. Prior to commencing work with the Defendant the Claimant had completed three medical questionnaires. These required him to disclose whether he was taking medication and whether he had suffered from fits. The Claimant realised that he would not be permitted to work as a sea-farer if he disclosed his previous history of epilepsy and so he did not disclose that he was taking anti-convulsive medication and had suffered from epileptic fits. The Claimant completed two further medical questionnaires[56] and, again, failed to disclose his medication and condition. The Defendant's response to the Claimant's loss of earnings claim was that an essential part of his claim that, but for the accident, he would have continued to work as a seaman, was that he would have had to continue to deceive his employer as to his epilepsy and medication (as he had in the past). The Claimant's claim for loss of earnings was dismissed at first instance and he appealed. The Court of Appeal commenced by observing that dishonesty in respect of one portion of the claim did not necessarily justify the dismissal of the entire claim (if it was possible to sever that part of the claim tainted by dishonesty). The issue was characterised as involving the

---

[53] [2002] EWCA Civ 591, para 14.
[54] Subject to deduction for the tax that should have been paid.
[55] [2002] EWCA Civ 1821.
[56] One before and one just after the index accident.

question whether the unlawful act of the Claimant was "*a collateral illegality in the performance of the contract*" or whether it formed part of his case.[57] Clarke LJ, delivering the leading judgment for the majority, relied on the following in dismissing the appeal. First, it would have been necessary for the Claimant to continue to deceive his employers in order to continue working as a seaman and that deception would have amounted to the criminal offence of obtaining a pecuniary advantage by deception.[58] The deception involved in the commission of the offence – while it might not lead to a severe criminal penalty – was central, rather than collateral, to the continuation of the Claimant's employment as a seaman. In the circumstances, the Claimant's deception,

> ...struck at the root of the contract under which he earned remuneration and ... would have done so in the future.[59]

Clarke LJ distinguished the *Duller* and *Newman* cases referred to above. He did not support his decision by appeal to the public conscience, although, incidentally, he did observe that the public conscience would be affronted by

> ... the notion that a claimant could recover earnings by way of damages which he could only have made by exercising a deliberate deception on employers (with consequent risk to others) and indeed by committing a criminal offence.[60]

3.030 *Hewison* was relied on by the Defendant in an appeal which was concerned with loss of earnings arising out of employment which had been dishonestly obtained some years after the index accident: *Major* v *Ministry of Defence*.[61] In this case the Claimant, a 13-year old girl, was permitted by the Defendant to drive a snow mobile. She injured herself and the persons riding on the snow mobile with her. Among other injuries the Claimant developed a serious post traumatic stress disorder, depression and alcohol dependency. She had self-harmed on occasions while in the grip of these illnesses. Several years after the accident the Claimant sought and obtained a post with the Royal Air Force. As part of her application for this post she was required to answer a question whether she had ever self-harmed. The

---

[57] A formula adopted by Clarke LJ at para 38 of his judgment and also adopted by Tuckey LJ at para 51 of his. Cf the dissenting judgment of Ward LJ.
[58] Tuckey LJ, who agreed with Clarke LJ that the appeal should be dismissed, did not base his judgment (at para 52) on the proposition that the Claimant had committed a criminal offence. Instead, he concentrated on the argument that a continuing deception had to lie at the heart of the claim.
[59] At para 45(vi).
[60] At para 45(viii).
[61] [2003] EWCA Civ 1433.

Claimant answered this question dishonestly, concealing past incidents of self-harm. If the Claimant had given an honest answer to that question then she would not have been admitted as a member of the armed services. The truth subsequently emerged and the Claimant was discharged from the armed services. She pursued a claim for past and future loss of earnings and the Defendant relied on *Hewison*. The Claimant's claim was dismissed at first instance and she appealed. *Hewison* was distinguished on appeal and the appeal was allowed. Buxton LJ, delivering the leading judgment, held as follows:

> [The Claimant's] complaint is that she is not, unlike Mr Hewison, a person who is congenitally unable to work without telling lies about his condition. She was put in the position of being unable to work by the tort of the defendants. The fact that in order to gain any employment she would have to behave deceitfully is a matter that she is entitled to complain of in respect of the tort of the defendants. This was not a matter on which Mr Hewison could rely in quantifying his damages.[62]

3.031 In other words, and by contrast with *Hewison*, the Claimant's lie was not an essential causal element in obtaining and retaining the earnings on which the claim was based. It was the Defendant, by its tortious conduct, that prevented the Claimant from working in the Royal Air Force without telling a lie.

4. FRAUD AS A DEFENCE IN CONTRACT

Basic principles

3.032 *Brown Jenkinson & Co Limited* v *Percy Dalton (London) Limited*[63] provides a useful illustration of the general approach. The Defendants wished to ship a large quantity of orange juice to Hamburg. The Claimants, the agents of the ship owner, told the Defendants that some of the containers to be used to store the juice during shipment were leaking and frail and that, accordingly, a qualified ("*claused*") bill of lading should be granted. The Defendants, however, required a clean bill of lading and the ship owners, at the Defendants' request and on provision of an indemnity by the Defendants (against all losses which might arise from the issue of clean bills of lading), signed bills stating that the barrels were "*shipped in apparent good order and condition.*" The barrels were leaking on arrival in Hamburg and the ship

---

[62] At para 12.
[63] [1957] 2 QB 621 (CA).

owners had to pay compensation for the loss. The Claimants sued the Defendants on the indemnity (the benefit of which had been assigned to them by the ship owner). The Defendants, refusing to pay an indemnity, raised a defence relying on the (unattractive) argument that the contract of indemnity was illegal in that it was based on a fraudulent misrepresentation. This case clearly involved some morally questionable conduct by both parties, save that the moral turpitude might be thought to have been stronger on the Defendants' side for the following reasons. First, it was found at first instance that the ship owner did not wish or intend to defraud anyone and, second, there was evidence that the supply of clean bills of lading (with corresponding indemnity) was a common occurrence in this context within the industry. The Claimants were successful at first instance and the Defendants appealed and were successful.

3.033 The Court of Appeal was clearly uncomfortable with the Defendants' stance which was variously described as one of "*singular ill grace*" and as "*lacking in merit.*" This did not prevent the Defendants' appeal, raising (as it did) questions of wider importance, from being successful. Morris LJ stated as follows:

> ... at the request of the defendants, the plaintiffs made a representation which they knew to be false and which they intended should be relied upon by persons who received the bill of lading, including any banker who might be concerned. In these circumstances, all the elements of the tort of deceit were present. Someone who could prove that he suffered damage by relying on the representation could sue for damages. I feel impelled to the conclusion that a promise to indemnify the plaintiffs against any loss resulting to them from making the representation is unenforceable. The claim cannot be put forward without basing it upon an unlawful transaction. The promise upon which the plaintiffs rely is in effect this: if you will make a false representation, which will deceive indorsees or bankers, we will indemnify you against any loss that may result to you. I cannot think that a court should lend its aid to such a bargain.[64]

3.034 It appears to have been key to the decision that all of the elements of fraud were present (would it have made any difference if some component of the tort of deceit was missing?) and that the fraudulent conduct formed the basis for the presentation of the claim.

3.035 A concentration upon the centrality of the fraud can also be detected in *Napier* v *National Business Agency Limited*[65] which involved a contract of

---

[64] At p 632. *Chitty on Contracts* (29th ed, 2004) 16-017 n 85, characterise this case as involving deceit without moral turpitude, although this seems a little generous to the Claimants' conduct.
[65] [1951] 2 All ER 264 (CA).

employment in which, to the knowledge of both employer and employee, the expenses paid were misrepresented in order to evade the payment of tax. The Claimant was summarily dismissed and brought an action against the Defendant employer for payment in lieu of notice. The claim was dismissed both at first instance and on appeal. The Court held that the Claimant's contract was based on defrauding the Inland Revenue and that this object so tainted the entirety of the contract that the objectionable portions of the contract could not be severed from the whole so that the Claimant could sue on and recover under the unobjectionable portions of the contract.[66] One wonders whether this robust approach to the defrauding of the Inland Revenue would survive the scrutiny of the appellate courts in the current legal environment where, as we have seen above in the tortious claims for loss of earnings, a more relaxed stance is evident.

Effects of fraud: repudiation and affirmation

3.036 The basic starting point is that where a contract is entered into on the basis of fraudulent representations, it is rendered voidable at the option of the innocent party, but will subsist until it is avoided by that party.[67] Once successfully avoided by the innocent party to a fraud it is tolerably clear that, the consent of the defrauded having been vitiated by the fraud, the contract is, "... *treated in law as never having come into existence.*"[68]

3.037 A good deal of the difficulty in this area has related to the exercise of the right to avoid the contract and, specifically, the problems which arise in circumstances where there has either been delay on the part of the innocent party (i.e. delay following the apprehension of the fraud) or where the parties' situations have changed with the result that they can no longer be put back in the position that they were in when the contract was entered.[69] Delay is relevant only insofar as it provides evidence to support the proposition that the defrauded party wishes to affirm, rather than to avoid,

---

[66] Cf. *Kwei Tek Chao* v *British Traders and Shippers Limited* [1954] 2 QB 459, 476 *per* Devlin J (QB).

[67] See among other cases, *Reese River Silver Mining Company Limited* v *Smith* [1869] 4 LR HL 64 (HL).

[68] *Johnson* v *Agnew* [1980] AC 367, 392H – 393A *per* Lord Wilberforce (HL(E)).

[69] "... *in the case of fraud the court will exercise its jurisdiction to the full in order, if possible, to prevent the defendant from enjoying the benefit of his fraud at the expense of the innocent plaintiff. Restoration, however, is essential to the idea of restitution. ... if a plaintiff who has been defrauded seeks to have the contract annulled and his money or property restored to him, it would be inequitable if he did not also restore what he had got under the contract from the defendant. Though the defendant has been fraudulent, he must not be robbed, nor must the plaintiff be unjustly enriched, as he would be if he both got back what he had parted with and kept what he had received in return.*" *Per* Lord Wright in *Spence* v *Crawford* [1939] 3 All ER 271, 288- 289 (HL (Sc)).

the contract. *Gordon* v *Street*[70] concerned an action brought on a promissory note. The Claimant was a money-lender who advertised his services under a fictitious name. The Defendant borrowed money and provided a promissory note in respect of the sum borrowed and the interest on the same. The Claimant brought an action on the promissory note and it was found, as a fact, that the Claimant had fraudulently concealed his identity in order to induce the Claimant to enter into the contract. An issue arose on the question whether the delay by the Defendant in repudiating the contract was such that the Claimant should, notwithstanding the fraud, be entitled to rely on it. The promissory note was dated 19 August. The Defendant discovered the fraud on 20 December and, on 28 December, the Claimant commenced the proceedings (before the Defendant sought to avoid the contract). The contract was formally repudiated in a letter from the Defendant's solicitors on 6 January. The Court of Appeal was unconvinced that the delay between the Defendant's discovery of the fraud and the repudiation prevented the Defendant from avoiding the contract (even though, by the date of avoidance, proceedings had commenced):

> The Exchequer Chamber in Clough v London and North Western Ry Co [LR 7 Ex 26] … held that, though lapse of time without rescinding will furnish evidence that the person defrauded has determined to affirm the contract, and when the lapse of time is great it probably would in practice be treated as conclusive evidence to shew that he has so determined, yet, as Mellor J said in delivering the judgment of the court … ' We cannot see any principle, and are not aware of any authority, for saying that the mere fact that one who is party to the fraud has issued a writ and commence an action before the rescission, is such a change of position (of the defrauding party) as would preclude the defrauded party from exercising his right to rescind. Neither can we see the principle or discover the authority for saying that it is necessary that there should be a declaration of his intention to rescind prior to the plea.'[71]

3.038 In *Peyman* v *Lanjani*[72] the Court of Appeal considered what the defrauded party was required to know before he would be treated as having affirmed the contract which the fraud had procured. The following principles emerged from the Court's comprehensive consideration of the authorities:

- The innocent party needs to have knowledge not only of the facts which gave rise to the right to rescind (or affirm), but also knowledge that he has the right to rescind or affirm:

---

[70] [1899] 2 QB 641 (CA).
[71] At pp 650 – 651 *per* A L Smith LJ.
[72] [1985] Ch 457 (CA).

> I do not think that a party to a contract can realistically or sensibly be held to have made this irrevocable choice between rescission and affirmation unless he has actual knowledge not only of the facts of the serious breach of the contract by the other party which is a pre-condition of his right to choose, but also of the fact that in the circumstances which exist he does have that right to make that choice which the law gives him.[73]

- Affirmation requires an unequivocal demonstration to the fraudulent party of the intention to proceed with the contract.

- Determining whether the defrauded party has elected to affirm the contract will be dealt with by reference to the facts of the instant case.

3.039 It should be borne in mind that any right to avoid the contract, where exercised, may be subject to rights acquired under the contract (in the period preceding repudiation) by innocent third parties.

---

[73] *Per* May LJ in *Peyman* at p 494E.

Chapter 4

EVIDENCE

1. BURDEN OF PROOF

4.001 In civil proceedings the legal or persuasive burden of proof lies with the party who asserts what *Phipson* refers to as "*the affirmative of the issue*".[1] There are two reasons for this rule. First, it is appropriate that the party who asserts a positive case and seeks, with respect to that assertion, a remedy in law should be required to discharge the burden of proof. Second, it is more difficult to prove a negative than a positive. In the light of these considerations, the law requires he who alleges to make good the allegation.

4.002 Accordingly, the party alleging fraud is required to prove it, as Lord Herschell made clear in *Derry* v *Peek*.[2] It is worth adding that where a Defendant or an insurer wish to raise fraud as a defence to a claim then they bear the burden of proof on that issue (see *Slattery* v *Mance*[3] and *The Alexion Hope*[4]).

2. STANDARD OF PROOF: Hornal v Neuberger Products Limited

4.003 In formal terms the standard of proof applicable to allegations of fraud is the ordinary civil standard of proof: fraud must be proved on the balance of probabilities. This has been defined as meaning that the court must be satisfied that the presence of fraud is "*more likely than not*."[5]

---

[1] *Phipson on Evidence* (16th ed, 2005) para 6-06 citing *Robins* v *National Trust Co Ltd* [1927] AC 515.
[2] *Derry* v *Peek* (1889) 14 App Cas 337, 374 (HL). See also *Glasier* v *Rolls* (1889) 42 Ch D 436, 458 (CA).
[3] [1962] 1 QB 676, 681 *per* Salmon J (QBD).
[4] [1988] 1 Ll Rep 311 (CA).
[5] See *In re H* [1996] AC 563, 586, *per* Lord Nicholls (HL).

4.004 The leading authority continues to be *Hornal* v *Neuberger Products Limited*.[6] The issue in this case was, at least superficially, a straightforward one. It was alleged that the director of a company had, in the course of negotiations for the sale of a used lathe, represented that the lathe had been reconditioned by a toolmaker; the representation was inaccurate. It was denied by the Defendant that the representation had been made. The Claimant brought a claim for breach of warranty and, in the alternative, for fraudulent misrepresentation. The judge at first instance found that the representation had no contractual status and the claim for breach of warranty was dismissed. The judge also found, applying the civil standard of proof, that the representation had been made and made fraudulently. However, the claim was dismissed on the basis that the Claimant could not prove that he had suffered loss by reliance on the fraudulent misrepresentation (the effect of the judge's finding that there had been fraud lay in the costs order that he made; the Claimant was ordered to pay only one quarter of the Defendant's costs of the action). Both parties appealed. On appeal, counsel for the Defendant suggested that the criminal standard of proof should apply to allegations of fraud. Denning LJ pointed out, in the course of argument, that where, as in *Hornal*, it was alleged that a statement was both a warranty and a fraud, a court might be driven to applying the lower standard of proof to the warranty and a higher standard of proof to the fraud (an approach which, he suggested, would "*be bringing the law into contempt*").[7] Denning LJ dealt with the matter in the following way:

> ... the standard of proof depends on the nature of the issue. The more serious the allegation the higher the degree of probability that is required: but it need not, in a civil case, reach the very high standard required by the criminal law. If Mr Neuberger did represent that the machine was ... reconditioned he did very wrong because he knew it was untrue. His moral guilt is just as great whatever the form of the action, no matter whether in warranty or in fraud. He should be judged by the same standard in either case.[8]

4.005 In *Hornal* the Court of Appeal resolved the problem that might have arisen out of the need to apply different standards of proof to the same factual issue; namely, whether the representation was made. The solution was to recognise that the seriousness of an allegation of fraud, involving, as it does, "*moral guilt*" on the part of the fraudster, requires more evidence and better quality evidence before the (conventional) civil standard of proof

---

[6] [1957] 1 QB 247 (CA).
[7] Given that the principal issue of fact in *Hornal* was whether or not the statement was made, the judge might have been driven to find that, on the issue of warranty, the statement was made and, in respect of the issue of fraud, the (same) statement was not made.
[8] [1957] 1 QB 247, 258 (CA).

will be discharged. In other words, the inherent flexibility of the civil standard of proof supplied its own solution. The Court of Appeal was satisfied that the trial judge had taken the correct approach to the standard of proof, but, on the facts, it was held that the Claimant had suffered damage and so his appeal was allowed. More recently, Lord Nicholls has explained that the *Hornal* approach, requiring stronger evidence, to discharge the burden of proof, is justified on the basis that the more serious the allegation, the less likely it is to have occurred:

> The more improbable the event, the stronger must be the evidence that it did occur before, on the balance of probability, its occurrence will be established...

and, Lord Nicholls suggested, "*Fraud is usually less likely than negligence.*"[9] The approach taken in *Hornal* has been adopted in a number of other common law jurisdictions.[10]

4.006 A finding of fraud will, to a large degree, depend on the view that the trial judge takes of the alleged fraudulent witness appearing before him. A corollary of this is that an appellate court should be slow to interfere with the trial judge's conclusions on the issue of fraud. This proposition was expressed in forceful terms by Cross LJ in *Gross* v *Lewis Hillman Limited*,[11]

> A Court of Appeal is not entitled to disturb findings of fact made by the trial judge, which depend to any appreciable extent on the view that he took as to the truthfulness or untruthfulness of a witness whom he has seen and heard, and the Court of Appeal will not do so unless it is completely satisfied that the Judge was wrong. It is not enough that it has doubts, even grave doubts, as to the correctness of the Judge's finding. It must be convinced that he was wrong.

---

[9] *In re H* [1996] AC 563, 586 (HL). In this case Lord Nicholls rejected the suggestion that a higher standard of proof should be applied to an application for a care order where serious allegations of sexual abuse were raised. He also dismissed, at p 587, a suggestion that the *Hornal* approach should be replaced with the formula, "*... the standard should be commensurate with the gravity of the allegation and the seriousness of the consequences.*" See also *Smith New Court Ltd* v *Scrimgeour Vickers* [1997] AC 254, 274 *per* Lord Steyn (HL). See also, applying *Re H* in the context of an insurance fraud, *Danepoint Ltd* v *Underwriting Insurance Ltd* [2006] Ll Rep IR 429, 437 *per* HHJ Peter Coulson QC (QB(TCC)) and, in the context of an RTA low velocity impact claim, *Humphries* v *Matthews* (2006) 16 June (Liverpool CC per Recorder Moran QC) (unreported, but available on Lawtel).

[10] See, e.g. the New Zealand case *Bromley* v *Attorney-General* [1968] NZLR 75

[11] [1970] Ch 445, 459. See also *Smith* v *Chadwick* (1884) 9 App Cas 187, 193 - 194 *per* Lord Blackburn (HL).

3. STANDARD OF PROOF: ELEMENTS OF THE TORT OF DECEIT

4.007 We have already looked at the separate elements of the tort of deceit. In *Hornal* it is not always wholly clear whether the Court of Appeal guidance is that the enhanced civil standard of proof should be applied to all of the elements of the tort. There seems no reason in principle why the *Hornal* approach to the civil standard of proof should be applied to all of the elements of the tort. Why, for example, should a Claimant be disadvantaged in a deceit action by being required to adduce stronger evidence (of the sort referred to in the *Hornal* line of authority) that a false statement was made which caused loss than might be required in an action for negligent misrepresentation. It is suggested that the proper approach is to apply the enhanced, *Hornal*, standard of proof only to the court's consideration of the fraudulent party's statement of mind (namely, whether the representor made a statement knowing it to be false or reckless as to whether it was true or false); the conventional standard of proof can be applied to the residual elements of the tort.

4. CRIMINAL CONVICTIONS

4.008 While it is conceivable, as a result of the difference in the standards of proof, that a party acquitted of a criminal offence of fraud in the criminal courts could be found liable of fraud, arising out of the same facts, in the civil courts, it is likely that a criminal conviction of fraud, where admissible in evidence, will in appropriate cases lead to a finding of civil fraud.

4.009 Section 11(2) of the Civil Evidence Act 1968 provides as follows:

> In any civil proceedings in which by virtue of this section a person is proved to have been convicted of an offence by or before any court in the United Kingdom or by a court-martial there or elsewhere – (a) he shall be taken to have committed that offence unless the contrary is proved; and (b) without prejudice to the reception of any other admissible evidence for the purpose of identifying the facts on which the conviction was based, the contents of any document which is admissible as evidence of the conviction; and the contents of the information, complaint or indictment or charge-sheet on which the person in question was convicted, shall be admissible in evidence for that purpose.

This provision was relied on in *Alliance & Leicester Building Society* v *Edgestop Limited*[12] where a Defendant was held liable for fraudulent misrepresentations made by an employee in circumstances where evidence of the employee's convictions for dishonesty offences (contained in section 20(2) of the Theft Act 1968) was admitted in the civil proceedings.

5. FAILING TO DISCHARGE THE BURDEN OF PROOF: CASE NOT PROVED

4.010 Most trial judges are reluctant to find that a witness has been dishonest. The reasons for this are obvious. A finding that a witness has lied on oath might have serious personal consequences for the witness. Equally, it may be personally embarrassing for a judge to record a finding that a witness has given false evidence (particularly when the witness is still present and sitting at the back of the court).

4.011 In circumstances where a claim is regarded as fraudulently presented or where a judge suspects the same, an express finding that the claim is dishonest may in any event be unnecessary. A judge might instead have recourse to the formula that the claim is dismissed because the Claimant has simply failed to discharge the burden of proof.

4.012 *The Popi M*[13] concerned the loss of a vessel at sea. The trial judge found that a submarine had collided with the vessel and caused its loss. On ultimate appeal to the House of Lords their Lordships held that no positive conclusions as to the cause of the vessel's loss could be reached and that, in the circumstances, the appropriate result was that the Claimant had failed to prove his case. Lord Brandon's speech contains the following:

> ... the Judge is not bound always to make a finding one way or the other with regard to the facts averred by the parties. He has open to him the third alternative of saying that the party on whom the burden of proof lies in relation to any averment made by him has failed to discharge that burden. No judge likes to decide cases on burden of proof if he can legitimately avoid having to do so. There are cases, however, in which, owing to the unsatisfactory state of the evidence or otherwise, deciding on the burden of proof is the only just course to take ... it is open to the judge to say simply that the evidence leaves him in doubt whether the event occurred or not, and

---

[12] [1993] 1 WLR 1462 (Ch D).
[13] *Rhesa Shipping Co SA* v *Edmunds ("The Popi M")* [1985] 1 WLR 948 (HL).

that the party on whom the burden of proving that the event occurred lies has therefore failed to discharge such a burden.[14]

4.013 The use of Lord Brandon's "*third alternative*" is common in cases where a judge is confronted with a claim that is (or at least appears to be) false.[15] It is equally common where an allegation of fraud is the centrepiece of a cause of action or defence (where the enhanced standard of proof increases the likelihood of a judge concluding that the case is not proved).

4.014 The *Popi M* formula was more recently applied in *Davis and Docherty v Balfour Kilpatrick Limited*[16] and a similar approach can also be discerned in the speech of Lord Hope in *Pickford* v *ICI Plc.*[17]

---

[14] At pp 955 -956.

[15] In *C (a Child)* v *First Choice Holidays & Flights Limited* (2004) (unreported) the trial judge concluded that the evidence for the Claimant as to the occurrence of an accident gave rise to "*considerable doubt*" as to its truthfulness and accuracy. Similarly, in *Hall* v *Jewel in the Crown Limited* (2004) (unreported) the trial judge, dismissing the claim, described the Claimant's evidence as "*wholly unreliable*" and such unreliability as tainting "*everything else he has to say*". However, no express finding was made in either case that the claim was dishonest; the conclusion was simply that the case was not proved (the Claimants having failed to discharge the burden of proof).

[16] [2002] EWCA Civ 736 paras 20-21 *per* Tuckey LJ.

[17] [1998] ICR 673, 686 (HL).

Chapter 5

PERJURY AND CONTEMPT

1. PERJURY: INTRODUCTION

5.001 This book deals with dishonesty in civil proceedings. It does not, save for what follows, deal with the many criminal offences for dishonest words and conduct. However, it is appropriate to consider in detail a specific criminal offence created by statute: namely, perjury. In a general sense this offence criminalises lies told in court. The elements of the offence which have to be proved in order to establish an offender's criminal liability share much in common with the tort of deceit and the other species of civil dishonesty which this book covers.

5.002 The offence of perjury is now enshrined in section 1 of the Perjury Act 1911, but it is an ancient offence with much older antecedents. Its history is helpfully summarised during the course of Lawton LJ's judgment in *R* v *Hamid & Hamid*.[1] Perjury was originally dealt with in the ecclesiastical courts before being taken over by the Royal Courts during the first half of the sixteenth century. Thereafter, the development of the offence was piecemeal (until the 1911 Act) and filtered through a large number of different statutes dealing with a very wide range of subjects (the schedule to the 1911 Act contains no fewer than eleven pages of repealed provisions in statutes dating as far back as the reigns of Henry VIII and Elizabeth I).

5.003 While the number of reported cases dealing with the offence of perjury are relatively scarce; it is by no means uncommon. Some statistics are gathered in an interesting recent article in the Criminal Law Review.[2] Between 1991 and 2000, no fewer than 1,024 Defendants stood trial in the Crown Court for perjury, of whom 830 were convicted and 437 were sentenced to imprisonment.

---

[1] (1979) 6 Cr App R 324, 327 (CA).
[2] Susan S M Edwards, "*Perjury and Perverting the Course of Justice Considered*" [2003] Crim LR 525. Table 1 at p 529.

2. THE OFFENCE: SECTION 1 OF THE PERJURY ACT 1911

5.004 This provides as follows:

> (1) If any person lawfully sworn as a witness or interpreter in a judicial proceeding wilfully makes a statement material in that proceeding, which he knows to be false or does not believe to be true, he shall be guilty of perjury, and shall, on conviction thereof on indictment, be liable to penal servitude for a term not exceeding seven years, or to imprisonment with or without hard labour for a term not exceeding two years, or to a fine or to both such penal servitude or imprisonment and fine.

5.005 Since the abolition of imprisonment with hard labour in 1948,[3] the sentencing powers under the Act are now imprisonment for a term not exceeding seven years or a fine or both.

5.006 It should be noted that the commission of the offence is not limited to false statements made within the jurisdiction. Section 8 of the 1911 Act expressly states that,

> Where an offence against this Act or any offence punishable as perjury or as subornation of perjury under any other Act of Parliament is committed in any place either on sea or land outside the United Kingdom, the offender may be proceeded against, indicted, tried, and punished ... in England ...

5.007 It should be noted that a person who, in sworn evidence before the European Court of Justice, makes a statement which he knows to be false or does not believe to be true shall, whether or not he is a British citizen, be guilty of perjury.[4] The wide territorial reach of the 1911 Act is confirmed by sections 1(4) and 1(5) of the Act which deal with rather different situations. First, the witness lawfully sworn within the jurisdiction for the purposes of evidence to be received overseas in: a dominion territory; a UK tribunal constituted overseas (whether on sea or land) or "*a tribunal of any foreign state.*" Statements made for the purposes of these tribunals are treated, by section 1(4) of the 1911 Act, "*as a statement made in a judicial proceeding in England*". Second, section 1(5) of the Act provides that a witness lawfully sworn in an overseas dominion or before a UK tribunal constituted overseas for the purposes of a judicial proceeding in England shall be treated as if actually made before the judicial proceeding in England.

---

[3] Criminal Justice Act 1948, ss 1(1) and 1(2).
[4] European Communities Act, s 11(1) (a).

5.008 The Defendant can be tried on separate counts in the same indictment where he has perjured himself on more than one occasion and the Defendant can be separately sentenced for each of several counts for a custodial term which, in aggregate, exceeds the statutory maximum for a single offence.

5.009 Section 14 of the 1911 Act sets out the manner in which the earlier trial (in which the perjured evidence was given) is to be proved. For trials on indictment, the requisite proof is obtained by a certificate signed by the clerk of the court or his deputy. The certificate should contain, "*the substance and effect (omitting the formal parts) of the indictment and trial*".[5] The Act is silent as to the appropriate manner of proof of the earlier trial where the perjured evidence was given in the course of civil proceedings. One assumes that a transcript of the evidence and judgment, signed by the trial judge and clerk of the court would suffice (supported by appropriate witness evidence).

3. ELEMENTS OF THE OFFENCE

"lawfully sworn"

5.010 Perjury can be committed in respect of evidence given under affirmations or declarations as well as under oath. Section 15 of the 1911 Act makes it clear that,

> 'oath' ... includes 'affirmation' and 'declaration,' and the expression 'swear' ... includes 'affirm' and 'declare'

and further provides that,

> For the purposes of this Act, the forms and ceremonies used in administering an oath are immaterial, if the court or the persons before whom the oath is taken has power to administer an oath for the purposes of verifying the statement in question, and if the oath has been administered in a form and with ceremonies which the person taking the oath has accepted without objection, or has declared to be binding on him.[6]

5.011 The Evidence Act 1851 contains, at section 16, a list of the persons with power to administer an oath; the list is expansive – every court, judge,

---

[5] Perjury Act 1911, s 14.
[6] s 15(1).

justice, officer, commissioner, arbitrator or other person having by law or consent of the parties authority to hear, receive and examine evidence.

5.012 It should be noted that a person who is sworn by mistake because he is not a competent witness will not have committed an offence with respect to any evidence that follows.[7]

"judicial proceeding"

5.013 Not every forum in which statements are read and evidence given will constitute a *"judicial proceeding"*, although, again, this phrase has been quite widely construed. The Act itself provides some definition of judicial proceeding. Section 1(2) states that judicial proceeding,

> ...includes a proceeding before any court, tribunal, or person having by law power to hear, receive, and examine evidence on oath.

In addition, where the statement made for the purposes of a judicial proceeding is not made before the tribunal itself, but is made on oath before a person who is authorised to administer the oath then that is treated, by virtue of section 1(3) of the Act, as a statement made in a judicial proceeding. Evidence given on oath by live link by a witness outside the jurisdiction will be treated as given in a judicial proceeding.[8] There is relatively little case law with respect to this element of the offence. It has been held that two special commissioners sitting, in pursuance of powers granted by the Income Tax Acts, constitute a tribunal and, therefore, a judicial proceeding for the purposes of section 1(2) of the Perjury Act 1911.[9] It also appears that evidence given in the course of a claim brought against a fictitious person on a fictitious claim may also have been given in a judicial proceeding.[10]

"wilfully makes a statement"

5.014 In common with certain aspects of the tort of deceit, the false statement has to be made deliberately, rather than through inadvertence or mistake. In *R* v *Millward*[11] the Appellant, a police officer, gave answers to questions in cross-examination at trial of two third parties for motoring offences. The Appellant later admitted that the answers that he gave were

---

[7] *R* v *Clegg* (1868) 19 LT 47.
[8] Criminal Justice Act 1988, s 32.
[9] *R* v *Hood-Barrs* [1943] KB 455 (CA).
[10] *R* v *Castiglione and Porteous* (1912) 7 Cr App R 233.
[11] [1985] QB 519 (CA).

lies. He stated that he had "*panicked*" during the course of cross-examination and had, therefore, lied. At trial on a charge of perjury a submission of no case to answer was made. The basis for the submission was that the Appellant lacked the state of mind required for the commission of the offence. This submission was rejected and, accordingly, the Appellant changed his plea to guilty. There was an appeal against the trial judge's ruling on matters of law. On appeal the Appellant's submission at first instance was repeated; namely, that

> ... the word 'wilfully' requires proof by the prosecution of knowledge or belief by the accused man that the question asked and the answer to be given are material. No offence is committed, it is submitted, if a person makes a statement even though he knows it to be false and even though it is in law material, if he does so in the honest though mistaken belief that it is not material in that proceeding.

5.015 This submission was rejected by the Court of Appeal. Lord Lane CJ stated as follows:

> It does not seem to us that as a matter of construction the words of section 1(1) of the Perjury Act 1911 can properly bear the meaning which counsel seeks to ascribe to them. If Parliament had intended that result, it would have been simple to say so, for example, by providing that 'if any person sworn as a witness in a judicial proceeding wilfully makes a statement which he knows to be material in that proceeding and which he knows to be false or does not believe to be true, he shall be guilty of the offence.'[12]

5.016 Lord Lane CJ went on to observe that if a statement could only be material within the meaning of section 1(1) of the Act when its maker believed it to be so then section 1(6) of the Act, which provides that materiality is a question of law to be assessed by the court,[13] would be rendered otiose (another reason for rejecting the Appellant's submission as to the proper construction of the Act). Accordingly, it is not necessary for the prosecution to prove that the witness believed the statement to be material.

5.017 If a witness gives evidence under duress then that may deprive it of the wilfulness necessary for the commission of the offence. In *R v Hudson, R v Taylor,*[14] the Appellants, young women aged 17 and 19 years respectively, were witnesses to a brawl in a public house. They were called as witnesses by the prosecution at the trial of one of the protagonists. They later admitted that their evidence at trial (which resulted in the acquittal of the accused

---

[12] At p 524B – C *per* Lord Lane CJ.
[13] This provision is considered below.
[14] [1971] 2 QB 202 (CA).

man) was false. At their own trial for perjury they raised a defence of duress (one of the Appellants claimed that she had been threatened with violence by an associate of the accused man in the event that she gave unfavourable evidence at his trial). At the subsequent perjury trial the jury were directed by the recorder that the defence of duress was not open to the two women. They were duly convicted and appealed. The appeal was allowed and the women's convictions were quashed. Lord Parker CJ held that the fact that the threat of violence might materialise the night after the women gave evidence, rather than while they were actually in the witness box, did not rob the defence of duress of the requirement that the threat be "*present and immediate*". It was, however, recognised that, for public policy reasons, it was necessary to keep the defence within reasonable bounds insofar as it applied to perjury. The following guidance was, therefore, given:

> In the opinion of this court it is always open to the Crown to prove that the accused failed to avail himself of some opportunity which was reasonably open to him to render the threat ineffective, and that upon this being established the threat in question can no longer be relied on by the defence. In deciding whether such an opportunity was reasonably open to the accused the jury should have regard to his age and circumstances, and to any risks to him which may be involved in the course of action relied upon.

There is some, albeit fairly antique, authority for the proposition that a statement of opinion can, insofar as the opinion is not honestly held, support a charge of perjury.[15]

"material in that proceeding"

5.018 Section 1(6) states, rather opaquely,

> The question whether a statement on which perjury is assigned was material is a question of law to be determined by the court or tribunal.

As indicated above, *R v Millward* is authority for the proposition that it does not need to be proved that the witness himself knew or believed that the false statement was material; the question whether or not a statement is material is to be assessed objectively – by the judge. The same case also establishes that the test whether a statement is material is based on whether a statement

---

[15] See *R v Pedley* (1784) 1 Leach 325; 168 ER 265 where, *per* Lord Mansfield, it was held that a statement of belief could found liability for perjury, although the almost equally early authority of *R v Crespigny* (1795) 1 Esp 280, 170 ER 357 (perjury cannot be maintained on the basis of an opinion as to the construction of a deed) would suggest the contrary. *R v Schlesinger* (1847) 10 QB 670, 116 ER 255 may resolve the matter (if a witness swears that he "*thinks*" a certain fact took place then this can give rise to a conviction for perjury).

might have affected the outcome of the proceedings, it is not necessary to prove that it would have done in order for the Defendant to be guilty of the offence: Lord Lane CJ characterised the test as based on the proposition that the perjured evidence "*might very well*" have affected the outcome of the case. A number of cases decided in the nineteenth century make it clear that the offence is widely cast. There is a focus on the extent to which the court receiving the evidence has or might have been, by reason of the false statement, caused to act in a particular way. In this regard there are, therefore, parallels that can again be drawn with the tort of deceit, although the tort of deceit requires proof of damage before it is committed; it cannot be committed by an attempt.

5.019 A statement which relates to a circumstantial matter can be material for the purposes of the offence if the court is induced by the statement to believe the greater part of a witness's evidence.[16] A statement can also be material if the court relies on it in order to justify the admission of other material evidence.[17] A false statement which is material only in the sense that it impacts on the credit of a witness can lead to the commission of the offence.[18] In *R v Hewitt*,[19] decided in 1913, it was established that a false statement which is given under oath during a plea in mitigation can be material for the purposes of the offence.

"he knows to be false or does not believe to be true"

5.020 The requirement that the statement be made with knowledge of its falsity or, as a corollary, a lack of belief in its truth provides another connection to the tort of deceit. Again, a reckless or conscious indifference to the truth of the statement can, it appears, give rise to criminal liability:

> ... a man may swear to a particular fact without knowing at the time whether the fact be true or false; it is as much perjury as if he knew the fact to be false, and equally indictable.[20]

There is also authority for the counter-intuitive proposition that the offence can be committed if the Defendant does not believe a statement to be true

---

[16] *R v Tyson* (1867) LR 1 CCR 107.
[17] *R v Phillpotts* (1851) 21 LJMC 18.
[18] *R v Baker* [1895] 1 QB 797 (CCR).
[19] (1913) 9 Cr App R 192 *per* Lord Isaacs CJ (CA). See also, *R v Wheeler* [1917] 1 KB 283 (CA) to like effect.
[20] *R v Mawbey* (1796) 6 Term Rep 619, 637 *per* Lawrence J; 101 ER 736.

when it is, in fact, true,[21] although in *R* v *Rider*[22] the Court of Appeal declined to express any concluded view on this issue.[23]

5.021 The offence of making a false declaration which is set out in section 5 of the Perjury Act 1911 (and is considered below) is committed when a Defendant "*knowingly and wilfully*" makes a statement which is false in a material particular. In *R* v *Sood*[24] the Appellant, a General Practitioner, signed the death certificate of one of his patients. There were no suspicious circumstances surrounding the death, but the form required the Appellant to state the cause of death and when the deceased had last been seen alive. The Appellant had not seen the deceased on the day of her death (she had been seen by a partner in the same practice), but the Appellant falsely stated that he had seen the deceased alive on the day of her death. A few days later the falsehood came to light and the Appellant was charged with and convicted of making a false statement under section 5 of the 1911 Act. On appeal it was argued that the prosecution had, in addition to proving that the Appellant had knowledge of falsity, to discharge an additional burden of proving that the Appellant had a positive intention to deceive. The Appellant's evidence at trial was that he genuinely believed that he was entitled to complete the death certificate in the manner in which he had even though he was aware that the information recorded was false. The appeal was dismissed. The Court of Appeal rejected the submission that there was any requirement that the prosecution adduce evidence to prove an additional *mens rea* element (intention to deceive) which found no expression in the Act itself.

4. FALSE STATEMENTS IN OTHER TYPES OF PROCEEDINGS

5.022 Perjury is an offence committed, as we have seen, by the making of a false statement in judicial proceedings. However, the Perjury Act 1911 also contains a number of additional offences, related to perjury itself, with

---

[21] See, e.g. Law Commission Report No 96, para 2.54 and discussion by R D Taylor, "*Complicity and Excuses*" [1983] Crim LR 656, 661.
[22] (1986) 83 Cr App R 207 (CA).
[23] At p 210 *per* Mustill LJ.
[24] [1998] Cr App R 355 (CA).

respect to false statements in other types of proceedings. They share a number of elements in common:

- they require a false statement;
- they require that the false statement be made knowingly and/or wilfully.

5.023 The specific additional offences are as follows:

- Section 2 of the Perjury Act 1911: the making of a false statement on oath otherwise than in a judicial proceeding – this offence bears the closest resemblance to perjury itself and consists of wilfully making a statement which is material and which the maker knows to be false or does not believe to be true.

- Section 3 of the 1911 Act: false oaths/declarations/notices/certificates with reference to marriage – the elements of this offence require a knowing and wilful oath etc. for the purpose of procuring a marriage, or certificate or licence for marriage. There are additional offences with respect to false entries in the marriage register and other related matters.

- Section 4 of the 1911 Act: false statements as to births or deaths – this offence is committed when a false answer is wilfully given to any question put by the Registrar of births and deaths or when a person wilfully gives false information to the Registrar. Again, there are related offences with respect to wilfully making any false certificate or declaration.

- Section 5 of the 1911 Act: false statutory declarations without oath – this offence is committed when,

  > …a person knowingly and wilfully makes (otherwise than on oath) a statement false in a material particular, and the statement is made in a statutory declaration … in an abstract, account, balance sheet, book, certificate, declaration, entry, estimate, inventory, notice, report, return or other document which he is authorised or required to make, attest, or verify, by any public general Act of Parliament …[25]

---

[25] See *R* v *Sood* [1998] Cr App R 355 (CA).

There is a related offence with respect to oral declarations or answers required by Act of Parliament.

- Section 6 of the 1911 Act: false declarations with a view to being registered on "*any register or roll of persons qualified by law to practise any vocation or qualification*" – this offence is aimed at those who seek to practise nursing, midwifery, medicine, veterinary science, law and so forth without the appropriate qualifications.[26] It requires the wilful,

> ...making or producing or causing to be made or produced either verbally or in writing, any declaration, certificate, or representation which he knows to be false or fraudulent.

5.024 The offences contained in sections 2, 3 and 4 of the Act carry the same penalty as perjury itself; namely, imprisonment for a term not exceeding seven years or a fine or both. The section 5 offence is punished by imprisonment for a term not exceeding two years or a fine or both. The section 6 offence is punished by a custodial sentence not exceeding 12 months or by a fine or by both.

5. COMPLICITY AND INCITEMENT

5.025 Section 7 of the Perjury Act 1911 provides:

> (1) Every person who aids, abets, counsels, procures, or suborns another person to commit an offence against this Act shall be liable to be proceeded against, indicted, tried and punished as if he were a principal offender
> (2) Every person who incites another person to commit an offence against this Act shall be guilty of a misdemeanour, and, on conviction thereof on indictment, shall be liable to imprisonment [for a term not exceeding 2 years], or to a fine, or to both such imprisonment and fine.

5.026 It should be noted that the accessorial liability to which the Act refers is committed not only in respect of the section 1 offence (perjury itself), but also in respect of the related offences described above. It seems likely that the general criminal law principles relevant to accessories and incitement will apply here. There does not appear to be any reported case law with respect to this section of the 1911 Act.[27]

---

[26] I.e. to take an example which periodically surfaces in the press: the person who has practised brain surgery for 25 years with only an "*O*" level in carpentry.
[27] Indeed, there are relatively few reported cases that deal with perjury at all.

6. EVIDENCE

5.027 Criminal liability under the Perjury Act 1911 cannot be established without corroboration. The Act makes specific provision for this in section 13 which reads as follows:

> A person shall not be liable to be convicted for any offence against this Act, or of any offence declared by any other Act to be perjury or subornation of perjury,[28] or to be punishable as perjury or subornation of perjury, solely upon the evidence of one witness as to the falsity of any statement alleged to be false.

5.028 Again, it should be noted that the requirement for corroboration applies not only to the section 1 offence (perjury), but also to, "*any offence against this Act.*" It should also be noted that the requirement for corroboration only applies to that element of the offence which requires that the statement be false and not to the other ingredients of the offence; for example, the Defendant's wilfulness or state of mind. Given that the Act requires that a single witness's evidence must be corroborated before there can be a conviction, the judge must provide a direction to the jury in these terms. In *R v Hamid and Hamid*[29] the judge's summing up was described by the Court of Appeal as "*outstandingly fair*", save for one "*very serious*" omission: the judge did not refer to section 13 of the Perjury Act 1911:

> ... in perjury cases nowadays the judge should approach the statutory requirement as one of corroboration and ... the ordinary practice rule about reminding juries of the need for corroboration should be followed. It is easy to see why this should be so. Occasionally in perjury trials those who prove the falsity of the material statement have no connection whatsoever with the defendant, but in many cases they have. The circumstances may be such that those who are relied upon by the Crown to prove the falsity may have motives of their own for making statements against the defendant which are not true.[30]

The convictions were, by reason of the omission in the summing up, quashed.

---

[28] A number of other Acts punish the making of false statements. The Prosecution has the option of prosecuting under the 1911 Act or under the other Act: Perjury Act 1911, s 16(3).

[29] (1979) 69 Cr App R 324 (CA). See also *R v Carroll, Perkins and Dickerson* (1994) 99 Cr App R 381 (CA) in which the approach of Lawton LJ in *Hamid and Hamid* was approved and the need for a reference to section 13 of the Act in the summing up was emphasised.

[30] *R v Hamid and Hamid* (1979) 69 Cr App R 324, 328 *per* Lawton LJ (CA)

5.029 *Phipson* suggests that, in policy terms, there are three justifications for this provision.[31] First, in the absence of the statutory requirement, a conviction would depend on weighing the evidence given under oath by one witness against the evidence, also given under oath, of another. Second, section 13 of the 1911 Act is a feature of a wider concern that witnesses be protected and feel able to speak freely when giving evidence in judicial and other proceedings. Third, witnesses called by the prosecution in a trial for perjury might have motives for lying. Other academic writers have questioned whether a requirement of corroboration is justified given that,

> A perjury is committed by a person making a statement which he does not believe to be true, even, apparently, if it is true[32]

(although there is, as we have seen above, little authority directly on this point). The Criminal Law Revision Committee considered the need for corroboration in perjury in its Sixth Report (as long ago as 1964) and, in 1973 JUSTICE suggested abolition of the corroboration requirement,[33] but no changes in the law followed.

5.030 There are a number of areas in which the courts have qualified the application of the statutory provision. First, a formal admission that the statement is false whether made prior to trial or in evidence at trial will, it seems, circumvent the statutory requirement. In *R* v *Rider*[34] the court stated that,

> ... if the defendant admits that the statement was untrue the prosecution need call no evidence to prove this fact.

In *R* v *Peach*[35] the index evidence was given to a Coroner's Court during the course of a treasure trove inquiry. The Appellant was a metal detecting enthusiast. The Appellant gave sworn evidence to the court that he had found two Celtic torcs in a property owned by his brother. Some years later the Appellant confessed to two archaeologists that the items in question had in fact been found at a quite different location. It was held that the evidence of the Appellant's confession was evidence of the falsity of the statement and that the provisions of section 13 of the Act were satisfied by the evidence of the two archaeologists as to the Appellant's admission of the falsity of the statement. Equally, a letter written by the Defendant which contradicts his

---

[31] *Phipson on Evidence* (16th ed, 2005) para 14-02.
[32] Editorial comment on *R* v *Carroll, Perkins and Dickerson* in [1993] Crim LR 613, 615.
[33] JUSTICE, *False Witness: the Problem of Perjury* (1973).
[34] *R* v *Rider* (1986) 83 Cr App R 207 (CA) and see also, *R* v *Stokes* [1988] Crim LR 110 (CA).
[35] [1990] 1 WLR 976 (CA).

sworn evidence may suffice to avoid the requirement of the Act. Therefore, in *R* v *Threlfall*[36] it was held that,

> ...the evidence of one witness and a confession [contained in a letter] may be enough, and ... [section 13] has been drafted so as to make this clear.

Clear statements by the accused which obviously contradict his sworn evidence may be treated in a similar way.[37] Concessions by the Defendant that his evidence was false, whether conscious or inadvertent, obviate the need for corroboration because, in these circumstances, it is not necessary for the prosecution to call any evidence on this issue.[38]

5.031 In *DPP* v *Humphrys*[39] it was held that there is no doctrine of issue estoppel known to the criminal law. Accordingly, evidence given at an earlier trial could be admitted in a subsequent trial for perjury notwithstanding the fact that it tended to suggest that the Defendant was guilty of the offence of which he had, at the earlier trial, been acquitted.

7. CONTEMPT OF COURT: INTRODUCTION

5.032 Contempt of court is a difficult topic to pin down. A full examination of the subject lies beyond the scope of this book and the brief excursion into the law of contempt which follows is intended only as the most gentle introduction to this area. Contempt has both criminal and civil aspects. It is enshrined in well established (if sometimes rather contradictory) common law principles and in legislation and its flexible qualities have long been recognised. In *Attorney-General* v *Newspaper Publishing Plc*[40] – a case involving an application to commit three newspapers for contempt of court for publishing extracts from the *Spycatcher* book in alleged breach of interim injunctions – Sir John Donaldson MR said this:

> The law of contempt is based on the broadest of principles, namely, that the courts cannot and will not permit interference with the due administration of justice. Its application is universal. The fact that it is applied in novel

---

[36] (1914) 10 Cr App R 112, 114 *per* Avory J in the course of argument (CA).
[37] *R* v *Hook* (1858) Dears & B 606; 169 ER 1138.
[38] *R* v *Rider* (1986) 83 Cr App R 207, 210 *per* Mustill LJ (CA).
[39] [1977] AC 1 (HL).
[40] [1988] Ch 333 (CA).

circumstances ... is not a case of widening its application. It is merely a new example of its application.[41]

5.033 Historically, it has been conventional to distinguish criminal from civil contempt. Criminal contempt is characteristically regarded as the publication of words (written or spoken) or the commission of acts which interfere with the administration of justice or give rise to a significant and substantial risk that the administration of justice will be compromised. Some examples of conduct which may be capable of amounting to criminal contempt may assist:

- the persistent and abusive interruption of court proceedings;
- a wilful and improper refusal to answer questions while giving evidence;
- the publication of material, perhaps in the media, which gives rise to a significant risk that a fair trial will be prejudiced;
- the harassment of a judge, witness, party or juror.

5.034 Civil contempt, by contrast, is primarily located in disobedience to judgments or other orders and rules of the Court. As we shall see, the Civil Procedure Rules have provided fertile new ground for the commission of civil contempt.

5.035 While there remains some justification for dealing separately with the two species of contempt[42] doubt has been expressed on a number of occasions about whether such separate treatment is justified. In *Attorney-General* v *Newspaper Publishing Plc*[43] the Master of the Rolls stated that he regarded the distinction as more apt to mislead than to assist in the light of the fact that they both used the same (criminal) standard of appeal and had a common right of appeal.[44] He went on to suggest reform based on reclassification of the law along the following lines,

---

[41] At p 368D-E. See also *Jennison* v *Baker* [1972] 2 QB 52 (CA) where Salmon LJ stated, at p 61D-G, that he regarded the phrase "contempt of court" as unfortunate and misleading and as capable of taking many forms.

[42] And this chapter adopts the same approach. Hearsay evidence can only be relied on in the context of civil contempt and the remedy of sequestration is, similarly, only available in respect of civil contempt.

[43] [1988] Ch 333 (CA).

[44] Under section 13 of the Administration of Justice Act 1960 (as amended). See also *Jennison* v *Baker* [1972] 2 QB 52, 61G-H *per* Salmon LJ (CA), "*Contempts have sometimes been classified as criminal and civil contempts. I think that, at any rate today, this is an unhelpful and almost meaningless classification.*" See more recently, Sir Richard Scott VC in *Malgar Limited* v *R E Leach (Engineering Limited)* [2000] *The Times*, February 17 (ChD), "*There are civil contempts and there are criminal contempts and the line between the two is not always easy to draw.*"

(a) conduct which involves a breach, or assisting in the breach, of a court order and (b) any other conduct which involves an interference with the due administration of justice, either in a particular case or, more generally, as a continuing process, the first category being a special form of the latter, such interference being a characteristic common to all contempts.[45]

5.036 The potential relevance of contempt in the context of proceedings which involve allegations of fraudulent conduct will, it is hoped, be clear. At the risk of stating the obvious, the following considerations might be borne in mind:

- Proceedings which involve an allegation that one or other party has committed or been a party to fraud will inevitably raise the courtroom temperature – there is considerably more scope for interruptions, interventions or improper refusals to assist or co-operate (and, therefore, more scope for conduct which approaches contempt) where fraud is alleged than there is in cases which involve less heated issues.

- A high profile case which contains an allegation of dishonesty or fraud is more likely to excite media attention than one with more mundane issues.

- A party who has committed a fraud is inherently less likely to be scrupulous in complying with court orders or in exhibiting the "*cards on the table*" approach which the Civil Procedure Rules require of the honest litigant.

8. CRIMINAL CONTEMPT

5.037 Criminal contempt is a strange beast and bears little resemblance to other criminal offences. Most striking is the fact that, procedurally, it is tried summarily without a jury and proceedings can be commenced by application for committal, rather than by summons or indictment. It is possible for the court to initiate proceedings of its own motion.[46] The origins of this, while

---

[45] [1988] Ch 333, 362C-D *per* Sir John Donaldson MR (CA).
[46] Contempt in the face of the court, where of sufficient gravity, may result in the contemnor being detained in custody without further formality: see *Balogh* v *St Albans Crown Court* [1975] QB 73 (CA) where Denning MR used the example of a person who assaults a judge to demonstrate this proposition. It is, however, always necessary, as a minimum procedural

obscure, are located in disobedience to the King's writ. Holdsworth states that such disobedience was a contempt of the King and was, from an early period, punishable summarily.[47] He goes on to state that it was possible for a contemnor to purge his contempt by payment of a fine and that,

> This power to imprison and fine those guilty of contempt seems to have been originally used, firstly, to punish direct disobedience to the process of the court, and, secondly, to punish all kinds of irregularities and misfeasances of officials of the Court.[48]

The notion of contempt of the King and the Royal writ seems to have been translated over time into the notion of contempt of judicial officers and the general administration of justice, although the use of this concept as a justification for the modern law of contempt has, more recently, been the subject of judicial criticism.[49]

5.038 The unusual nature of criminal contempt, when compared with more conventional criminal offences, finds expression in other ways. The strict rules of evidence are not followed and evidence is generally given on affidavit. Equally, the full range of sentences available to a judge dealing with an ordinary criminal offence are not available to dispose of the offender found guilty of contempt. There are further unusual features connected with the identification of the *actus reus* and *mens rea* of criminal contempt. The *actus reus* is generally regarded as conduct which interferes with or impedes the administration of justice.[50] At common law this is accompanied by the *mens rea* of an intent to interfere (or, at the very least, recklessness as to the same).[51] However, the Contempt of Court Act 1981 introduces a strict liability element to the commission of certain types of contempt in which conduct will be treated as amounting to contempt, regardless whether this is accompanied by intent.

---

safeguard, to state the conduct alleged to constitute the offence and to give the alleged contemnor the opportunity of answering it.

[47] W S Holdsworth, *A History of English Law* (3rd ed, 1923), vol III, p 391.

[48] At p 391.

[49] See *Jennison* v *Baker* [1972] 2 QB 52, 61E *per* Salmon LJ (CA), " '*Contempt of court*' is an unfortunate and misleading phrase. It suggests that it exists to protect the dignity of the judges. Nothing could be further from the truth."

[50] It is not wholly clear whether there is an inchoate variant of the offence: an *attempt* to commit contempt. See *Balogh* v *St Albans Crown Court* [1975] QB 73 (CA).

[51] The case law is not wholly clear whether this means an intention to interfere with the course of justice or whether it is sufficient that there be an intention to commit the acts which interfere with the course of justice. However, "... *it must in every case be shown that the individual knew that what he was saying was false and that his false statement was likely to interfere with the course of justice.*" *Per* Sir Richard Scott VC in *Malgar Limited* v *R E Leach (Engineering) Limited* [2000] *The Times*, February 17 (ChD).

5.039 Criminal contempt is punishable by imprisonment for a term not exceeding two years (one month in the case of an inferior court – which includes the county court)[52] or by a fine or by an order for security for good behaviour. As an alternative to these forms of disposal the court may order an injunction to prevent the offending behaviour from being repeated. Procedural rules with respect to sanctions for criminal contempt, where committed in the civil courts, appear in the Rules of the Supreme Court[53] and in the County Courts Act 1984.[54] Ordinarily, evidence will be given by Affidavit and any hearing will take place in open court. It should be noted, as observed above, that contempt in the face of the court is generally dealt with summarily by the court of its own motion (either by immediate committal) or by committal at the conclusion of the proceedings. Jurisdiction to punish for contempt committed outside court is vested in the superior courts and is generally dealt with by the Divisional Court of the Queen's Bench Division. Where proceedings for criminal contempt committed outside court involve an allegation of conduct for which the offender is or would be strictly liable (by virtue of the Contempt of Court Act 1981) the institution of proceedings generally requires the consent of the Attorney-General.[55]

5.040 As indicated above, it is conventional to divide criminal contempts into conduct which is, archaically, characterised and described as a contempt "*in the face of the court*" and conduct which is committed outside the court by publication of prejudicial material or interference with a witness.

Contempt in the face of the court

5.041 An exhaustive classification of the categories of conduct which are capable of being described as contempt in the face of the court is impossible. The net is widely cast and may catch any conduct inside court or, conceivably, within the precincts of the court[56] which is capable of

---

[52] Contempt of Court Act 1981, s 14. See also the County Courts Act 1981, s 118. In the county court the power to commit for contempt is available to the district judge, as well as the circuit judge.

[53] RSC 52 PD which stipulates that proceedings for committal for contempt (whether criminal or civil contempt) are commenced by issue of Part 8 Claim Form or, if the application is made in the context of existing proceedings, by filing of an Application Notice.

[54] See sections 14 and 118 of the County Courts Act 1984 which deal, respectively, with the penalties for assaulting an officer of a court in the execution of his duty and the power to commit for contempt.

[55] Contempt of Court Act 1981, s 7.

[56] See, e.g. *In re Johnson* (1887) 20 QBD 67 (CA) which concerned a solicitor who conducted himself "*disgracefully*" by the use of "*violent language of the lowest description to the solicitor opposed to him*" while both made their way from the judge's chambers where they had appeared on a contested matter to the entrance gate of the courtroom. The report records that

amounting to what has been broadly referred to as a *"contempt in the cognizance of the Court"*.[57] The best that one can do is identify (by a non-exhaustive list) some examples of conduct which have, in the past, been held to give rise to a contempt in the face of the court (an approach which has been adopted by at least one very distinguished judge).[58] Accordingly, the following has been held to constitute contempt in the face of the court:

- the interruption or disturbance of court proceedings whether by conduct or words or some combination of the two;[59]

- an assault or threatened assault of a judge, witness, advocate or other party to proceedings;[60]

- the use of insulting language or behaviour;[61]

- the taking of photographs of the proceedings or drawing pictures of the same;[62]

- the tape recording of proceedings (save for tape recording for the purposes of producing approved transcripts);[63]

- the intentional refusal by a witness, in the absence of lawful excuse, to answer a summons to attend court, to be sworn or, after being sworn, to refuse to answer proper questions;[64]

- misbehaviour by litigants, counsel, solicitors or lay advocates;

- misbehaviour by jurors.

---

the contemnor referred to his opponent as a *"damned perjured scoundrel"*. This was held to be a contempt.

[57] *Balogh v St Albans Crown Court* [1975] QB 73, 84B *per* Lord Denning MR (CA), *"… I find nothing to tell us what is meant by 'committed in the face of the Court'. It has never been defined. Its meaning is, I think, to be ascertained from the practice of the judges over the centuries. … It covered all contempts for which a judge of his own motion could punish a man on the spot."*

[58] See Lord Denning MR in *Balogh* at pp 84-85 where a list of *"instances"* of contempt in the face of the court is given (as an alternative to providing some *"catch-all"* definition).

[59] See, e.g. *Morris v Crown Office* [1970] 2 QB 114 (CA) which involved a group of Welsh students who disrupted a libel action in the High Court by shouting slogans, scattering leaflets and singing songs. See also, County Courts Act 1984, s 118(1)(b).

[60] See, e.g. *Balogh v St Albans Crown Court* [1975] QB 73, 84D *per* Lord Denning MR (CA), *"… throwing a missile at the Judge, be it a brickbat, an egg or a tomato."*

[61] See, e.g. *In re Johnson* (1887) 20 QBD 67 (CA) and County Courts Act 1984, s 118(1)(a).

[62] Dealt with by Criminal Justice Act 1925, s 41.

[63] Dealt with by Contempt of Court Act 1981, s 9.

[64] *In re Maria Annie Davies* (1888) 21 QBD 236, 238 *per* Mathew J (QBD).

Contempt outside court: publication and interference

5.042 This has sometimes been referred to as "*indirect*" contempt. Again, an attempt can be made to list the conduct which might give rise to the offence:

- publication of material which gives rise to a significant risk that the administration of justice will, in a particular case, be prejudiced (where there is, by virtue of the Contempt of Court Act 1981, no requirement that the relevant conduct be committed with intent (on which, see below));

- publication of material with the intention of prejudicing the administration of justice;[65]

- publication of material in breach of a court order which restrains such publication;

- interference with witnesses, parties, court officers, jurors or court documents;

- acts which scandalise the process of the court.[66]

---

[65] This includes, among other categories of conduct, material which is published *sub judice*. It is necessary that there be a real or substantial risk that publication will interfere with the administration of justice and it is necessary that the material be published with the intention of interfering with the same.

[66] Conduct in the form of any act or publication of any writing which is intended to bring a judge or a court into contempt or otherwise to lower his or her authority. There is clearly a considerable latitude given here when it comes to criticism (even where expressed in the most robust terms) of judicial conduct. It may be that this category of contempt is now synonymous with contempt in the face of the court and may only be committed where the conduct is of a particularly extreme kind.

9. STRICT LIABILITY: CONTEMPT OF COURT ACT 1981

5.043 The Act identifies the "*strict liability rule*" as meaning the rule of law

> ...whereby conduct may be treated as a contempt of court as tending to interfere with the course of justice in particular legal proceedings regardless of intent to do so.[67]

It goes on to limit the scope of the rule in the following terms:

> (1) The strict liability rules applies only in relation to publications, and for this purpose 'publication' includes any speech writing, programme included in a service or other communication in whatever form, which is addressed to the public at large or any section of the public. (2) The strict liability rule applies only to a publication which creates a substantial risk that the course of justice in the proceedings in question will be seriously impeded or prejudiced. (3) The strict liability rule applies only if the proceedings in question are active within the meaning of this section at the time of the publication.

5.044 Schedule 1 to the 1981 Act defines when proceedings are "*active*" for the purposes of the strict liability rule. It should be noted that there is a defence to the liability which would otherwise arise under the strict liability rule if the alleged offender did not and had no reason to suspect that the proceedings are active or if he did not know or have any reason to suspect that the published material created a substantial risk that the course of justice in the proceedings in question would be seriously impeded or prejudiced.[68] The 1981 Act further provides that liability under the strict liability rule will not attach in respect of material published,

> ...in respect of a fair and accurate report of legal proceedings held in public, published contemporaneously and in good faith,[69]

nor where published,

> ...as part of a discussion in good faith of public affairs or other matters of general public interest.[70]

---

[67] Contempt of Court Act 1981, s 1.
[68] Contempt of Court Act 1981, s 3.
[69] Contempt of Court Act 1981, s 4.

10. CIVIL CONTEMPT

Introduction

5.045 This has been described as follows,

> Civil contempt of court exists ... to provide the ultimate sanction against a person who refuses to comply with the order of a properly constituted court. In English law the form of the sanction is typically committal to prison or, in the case of a body corporate, a fine or the sequestration of assets.[71]

Therefore, civil contempt can be committed by:

- a failure to comply with a court order;[72]

- breaching an undertaking given to the court;

- making a false statement of truth or false disclosure statement.

5.046 In the context of a book that deals with fraud the most obvious conduct giving rise to civil contempt will be a false statement of truth and, accordingly, this section concentrates on this.

5.047 The procedure for imposing a sanction for contempt can, as indicated above, be found in Rules of the Supreme Court, Order 52 (and the Practice Direction thereto) and, in respect of committal for breach of an order or undertaking, County Court Rules, Order 29.[73]

5.048 The sanctions for civil contempt consist of:

- imprisonment for a fixed term not exceeding two years where sentencing is by a superior court or one month where sentencing is by an inferior court (the sentence can be suspended);

- the imposition of a fine (unlimited in respect of a superior court, but limited to £2,500 in respect of an inferior court);

- sequestration of assets;

---

[70] Contempt of Court Act 1981, s 5.
[71] C J Miller, *Contempt of Court* (3rd ed, 2000) para 1.07.
[72] See *Re P (a Child)* [2006] EWCA Civ 179 where repeated failures to comply with court orders led to the refusal of an application for an adjournment and the imposition of a suspended order for committal even though the contemnor was absent from court.
[73] Both preserved by the Civil Procedure Rules.

- the requirement of security against a repetition of the offending conduct;

- the grant of injunctive relief restraining any continuance or repetition of the offending conduct.

5.049 In practice, the harshness of the sanctions for civil contempt is substantially mitigated by the civil courts. It is far more common for the court to impose a costs sanction, strike out a statement of case,[74] refuse to admit a witness statement or other document in evidence,[75] reach a summary determination or impose an unless order, than it is for an offending party to be committed.

False statements of truth: CPR 32.14

5.050 The following documents are required, by Part 22 of the Rules, to be accompanied by a statement of truth:

- a statement of case;

- a response complying with a request for further information under Part 18 of the Rules;

- a witness statement;

- an acknowledgement of service of a claim commenced under the Part 8 procedure;

- a certificate stating the reason for bringing a possession claim or a landlord and tenant claim in the High Court under rules 55.3(2) and 56.2(2);

- a certificate of service;

- an amended statement of case;

- evidence relied on in support of an application and set out in Part C of an Application Notice.

---

[74] See, e.g. CPR 22.2(2) which provides that a consequence of a failure to verify a statement of truth may be the striking out of the statement of case.
[75] CPR 22.3.

5.051 As an addition to the list, it should be noted that a list for disclosure should be accompanied by a disclosure statement.[76] The rules also require an expert's report to be accompanied by an appropriate declaration and statement of truth.[77]

5.052 Part 22 goes on to provide that where the statement of truth appears on a statement of case, reply to a Part 18 request or application notice, it must be signed by the party or litigation friend or by the legal representative on behalf of the party or litigation friend.[78] In the case of a witness statement the statement of truth is signed, obviously enough, by the maker of the statement.

5.053 In *Hughes* v *Caerphilly Borough Council*[79] the court accepted the following as an accurate summary of the law in this area,

> In order to establish each contempt alleged the Claimant must prove beyond a reasonable doubt in respect of each statement (a) the falsity of the statement in question, (b) that the statement has or, if persisted in, would be likely to have interfered with the course of justice in some material respects, and (c) that at the time it was made the maker of the statement had no honest belief in the truth of the statement and knew of its likelihood to interfere with the course of justice.

5.054 The sanction for making a false statement and the procedure for initiating contempt proceedings in respect of the same are also prescribed by the Rules:

> **False statements** (1) Proceedings for contempt of court may be brought against a person if he makes, or causes to be made, a false statement in a document verified by a statement of truth without an honest belief in its truth. (2) Proceedings under this rule may be brought only – (a) by the Attorney-General; or (b) with the permission of the court.[80]

5.055 The Practice Direction to Part 32 provides[81] that:

- Where a party alleges that a false statement of truth or disclosure statement has been made then it should refer that allegation to the court which dealt with the claim in which the statement was made.

---

[76] CPR 31.10.
[77] Set out in CPR 35.10 and in CPR 35, PD paras 2.3-2.4.
[78] CPR 22.1(6).
[79] (2005) 6 December (unreported) (QBD).
[80] CPR 32.14.
[81] CPR 32, PD paras 28.1-28.4.

- The court can then (a) exercise any power that it has under the Rules; (b) initiate steps to consider whether there has been a contempt of court and consider whether to punish the same;[82] or, (c) direct the party making the complaint to refer the matter to the Attorney-General with a request for him to consider whether to bring proceedings for contempt of court.

- An application to the Attorney-General[83] should be in writing and accompanied by (a) an order recording the direction of the judge to refer the matter to him; (b) information where and why the statement is false and explaining why the maker knew it to be false at the time that it was made; and, (c) explaining why contempt proceedings would be appropriate (having regard to the overriding objective).

- The Practice Direction states, in terms (and for understandable reasons), that the Attorney-General's preference is to receive an application from the court (i.e. an application which reaches him after consideration by a judge, rather than an application which arrives direct from a party – *"An application to the Attorney-General is not a way of appealing against, or reviewing, the decision of the judge."*

5.056 It is clear that the provisions of Part 32 of the Rules, insofar as they deal with contempt arising out of the making of false statements, are not intended to override or to add new categories to the general law of contempt.[84]

5.057 CPR 32.14 was considered – in the context of its application to statements of case and witness statements – in *Malgar Limited* v *R E Leach (Engineering) Limited*:[85] a case decided within a year of the Civil Procedure Rules coming into force.[86] The case concerned a commercial dispute in which, among a number of other allegations, it was claimed that the Defendants were liable for breach of copyright, breach of design rights and passing off. The claim was defended; the Defendant filed and served a Defence containing a statement of truth. The Claimant made an application

---

[82] In accordance with RSC, Ord 52 or CCR, Ord 29.
[83] At Attorney-General's Chambers, 9 Buckingham Gate, London SW1E 6JP.
[84] CPR 32, PD para 28.4 makes this explicitly clear.
[85] [2000] *The Times*, February 17 (ChD).
[86] On 1 November 1999. Sir Richard Scott VC stated that this case was the first application made under CPR 32.14.

for summary judgment and a representative of the Defendant filed a witness statement resisting the same. The witness statement was also accompanied by the requisite signed statement of truth. The case came before a judge and the Defendant submitted to judgment in respect of a number of the matters alleged against it; the remainder of the matters alleged were left to be resolved at trial. The summary judgment application did not proceed and was disposed of by means of a consent order. The matter did not rest there. The Claimant made an application under CPR 32.14 seeking permission to proceed against the representatives of the Defendant who had signed the statements of truth on, respectively, the Defence and the witness statement. The application came before the Vice-Chancellor (Sir Richard Scott). Sir Richard did not reach any concluded view on the alleged falsity of the statements made on the Defendant's behalf, although he expressed incredulity at some of the matters that were stated. He did, however, make a number of broadly drawn points about the proper ambit of CPR 32.14.

5.058 The Vice-Chancellor commenced by stating that the Civil Procedure Rules had made a particular innovation in: (a) requiring statements of case to be accompanied by a statement of truth; and (b) replacing the *jurat* on an affidavit with the statement of truth on a witness statement. It was further observed that the Rules encouraged the use of witness statements as an alternative to the swearing of an affidavit in the context of interim applications. It was made clear in the course of the judgment that Part 22 statements in statements of case performed a more important function than statements of truth in witness statements. Sir Richard went on to state that the swearing of an affidavit knowing it to be false rendered its maker liable to a prosecution for perjury.[87] The CPR sought to ensure that false witness statements were punished by means of CPR 32.14. The following general guidance was given about the effects and ambit of CPR 32.14:

- CPR 32.14 does not make any change to the general or substantive law;

- the role of CPR 32.14 is to provide for the possibility of a person being prosecuted for contempt, but it does not predict the outcome because that is left to the general law – in other words, it is a procedural device;

- contempt proceedings for which application is made under CPR 32.14, while civil proceedings and, therefore, subject to the overriding objective, consist of an allegation of a public wrong –

---

[87] Although the use of this as a sanction is very rare.

accordingly, it is right that there should be public control of the same (through the role and function of the Attorney-General);

- *"... flagrant breaches of the obligation to be responsible and truthful in verifying witness statements of case and in verifying witness statements should be policed and enforced if necessary by committal proceedings."*

5.059 The Vice-Chancellor dismissed the application for permission under CPR 32.14. He felt that, on application of the overriding objective (including the principle of proportionality) and in consideration of the public interest, a prosecution for contempt was inappropriate. He based this conclusion primarily on the fact that the evidential material attested to by statements of truth had not been persisted in by the Defendant which had submitted to judgment. He also held that the trial of the residual issues between the parties may well be prejudiced by the grant of permission under CPR 32.14.

5.060 *Malgar* was considered and applied in *Kabushiki Kaisha Sony Computer Entertainment & Others v Ball.*[88] In this case the Claimants, rather than the Attorney-General, brought proceedings to commit the First Defendant for contempt pursuant to CPR 32.14. Permission was granted and the substantive application came before Blackburne J. Blackburne J held that the need for permission, where proceedings were brought other than by the Attorney-General, enabled the courts to direct the grant of such permission to those cases where there was a *"real prospect"*, as distinct from a certainty, that the applicant can establish:

(a) the falsity of the statement in question;

(b) that the statement has or will, if persisted in, be likely to interfere with the course of justice in some material respect; and,

(c) that at the time that the statement was made its maker lacked an honest belief in the truth of the statement and knew of its likelihood to interfere with the course of justice.

5.061 In *Kabushiki Kaisha Sony Computer Entertainment & Others v Ball* the contempt proceedings succeeded; the following factors influenced the judge's decision:

---

[88] [2004] EWHC 1984 (ChD).

- the significance of signing the statements of truth (on a Defence, an amended Defence and a reply to a Part 18 request for further information) and the consequences of signing false statements had been fully brought home to the First Defendant;

- the First Defendant had repeated the offence involved in signing the first false statement in the Defence by signing false statements in an amended Defence and in a Part 18 reply;

- the First Defendant had sought, in correspondence advancing Part 36 offers, to disguise the full extent of his involvement in the activities which had prompted the Claimants to bring breach of copyright proceedings against him;

- the First Defendant had sought to influence the course of the litigation by making statements which he knew to be false.

Blackburne J imposed a fine on the First Defendant as an alternative to a custodial penalty.[89]

5.062 Every story should have a happy ending or, at least, a moral. *Hughes v Caerphilly Borough Council*,[90] a claim for personal injury and other losses, arose out of an alleged tripping accident on the public highway. The Claimant, Matthew Hughes, brought a relatively low value (£10,000) claim against the Defendant local highway authority in respect of its alleged failure to maintain the relevant pavement.[91] His case was that he had sustained a serious knee injury as a result of tripping over a pothole and that this had prevented him from indulging in his favourite hobby of playing football. The Claimant relied on evidence from two friends. In fact, it emerged that the Claimant had played football within two hours of his alleged tripping accident, had scored a goal and had left the field following a tackle on the field which had caused him to sustain a knee injury. The Council produced team sheets for two seasons which showed that the Claimant had played 29 matches at a time when he alleged that he had been so seriously injured that he had been unable to play football at all. To add to the comedic value of the

---

[89] See also, *Daltel Europe Limited v Makki* [2005] EWHC 749 (ChD) where a committal for contempt succeeded in the context of deliberate breaches of freezing injunctions and search orders and where Defences signed by the contemnors contained false statements which were known to be false at the time that they were signed. It was held that the intention of raising the false Defences had been to interfere with the administration of justice.
[90] (2005) 6 December (unreported, save on Lawtel, in *The Daily Mail* " *The £10,000 Own Goal*" and other media) (QBD).
[91] Highways Act, s 41.

Claimant's deceit a photograph of the Claimant from a local newspaper was produced which showed him, in football team colours and only one hour after the alleged tripping accident, kneeling on the knee which he alleged that he had injured. The Claimant's action was discontinued. However, the notice of discontinuance was set aside and the Defendant brought contempt proceedings against the Claimant which were heard by Silber J. The judge held that the Claimant should be sentenced to two weeks' custody for contempt in order that this might act as a deterrent to others considering making false personal injury claims.[92] The Claimant's two friends, who had made false statements on his behalf, were sentenced to pay fines of £1,500 each. The Claimant is reported as having denied, in the course of his evidence, that he had lied about being unable to play football following the fictitious accident. His reported evidence betrays a sophisticated grasp of the moral distinctions between a lie and something which is merely untrue:

> I would not call it a lie. It was wrong. It was just misleading ... When I was writing down my statement I did not put it down correctly. I meant to say I was not playing regularly.[93]

---

[92] Silber J is reported as having indicated that, in future, longer immediate custodial sentences should be expected by those guilty of contempt for making false statements. He had identified a number of mitigating factors which justified a shorter sentence in the Claimant's case; namely, that he had paid over £11,000 in costs, that there were outstanding costs liabilities for the Claimant to discharge (which would remain after he left prison), that he had no previous convictions and an impressive work record and that his "*intellectual powers*" were such that he had not appreciated the seriousness of what he had done.

[93] See also, *Humphries* v *Matthews* (2006) 16 June (Liverpool CC *per* Recorder Moran QC) (unreported, but available on Lawtel). This case, arising out of a low velocity RTA collision, resulted in a finding by the trial judge that the Claimant had embarked on a fraudulent attempt to obtain damages for personal injury which had led him to make false statements and to give false evidence. The judge identified three options: (1) to give the Defendant permission to bring proceedings for contempt in the Queen's Bench Division; (2) to direct that the papers in the case be sent to the Attorney-General to consider proceedings for contempt under CPR 32.14; and (3) to direct that the papers and a transcript of the judgment be sent to the Chief Constable of the Police Force with jurisdiction to decide whether a criminal investigation should take place.

Chapter 6

REGULATING FRAUD AND ITS PROFITS: THE PROCEEDS OF CRIME ACT 2002

1. INTRODUCTION

6.001 The Proceeds of Crime Act 2002, described by Jack Straw MP (the then Home Secretary) as *"large, complex and innovative"* grew from earlier legislative efforts aimed at similar mischiefs,[1] from a Home Office report published for consultation in November 1998 and a subsequent Cabinet Office report published in June 2000.[2] A commitment to present a Bill was included in the Queen's Speech on 6 December 2000 and the Act received the Royal Assent on 24 July 2002. The key provisions in the Act (which are the subject of consideration below) came into force on 24 February 2003. It should also be noted that the genesis of the money laundering provisions in the Act can be found in two European Union Directives.[3]

6.002 The principal achievements of the 2002 Act are to strengthen and extend the powers of the court to make confiscation orders, the introduction of an Assets Recovery Agency and the institution of High Court civil proceedings for the forfeiture of assets where there are, on application of the civil standard of proof, reasonable grounds to suspect that the assets are the proceeds of, or are to be used in, criminal activities. Finally, the Act introduces a set of key money laundering offences and this chapter concentrates on these provisions. The Home Secretary's description of the 2002 Act as *"large"* is fully justified. There is not room within the ambit of this work to consider all, or even most, of the regulatory machinery which the Act contains and readers with an interest in this detail are referred to the specialist literature and the various annotated guides to the legislation. This

---

[1] See, Drug Trafficking Act 1994 and the Criminal Justice Act 1988 (as amended by the Proceeds of Crime Act 1995).
[2] HO Organised and International Crime Directorate Working Group on Confiscation (3rd report), *Criminal Assets* (1998) and Cabinet Office Performance and Innovation Unit, Recovering the Proceeds of Crime (2000).
[3] Council Directive of 10 June 1991 (91/308/EEC) and Council Directive of 4 December 2001 (2001/97/EC).

chapter intends, instead, to concentrate on the connections that can be drawn between fraud as it is discussed in this work and the contents of the 2002 Act.

2. PROCEEDS OF CRIME ACT 2002

Money laundering offences

6.003 "*Money laundering*" describes the process by which illegal or illicitly obtained funds are clothed with (apparent) legitimacy. The Act contains a definition of this term at section 340(11) which provides that money laundering is tied to the offences set out in Part 7 of the Act and, specifically, that it takes place when the offences in sections 327-329 are committed, when an inchoate variant of these offences is committed, when there is aiding, abetting, counselling or procuring of the commission of an offence under sections 327-329 or, finally, where an act would constitute an offence under these sections of the Act if committed in the United Kingdom.

6.004 The offences set out in sections 327-329 of the Act are as follows:

- the section 327 offence covers the concealment, disguise, conversion, transferral or removal (from England or Wales) of "*criminal property*";

- section 328 provides that an offence is committed if a person

   > ...enters into or becomes concerned in an arrangement which he knows or suspects facilitates ... the acquisition, retention, use or control of criminal property by or on behalf of another person;

- the section 329 offence covers the acquisition, use or possession of criminal property.

6.005 Clearly, the definition of criminal property is important in this context and this is very widely defined in section 340 of the 2002 Act which provides as follows:

> (2) Criminal conduct is conduct which – (a) constitutes an offence in any part of the United Kingdom, or (b) would constitute an offence in any part of the United Kingdom if it occurred there. (3) Property is criminal property

if – (a) it constitutes a person's benefit from criminal conduct[4] or it represents such a benefit (in whole or in part and whether directly or indirectly), and (b) the alleged offender knows or suspects that it constitutes or represents such a benefit. (4) It is immaterial – (a) who carried out the conduct; (b) who benefited from it; (c) whether the conduct occurred before or after the passing of this Act. (5) A person benefits from conduct if he obtains property as a result of or in connection with the conduct.

6.006 An intriguing feature of the definition of "*criminal property*" is that it captures, by virtue of section 340(3)(b), circumstances where the offender "*knows or suspects*" that it constitutes benefit from criminal conduct. The *mens rea* of the money laundering offences is, it should be noted, directed towards (*subjective*) knowledge or suspicion that the property is "*criminal property*", rather than to knowledge or suspicion of the activities of the person with whom the alleged offender has been dealing (although, in an evidential sense, there may, of course, be considerable overlap between these categories). It is immaterial who carried out the (initial) criminal conduct as is the identity of the person who benefited from it (and it should be noted that it is also immaterial whether the criminal conduct was before or after the passing of the 2002 Act). The offender under the Act may, therefore, be several steps away from the original criminal conduct.

6.007 There has been some discussion in recent case law of the meaning of "*suspicion*" in the context of the money laundering offences and, in particular, the offence contained in section 328 of the Act. The Act does not require, at least on first reading, any suspicion to be based on reasonable grounds. While Laddie J discussed this issue, but declined to reach conclusions in respect of it in *Squirrell Limited* v *National Westminster Bank Plc & HM Customs & Excise,*[5] the Court of Appeal provided a little more assistance in *K Limited* v *National Westminster Bank Plc & another.*[6]

6.008 The *K Limited* appeal arose out of two contracts which the Claimant made. The first was for the purchase of a consignment of mobile telephones. The second was for the telephones to be sold on to a Swiss registered company. The Swiss company paid a sum of money into the Claimant's bank account and, on the same day, the Claimant instructed the Defendant bank to make a payment to the seller of the mobile telephones. The Defendant informed the Claimant that it could not comply with the instruction and that

---

[4] Section 340(5) and (8) provide, respectively, that, "*A person benefits from conduct if he obtains property as a result of or in connection with the conduct*" and "*If a person benefits from conduct his benefit is the property obtained as a result of or in connection with the conduct.*"
[5] [2005] EWHC 664, paras 13-15 (Ch D).
[6] [2006] 4 All ER 907 (CA).

it could not enter into any further discussion of the matter. The Claimant applied for an injunction requiring the Defendant to comply with its instructions and the Defendant's solicitors wrote a letter to the court stating that it had made an authorised disclosure to Customs & Excise in accordance with its duty under section 328 of the 2002 Act. The judge dismissed the application for injunctive relief and the Claimant appealed. Among other arguments raised in support of the appeal the Claimant contended that if the Defendant was going to rely on a suspicion that that the money which was in the Claimant's account was criminal property then it should have provided the court with admissible evidence in support of that suspicion in order that there could be cross-examination first on whether the suspicion was actually held and, second, on whether there were (reasonable) grounds for that suspicion. The Court of Appeal was urged by counsel for the Defendant bank and for Serious and Organised Crime Agency ("SOCA") to resist the temptation to provide any guidance on the meaning of "*suspects*" as it is used in Part 7 of the 2002 Act; it was argued that this was an ordinary English word and that any definition was apt to mislead. The Court of Appeal declined this invitation and held as follows:

> In *R* v *Da Silva* ... [2006] 4 All ER 900 this court has said that for a defendant to be convicted of an offence under section 93(A)(1)(a) of the Criminal Justice Act 1988 (the earlier equivalent of s 328 of the 2002 Act), he or she must think that there is a possibility, which is more than fanciful, that the relevant facts exist. This is subject, in an appropriate case, to the further requirement that the suspicion so formed should be of a settled nature. If that definition is sufficient for criminal cases, so also should it be for civil cases.[7]

6.009 The Court of Appeal was unimpressed by the argument for the Claimant in *K Limited* that there should be an opportunity to cross-examine the Defendant on the grounds for suspecting that the funds in the account were criminal property. Longmore LJ feared that the disclosure of evidence necessary for fruitful cross-examination may lead to the commission of other offences under the Act; for example, tipping off or prejudicing an investigation (which are discussed below). Equally, Parliament had struck a "*precise and workable balance of conflicting interests in the 2002 Act*" in which notice and moratorium periods (see below) ensured that any interference with the free flow of trade was only on a limited basis. In *K Limited* the Court of Appeal dismissed the Claimant's appeal against the judge's order at first instance.

---

[7] At p 913d *per* Longmore LJ.

6.0010 It should be noted, in respect of the money laundering offences, that the offences apply to conduct overseas if the same would be criminal conduct in the United Kingdom and, further, that there are no "*degrees of conduct*" or, to put the matter another way, there is no minimum amount to provide a threshold for criminal liability under Part 7 of the Act: a feature of the legislation to which the President of the Family Division made particular reference in *P* v *P*[8] (considered in more detail below).

6.011 Penalties for the money laundering offences (sections 327-329 of the Act) are prescribed by section 334(1) of the 2002 Act which indicates that the offences are triable either way and are punishable, on summary conviction, by a sentence of six months' imprisonment or a fine not exceeding the statutory maximum or both and, on conviction on indictment, by a sentence of imprisonment not exceeding 14 years or a fine or both.

Concealing criminal property: the section 327 offence

6.012 As indicated above the offence can be committed in no less than five different ways, although there is clearly some considerable overlap between the various methods of commission and, in particular, between concealment and disguise of the criminal property. The essence of the offence is the commission of one of the acts spelt out in section 327(1)(a)-(e) (the *actus reus*) with accompanying *mens rea* in the form of knowledge or suspicion as defined in section 340 and discussed above.

6.013 Concealment and disguise are further defined (it will be noted that the Act accretes multiple definitions) by section 327(3) which treats these terms synonymously and states,

> Concealing or disguising criminal property includes concealing or disguising its nature, source, location, disposition, movement or ownership or any rights with respect to it.

The removal of criminal property from one part of the United Kingdom to another will, if committed with the requisite *mens rea*, constitute an offence by virtue of section 327(1)(e) of the Act.

6.014 Sections 327(2) provides that liability for the commission of an offence under section 327 will be avoided in defined circumstances: primarily, where there has been an "*authorised disclosure*" of the sort

---

[8] [2004] 1 Fam 1, 14 (Fam).

described in section 338 of the Act (on which, see section on disclosure below):

> ... a person does not commit ... an offence [under section 327 of the Act] if – (a) he makes an authorised disclosure under section 338 and (if the disclosure is made before he does the act mentioned in subsection (1)) [viz. the concealment, disguise, conversion etc] he has the appropriate consent; (b) he intended to make such a disclosure but had a reasonable excuse for not doing so; (c) the act he does is done in carrying out a function he has relating to the enforcement of any provision of this Act or of any enactment relating to criminal conduct or benefit from criminal conduct.

Arrangements for the acquisition of criminal property: the section 328 offence

6.015 This offence casts its net wide. The essence of the offence is expressed in the width of the word "*arrangements*" with the accompanying *mens rea* of knowledge or suspicion that such arrangements facilitate "*by whatever means*" the "*acquisition, use or control of criminal property*" whether by or on behalf of another person. In other words, the offence contained in section 328 relates to arrangements made to assist another person to acquire, use or control criminal property. There is provision, in section 328(2), for the avoidance of criminal liability which is similar to that contained in section 327(2): namely, authorised disclosure (or obtaining advance consent), intention to make authorised disclosure in circumstances where there is a reasonable excuse for not doing so and, as a final alternative, committing an act which constitutes the carrying out of a function relating to the enforcement of any provision of the Act.

6.016 This section of the Act (and a related provision containing an offence of "*tipping off*" – on which, see below) have caused considerable concern for legal professionals dealing with and negotiating settlements on behalf of and with persons suspected of fraud. Two of the leading cases in this area directly consider section 328: *P* v *P*[9] and *Bowman* v *Fels*.[10] These cases and the issues to which they give rise are considered below.

---

[9] [2004] 1 Fam 1 (Fam).
[10] [2005] 1 WLR 3083 (CA).

Acquisition, use and possession of criminal property: the section 329 offence

6.017 The *actus reus* of this offence is quite straightforward; it is located in the acquisition, use or possession of criminal property. The *mens rea* is, again, found in the conjoined definitions of criminal conduct and criminal property found in section 340 of the Act: namely, the offender's (subjectively determined) knowledge or suspicion that the property in question constitutes criminal property (as defined).

6.018 There is provision, in section 329(2), for the avoidance of liability in the same manner set out in sections 327 and 328; that is, authorised disclosure (or obtaining advance consent), intention to make authorised disclosure in circumstances where there is a reasonable excuse for not doing so and, committing an act which constitutes the carrying out of a function relating to the enforcement of any provision of the Act or of any other enactment relating to criminal conduct or benefit from criminal conduct. There is a further provision with respect to the avoidance of liability (section 329(2)(c)):

> ... a person does not commit ... an offence if – (c) he acquired or used or had possession of the property for adequate consideration ...

This provision is intended to protect those who purchase property with funds about which they are suspicious and ensures that criminal liability will only attach in circumstances where the consideration is inadequate. Again, there is a further definition, for these purposes, which is provided by section 329(3):

> (a) a person acquires property for inadequate consideration if the value of the consideration is significantly less than the value of the property; (b) a person uses or has possession of property for inadequate consideration if the value of the consideration is significantly less than the value of the use or possession; (c) the provision by a person of goods or services which he knows or suspects may help another to carry out criminal conduct is not consideration.

Disclosure and appropriate consent

6.019 Disclosure is governed by section 338 of the 2002 Act. This provision is intended to ensure that information is provided by disclosure to the relevant authorities while at the same time enabling a relevant money transfer or other transaction to be completed. The essence of "*authorised* *disclosure*" is that it immunises the person disclosing from the imposition of criminal liability for the money laundering offences considered above.

6.020 Section 338 of the Act makes it clear[11] that, in order to be "*authorised*", disclosure (the definition of which is considered below) is either made before the alleged offender commits a prohibited act (which is defined by section 338(6) as an act mentioned in sections 327-329 of the 2002 Act) (condition 1) or is made after the commission of the prohibited act (condition 2). Section 338(3)(b) makes it abundantly clear that the preferred route is to disclose before the making of the prohibited act because if the disclosure is left until after the act is committed it is necessary for there to be "*a good reason for ...* [the alleged offender's] *failure to make the disclosure before he did the act*". In addition, disclosure after the commission of the prohibited act has to be made on the alleged offender's "*own initiative and as soon as it is practicable for him to make it.*"

6.021 Section 338(1) defines authorised disclosure in the following terms:

> (a) ... a disclosure to a constable, a customs officer or a nominated officer by the alleged offender that property is criminal property; (b) ... [a disclosure] made in the form and manner prescribed for the purposes of this subsection by order under section 339 ...

It is an additional requirement that condition 1 or condition 2 (described above) be satisfied. It will be noted that "*criminal property*" (with the *mens area* element that property is known, or suspected to be, the benefit from criminal conduct) lies at the heart of the 2002 Act's disclosure regime. Disclosure is made on what is referred to as a suspicious activity report or "*SAR*" and is generally made to the National Criminal Intelligence Service ("*NCIS*") which now forms part of SOCA. A *pro forma* SAR can be downloaded from the SOCA website; it is a nosy and detailed document containing, among other things, sections dealing with the name, identity, address of the main (and any associated subjects), the disclosed account details and, most importantly perhaps, the reasons for suspicion.

6.022 For those in employment, the 2002 Act provides an alternative method for authorised disclosure.[12] Section 338(5) defines "*nominated person*" for the purposes of authorised disclosure under the Act. It provides that an authorised disclosure is made (for the purposes of section 338(1)(a)) where disclosure is to a

---

[11] At ss 338(2) and (3).
[12] That is, an alternative to disclosure direct to NCIS.

> ...person nominated by the alleged offender's employer to receive authorised disclosures and ... is made in the course of the alleged offender's employment and in accordance with the procedure established by the employer for that purpose.

The Act characteristically contains a wide definition of "*employment*" for the purposes of this provision and expressly states[13] that, for the purposes of disclosure to a nominated officer,

> ... references to a person's employer include any body, association or organisation (including a voluntary organisation) in connection with whose activities the person exercises a function (whether or not for gain or reward).

It should be noted that, by virtue of section 336 of the 2002 Act, the nominated officer must pass on any SAR to NCIS and obtain the necessary consents before he provides consent to the commission of the act which would otherwise be prohibited under sections 327-329 of the Act. A criminal penalty is imposed on the nominated officer in the event that consent is given to the employee without satisfying the condition in section 336 (namely, disclosure to NCIS). Accordingly, the disclosure provisions of the Act absolve the individual employee of the duty to report direct to NCIS provided that there is a nominated officer to whom they can report and who can then act as intermediary. However, the burden of disclosing to NCIS is simply passed on to the nominated officer and is backed by the possible sanction of criminal liability. It is difficult to envisage many employees in smaller workplaces volunteering to take on the administrative burden of being nominated officer in the light of this.

6.023 It will be noted from the discussion above that liability for the offences contained in sections 327-329 of the Act can be avoided if the alleged offender obtains appropriate consent in advance (following authorised disclosure) with respect to the commission of the prohibited act.[14] It has been argued, in the context of the disclosure provisions in sections 327-329 of the Act, that these offences constitute "*reverse onus*" provisions with the result that, at trial,

---

[13] At s 340(12).

[14] The alternative to obtaining appropriate consent in advance is making authorised disclosure after the act is committed. In the event that authorised disclosure is not made, the *alleged offender will need an "intention to make such a disclosure"* and *"a reasonable excuse for not doing so"* in order to avoid liability.

> ... it is for the defendant to prove on the balance of probabilities that he had made a s 338 disclosure or had a reasonable excuse for not doing so;[15]

it may, however, be more accurate at this early stage in the life of the Act to observe that the precise scope of the money laundering offences as to *actus reus* and *mens rea* (and the incidence of the burden of proof) will be worked out through the case law.

6.024 The scheme of the Act acknowledges (at least tacitly) concerns about the delay that might be involved in receiving appropriate feedback (following disclosure) from NCIS.[16] This is dealt with in section 335 of the Act which provides that appropriate consent will be present if the alleged offender makes an authorised disclosure to a constable or a customs officer and one of two conditions is satisfied; namely, *either* he does not receive notice that consent is refused before the end of seven working days following the day on which disclosure is made (i.e. if no refusal of consent is received during this short period then consent is deemed to have been given) *or*, in the event that consent has been refused, 31 days have passed since the day when notice was received that such consent was refused. In other words, and in respect of the second alternative, the refusal of consent provides only a moratorium on the carrying out of the transaction which would otherwise be proscribed by the Act. A like provision (containing the same notice and moratorium periods) with respect to disclosures to NCIS by nominated officers appears in section 336 of the 2002 Act.

6.025 The Act provides immunity for those making authorised disclosures from actions for breach of confidence or contract. Section 338(4) of the Act states that,

> An authorised disclosure is not to be taken to breach any restriction on the disclosure of information (however imposed).

This is expanded upon by section 337 which is headed "*Protected disclosures*" and provides that if three conditions are satisfied then the subject disclosure is not to be taken "*to breach any restriction on the disclosure of information (however imposed)*." The conditions are as follows:

---

[15] S Biggs, S Farrell and N Padfield *The Proceeds of Crime Act 2002* (2002), para 8.7.

[16] Although counsel for NCIS in *Bowman* v *Fels* [2005] 1 WLR 3083 (CA) indicated, at p 3089, that in 75% of cases involving disclosure to NCIS by lawyers the appropriate consent is forthcoming within 24 hours.

- that the information disclosed came to the discloser in the course of his trade, profession, business or employment;

- that the information causes the discloser to know or suspect or gives him reasonable grounds for knowing or suspecting that another person is engaged in money laundering; and,

- that the disclosure is made to a constable, customs officer or nominated officer as soon as possible after the index information comes to the discloser.

Disclosure offences

6.026 Section 330 provides that an offence is committed if a person:

- knows or suspects or has reasonable grounds for knowing or suspecting that another person is engaged in money laundering;

- the information on which such knowledge or suspicion is based came to him in the course of a business in the regulated sector; and

- *"...he does not make the required disclosure as soon as is practicable after the information ... comes to him".*[17]

Required disclosure is defined in terms closely allied to *"authorised disclosure".*[18]

6.027 The requirement that the discloseable information reaches the discloser *"in the course of a business in the regulated sector"* imposes an onerous burden on those working in this sector given that the penalty for non-compliance is liability for a criminal offence (the draftsman's intention was clearly to require an even more conscientious approach to disclosure from those employed in the regulated sector businesses than those employed in other areas of the economy). It should be noted that, in respect of the section 330 offence, the *mens rea* can be founded on objective (as well as subjective) grounds: *reasonable grounds* for knowing or suspecting that another person is engaged in money laundering. Concern about the apparent width of this potential criminal liability may (or may not) be allayed by

---

[17] Proceeds of Crime Act 2002, s 330(4).
[18] Proceeds of Crime Act 2002, s 330(5).

sections 330(6) and (7) of the Act which, respectively, provide that the offence is not committed:

- if there is a reasonable excuse for not disclosing;

- if the alleged offender is a professional legal adviser and the information reached him in "*privileged circumstances*";

- if the alleged offender does not (subjectively) know or suspect that the other person is engaged in money laundering and

> ...he has not been provided by his employer with such training as is specified by the Secretary of State for the purposes of this section.[19]

6.028 A restricted definition of "*privileged circumstances*" is set out in section 330(10) of the 2002 Act; essentially, information will only reach a legal adviser in such circumstances where it is communicated or given to him in connection with the giving of legal advice or where it emanates from a person seeking legal advice or, finally, where communicated or given in connection with legal proceedings or contemplated legal proceedings (it is a further condition, by virtue of section 330(11) that such information is not communicated or given "*with the intention of furthering a criminal purpose*"). The absence of training as a potential defence to the commission of a section 330 offence might be regarded, counter-intuitively, as an incentive not to provide training to staff. However, this apparent loophole is closed by regulation 3 of the Money Laundering Regulations 2003 which imposes an obligation on employers to provide such training and stipulates that an offence is committed if this obligation is not complied with.[20]

6.029 There is a further layering of protection afforded to those charged with failing to disclose within the regulated sector, although this damages the certainty (the "*clear labelling*") of the conduct which is proscribed. Section 330(8) provides that,

> In deciding whether a person committed an offence under this section the court must consider whether he followed any relevant guidance which was at the time concerned ... issued by a supervisory authority or any other appropriate body, ... approved by the Treasury, and ... published in a manner it approved as appropriate in its opinion to bring the guidance to the attention of persons likely to be affected by it.

[19] Proceeds of Crime Act 2002, s 330(7)(b).
[20] SI 2003/3075.

6.030 It is striking that the Act appears to acknowledge that its provisions may require further explanation in the form of "*relevant guidance*" and that the commission of a criminal offence may depend on whether such guidance has been followed (particularly when such guidance may be wrong or inaccurate – even when given by a body responsible for the enforcement of these provisions of the Act).[21] Supervisory authorities are the Bank of England, the Council of Lloyds and the Office of Fair Trading and it appears that the Bar Council and Law Society will constitute "*any other appropriate body*" insofar as legal professionals are concerned.[22]

6.031 Section 331 of the Act contains a like offence (to that contained in section 330) for failures to disclose by nominated officers in the regulated sector.

6.032 It is central to the failure to disclose offences contained in sections 330 and 331 that the failure to disclose be in the "*regulated sector*" and this is defined by Schedule 9 to the Act as a business which engages in any of the following activities:

> (a) accepting deposits by a person with permission under Part 4 of the Financial Services and Markets Act 2000 (c. 8) to accept deposits (including, in the case of a building society, the raising of money from members of the society by the issue of shares); (b) the business of the National Savings Bank; (c) business carried on by a credit union; (d) any home-regulated activity carried on by a European institution in respect of which the establishment conditions in paragraph 13 of Schedule 3 to the Financial Services and Markets Act 2000, or the service conditions in paragraph 14 of that Schedule, are satisfied; (e) any activity carried on for the purpose of raising money authorised to be raised under the National Loans Act 1968 (c. 13) under the auspices of the Director of Savings; (f) the activity of operating a bureau de change, transmitting money (or any representation of monetary value) by any means or cashing cheques which are made payable to customers; (g) any activity falling within sub-paragraph (2); (h) any of the activities in points 1 to 12 or 14 of Annex 1 to the Banking Consolidation Directive, ignoring an activity described in any of sub-paragraphs (a) to (g) above; (i) business which consists of effecting or carrying out contracts of long term insurance by a person who has received official authorisation pursuant to Article 6 or 27 of the First Life Directive.

---

[21] See, e.g. *P* v *P* [2004] 1 Fam 1 (Fam) where Dame Elizabeth Butler-Sloss P took the view that guidance provided by telephone to a party's legal advisers by a duty officer at NCIS was, in a number of respects, wrong. The requirement that the Guidance be approved by the Treasury may provide a safeguard.

[22] The Bar Council has published guidance which was updated in the light of the Court of Appeal's decision in *Bowman* v *Fels* [2005] 1 WLR 3083.

6.033 Sub-paragraph (2) (to which sub-paragraph 1(1)(g) of Schedule 9 refers) provides that an activity is regulated if it constitutes any of the following kinds of activity in the United Kingdom:

> (a) dealing in investments as principal or as agent; (b) arranging deals in investments; (c) managing investments; (d) safeguarding and administering investments; (e) sending dematerialised instructions; (f) establishing (and taking other steps in relation to) collective investment schemes; (g) advising on investments.

6.034 There is a final failure to disclose offence contained in the Act: section 332. This offence imposes a liability on nominated officers outside the regulated sector. It is expressed in similar terms to the offences contained in sections 330 and 331. However, the offence is committed only when the nominated officer (subjectively) "*knows or suspects that another person is engaged in money laundering*". By contrast to the offences that may be committed by those working in the regulated sector, there will be no liability where, in the absence of a subjective knowledge or suspicion of money laundering, there are simply "*reasonable grounds*" on which such knowledge or suspicion might be based.

6.035 For the offences of failing to disclose and tipping off (sections 330-333 of the Act) the penalties are prescribed by section 334(2): on summary conviction, a sentence of six months' imprisonment or a fine not exceeding the statutory maximum or both and, on conviction on indictment, by a sentence of imprisonment not exceeding five years or a fine or both. The same penalties are prescribed, by section 342(7) of the Act, for the offence of prejudicing an investigation.

Tipping off and prejudicing an investigation

6.036 The offence is contained in section 333(1) of the Act which reads:

> A person commits an offence if – (a) he knows or suspects that a disclosure falling within section 337 or 338 has been made; and (b) he makes a disclosure which is likely to prejudice any investigation which might be conducted following the disclosure referred to in paragraph (a).

6.037 The Act provides that no offence will be committed where the alleged offender neither knew nor suspected that the disclosure which he made was likely to be prejudicial to an investigation.[23]

---

[23] Proceeds of Crime Act 2002, s 333(2)(a).

6.038 There is further provision in the 2002 Act for the avoidance of criminal liability under section 333. The tipping off offence is not committed if,

> ... the disclosure is made in carrying out a function [the alleged offender] ... has relating to the enforcement of any provision of this Act or of any other enactment relating to criminal conduct or benefit from criminal conduct

or if the alleged offender "... *is a professional legal adviser and the disclosure falls within subsection (3)*."[24] The legal professional privilege exception is, of course, likely to be of most interest to practitioners and is defined by section 333(3) which provides that a relevant disclosure for the purposes of avoiding liability is a disclosure:

> (a) to (or to a representative of) a client of the professional legal adviser in connection with the giving by the adviser of legal advice to the client, or (b) to any person in connection with legal proceedings or contemplated legal proceedings.

However, this provision cannot be relied on where the disclosure is made with the intention of furthering a criminal purpose.[25]

6.039 Part 8 of the 2002 Act contains a criminal offence which is related to the tipping off offence: prejudicing an investigation. This differs from tipping off in that the section 333 offence is aimed at the alleged offender who knows or suspects that a disclosure has been made under sections 337 or 338; in other words, the tipping off offence is tied to the protected or authorised disclosure and aims to protect the investigation which follows. Section 342, by contrast, has a broader remit and is intended to protect investigations into confiscation, civil recovery or money laundering. Sections 342(1)-(2) of the Act provide as follows:

> (1) This section applies if a person knows or suspects that an appropriate officer ... is acting (or proposing to act) in connection with a confiscation investigation, a civil recovery investigation or a money laundering investigation which is being or is about to conducted. (2) The person commits an offence if – (a) he makes a disclosure which is likely to prejudice the investigation, or (b) he falsifies, conceals, destroys or otherwise disposes of, or causes or permits the falsification, concealment, destruction or disposal of, documents which are relevant to the investigation.

---

[24] Proceeds of Crime Act 2002, section 333(2)(b) and (c).
[25] Proceeds of Crime Act 2002, s 333(4).

6.040 Section 342 goes on to provide means by which criminal liability is avoided and these mirror the provisions in section 333(2)-(4) which are discussed, in the context of tipping off, above. There is a further escape clause in section 342(6) which provides that the offence of falsifying, concealing, destroying or otherwise disposing of relevant documents is not committed (section 342(2)(b)) where the alleged offender neither knows nor suspects that the documents are relevant to the investigation or where he lacks intention to conceal from the investigator any facts disclosed by the documents. Clearly, this provision reflects the policy which informed the insertion of section 333(2)(a) into the Act (with respect to the tipping off offence).

Legal professionals and POCA

6.041 Even the most cursory perusal of Part 7 of the 2002 Act will reveal that it gives rise to particular anxiety for legal practitioners – anxiety which is heightened by the fact that the 2002 Act contains a number of widely drawn penal provisions:

> The provisions of Part 7 and section 342 of POCA have become of increasing concern to the legal profession practising civil litigation and, more particularly, in the field of family law. The Bar and solicitors dealing with financial relief disputes of clients with substantial assets or making ancillary relief claims in such cases have been unsure as to their obligations under POCA and the extent to which the provisions of POCA might be a barrier to the resolution of financial disputes.[26]

6.042 The framework for the proper interpretation of the Act in this regard is largely set by two fairly recent decisions: one at first instance and the second, and more recent, on appeal: *P v P (Ancillary Relief: Proceeds of Crime)*[27] and *Bowman v Fels*.[28] The importance of these decisions, and the issues to which they give rise, is reflected by the fact that, in both cases, the Law Society and Bar Council were given permission to intervene and make submissions.

6.043 *P v P* arose out of ancillary relief proceedings in the Family Division. Lawyers acting for the wife were concerned that part of the assets of the husband resulted from untaxed income which fell within the definition of "*criminal property*" for the purposes of the Proceeds of Crime Act 2002. Their more immediate concern was that, in acting for the wife in the course

---

[26] *P v P* [2004] 1 Fam 1, 11 *per* Dame Elizabeth Butler-Sloss P (Fam).
[27] [2004] 1 Fam 1 (Fam).
[28] [2005] 1 WLR 3083 (CA).

of proceedings, they might be entering into or becoming concerned in an arrangement within the meaning of section 328(1) of the 2002 Act. Accordingly, the wife's advisers made an authorised disclosure to NCIS pursuant to section 328(2)(a) of the Act in order to protect both themselves and their lay client. They were advised by NCIS that they were not permitted to inform the husband, his advisers or the wife of the disclosure in order to avoid tipping off and/or prejudicing the investigation (sections 333 and 342 of the 2002 Act). The notice period passed without a response from NCIS in respect of the authorised disclosure. The wife's advisers remained concerned that it was impossible to reconcile their duties to their client with the scheme of the Act. They therefore made application to the court for declarations as to their ambit of their obligations under the Act. The application was heard, by the President of the Family Division,[29] in unusual circumstances. The application was made on a without notice basis, but its existence and subject matter became known to the husband's solicitors as a result of the consequential adjournment of another hearing in the same proceedings. The President permitted the husband's solicitors to attend and to participate in the hearing of the application for declaratory relief on condition that they did not inform their lay client.

6.044 The President held that section 328 contained a straightforward offence:

- "*arrangement*" was widely drawn and there were a range of ways in which a legal professional might become "*concerned in*" an arrangement;

- there was nothing to suggest that the offence could only be committed at the "*point of execution*" of the arrangement and, therefore, the offence could be committed by negotiating an arrangement;

- in the circumstances, authorisation (disclosure and consent) should be sought where the legal professional knew or suspected that he or his client were, in seeking an arrangement from the court or in negotiating a settlement with the other side, becoming concerned in an arrangement of the sort prohibited by the Act;

- no issue of legal professional privilege arose in respect of the money laundering offences contained in sections 327-329 of the 2002 Act

---

[29] Dame Elizabeth Butler-Sloss P.

(because there was, for these offences, no escape clause of the sort found, for example, in sections 330 and 333).

6.045 The President was clearly aware of the draconian effect of Part 7 of the 2002 Act, but reminded herself that the notice and moratorium periods meant that, in practice,

> ...the longest possible time for which a person could be prevented from taking steps in relation to an arrangement, after sending a notice to the NCIS, will be 31 days plus seven working days.[30]

Notwithstanding this, she remained concerned that the overall effect of the Act, as interpreted by her, was disproportionate given that the Act drew no distinction between "*degrees*" of criminal property and, therefore, treated an illegally-obtained £10 in the same manner as an illegally obtained £1,000,000. In the light of this she observed that if the approach which she had set out was

> ... scrupulously followed by the legal advisers, the result is likely to have a considerable and potentially adverse impact upon the NCIS and would create serious consequential delays ... [31]

6.046 Having dealt succinctly with the section 328 offence, the President turned to consideration of tipping off and prejudicing an investigation. She described the implications of these offences as "*Of much greater concern to the legal profession.*" The President relied heavily on the protection expressly afforded to legal professionals by sections 333(2)(c)-(3) and 342(3)(c)-(4) of the 2002 Act. Much of the discussion in the judgment is taken up with the interface between the provisions dealing with legal professional privilege and subsections which make it clear that privilege cannot be relied on where tipping off or disclosure is made "*with the intention of furthering a criminal purpose*".[32] The difficulty identified by the President was that a central component of the duty to one's lay client was to keep him informed and not to withhold information from him, whereas in every circumstance where a solicitor took the view that a disclosure to NCIS was required there must, inevitably, be some suspicion of criminal activity. Counsel for NCIS had submitted that wherever such suspicion arose and tipping off took place or disclosure was made then the legal professional exemption would be inoperative. The President was not prepared to accept this submission because to do so would render the legal professional privilege escape

---

[30] [2004] 1 Fam 1, 14 (Fam).
[31] At p 15.
[32] Section 333(4) and 342(5).

provisions in the Act meaningless. She preferred to solve the conundrum by a different method:

> ... there may well be instances where a solicitor's disclosure to a client is in breach of section 333(4) or section 342(5) of the 2002 Act, because the solicitor makes the disclosure with an improper purpose. In such a case the legal professional exemption would, of course, be lost. I cannot ... give a blanket guarantee to all family practitioners that they will never lose the protection of the exemption. But unless the requisite improper intention is there, the solicitor should be free to communicate such information to his/her client or opponent as is necessary and appropriate in connection with the giving of legal advice or acting in connection with actual or contemplated proceedings.[33]

6.047 It therefore appears that the solicitor's "*intention*" in tipping off or disclosing will determine whether or not the criminal offences contained in sections 333 and 342 are committed. The President further directed herself that the notice and moratorium periods contained in sections 327-329 of the Act are independent of the provisions of section 333 and 342 of the Act and that, accordingly, once a solicitor has made an authorised disclosure and obtained the appropriate consent in accordance with section 328 there is no reason for him to delay in informing his client provided that he can take advantage of the legal professional privilege exemption. Conversely, if section 333(4) or 342(5) is engaged then he is not entitled to inform his client at all, "*There is no middle ground*". On the facts of *P* v *P* itself, the President held that the wife's solicitors had been right to make an authorised disclosure to NCIS and that the fact that there had been a delay beyond the notice period meant that they were free to communicate the fact of an authorised disclosure to the husband's advisers. Given that they lacked any intention to further a criminal purpose there was no question of the commission of any offence under sections 333 or 342.

6.048 In the light of the strict approach that the President took with respect to the section 328 offence (in spite of the concerns that she freely expressed about its disproportionate and draconian effects) it is hardly surprising that *P* v *P* did not turn out to be the last word on the ambit of the offence; in 2004 *Bowman* v *Fels*[34] reached the Court of Appeal. This case arose out of civil litigation with respect to beneficial ownership of a house lived in by the Claimant and Defendant who had been in a relationship for a number of years. Following disclosure and inspection the Claimant's solicitors became aware of the existence of documents which tended to suggest that the

---

[33] [2004] 1 Fam 1, 17 (Fam).
[34] [2005] 1 WLR 3083 (CA).

Defendant had included the cost of works done at the house within his business accounts and VAT returns, even though these works were, in fact, unconnected to the business. The knowledge acquired by the Claimant's solicitors was disclosed by them to NCIS on the basis that they believed this was required by section 328 of the 2002 Act. They also took the view that they were prohibited from telling the Defendant's solicitors what they had done. At the time that disclosure to NCIS took place a trial date was fast approaching; the solicitors were informed by an officer at NCIS that it was unlikely that consent would be granted prior to the date of the trial. Therefore, the Claimant's solicitors made a without notice application to a circuit judge for vacation of the trial date. The judge granted the Order and the Defendant's solicitors were then informed that the trial date had been vacated (they were not informed of the reason why the application to vacate had been made, but correctly guessed the reason in any event). The Defendant's solicitors responded to this information by making an application to set aside the without notice Order and for a direction that the Claimant's solicitors be required to disclose the reason for their application and the evidence relied on in support of it. The Defendant's application was heard by a different circuit judge. He determined, in reliance on the legal professional exemption contained in section 333(2)(c) of the 2002 Act, that there was no reason why the Claimant's solicitors could not have disclosed both to the court and, more importantly perhaps, the Defendant's solicitors the reasons for the making of the application to vacate. The Order vacating the trial date was set aside. The Claimant appealed against this Order. By the time of the hearing the litigation had been settled, but, in the light of the public importance of the issues raised by the appeal, the Court of Appeal decided that it had jurisdiction to consider the appeal.

6.049 The Court of Appeal dismissed the Claimant's appeal and disapproved the approach taken by the President in *P* v *P*. Brooke LJ, who delivered the judgment of the Court, identified the question raised by the appeal as follows:

> ... whether section 328 ... means that as soon as a lawyer acting for a client in legal proceedings discovers or suspects anything in the proceedings that may facilitate the acquisition, retention, use or control (usually by his client or his client's opponent) of 'criminal property', he must immediately notify NCIS of his belief if he is to avoid being guilty of the criminal offence of being concerned in an arrangement which he knows or suspects facilitates such activity (by whatever means).[35]

---

[35] At p 3091.

6.050 The Court commenced answering this question by considering the EU Directives which gave rise to the money laundering offences and the domestic legislation which translated the EU legislation into English law. The concern, articulated by Brooke LJ in conducting this exercise, was whether Parliament could, without making it clear, have intended to override long established principles of legal professional privilege in the conduct of ordinary civil litigation. It was concluded, for the following reasons, that it was "*improbable*" that Parliament, in passing the 2002 Act, had this intention:

- If civil litigation resulted in a judgment or Order of the court then the resultant Order could not properly be described as an "*arrangement which … facilitates*" within the meaning of section 328 of the Act and it would be absurd to describe the judge granting the judgment or making the Order as "*a person … concerned in an arrangement*".

- The absurdity of describing a judge as "*a person … concerned in an arrangement*" must, logically, extend to legal professionals acting for lay clients who had a hand in procuring the judgment or Order in the course of civil proceedings.

- "*… if a judgment or order is outside the concept of an arrangement under section 328, we see equally little basis in ordinary language for treating any step taken to issue or pursue legal proceedings with a view to obtaining a judgment or order as an 'arrangement'*".[36]

- The money laundering offences contained in sections 327-329 of the Act referred, in specific terms, to the commission of an act which was suggestive of a particular point in time – entering into or becoming concerned in an arrangement indicated a single act at a single point in time. Accordingly, the ordinary conduct of civil proceedings would not result in criminal liability under section 328 in respect of the taking of any intermediate step in the proceedings which did not result in the acquisition, retention, use or control of criminal property.

- There were, moreover, important policy reasons why legal professional privilege should continue to operate in the conventional manner – not least, the importance of a consensual approach to litigation and the "*cards on the table*" stance which the Civil Procedure Rules and the overriding objective encouraged.

---

[36] At p 3106.

6.051 The Court of Appeal expressed its conclusions as follows:

> ... the proper interpretation of section 328 is that it is not intended to cover or affect the ordinary conduct of litigation by legal professionals. That includes any step taken by them in litigation from the issue of proceedings and the securing of injunctive relief or a freezing order up to its final disposal by judgment. We do not consider that either the European or the United Kingdom legislator can have envisaged that any of these ordinary activities could fall within the concept of 'becoming concerned in an arrangement which ... facilitates ... the acquisition, retention, use or control of criminal property.'[37]

6.052 The Court left open the question whether a person carrying out some earlier act, for example, giving advice or conducting negotiations, could be treated as having retroactively committed an offence *by that act* under section 328 when an arrangement was subsequently entered into.[38] In *P* v *P* the President had indicated that the offence could only be committed when the arrangement was made or at some subsequent stage,[39] but the Court of Appeal declined to be drawn on this subject. In the wake of the decision of the Court of Appeal in *Bowman* v *Fels* the Bar Council immediately issued revised guidance to the Bar[40] and posted the decision on its website.

Assets Recovery Agency

6.053 Part 1 of the Act creates the Assets Recovery Agency ("ARA") as a corporation sole under a Director appointed by the Home Secretary. The ARA has three functions. First, criminal confiscation, second civil recovery and, third, the taxation of income related to crime. In respect of its function of civil recovery the 2002 Act is similarly innovative in creating a new jurisdiction for the High Court in the making of orders for the recovery,

> ...in civil proceedings ... property which is, or represents, property obtained through unlawful conduct.[41]

The power to apply for such orders is vested by the Act in "*the enforcement authority*": the Director of the ARA.

---

[37] At p 3110.
[38] At p 3106.
[39] [2004] 1 Fam 1, 13 (Fam).
[40] General Council of the Bar, "*The Proceeds of Crime Act 2002: Note to the Bar*" 8 March 2005.
[41] Proceeds of Crime Act 2002, s 240(1)(a).

6.054 The 2002 Act defines unlawful conduct as conduct which is unlawful according to the criminal law of any part of the United Kingdom and as conduct which occurs outside the United Kingdom which is unlawful under the criminal law of the country where it occurs, provided that it is also unlawful according to the criminal law of the index part of the United Kingdom.[42] Property is obtained through unlawful conduct if obtained "*by or in return for the conduct.*"[43]

6.055 The Act contains detailed material on the machinery by which such orders are to be obtained and this lies beyond the scope of this work. It is worth pointing out, however, that considerable unease was expressed at the time of the passage of the Bill through Parliament about the wide-ranging powers proposed for the ARA:

> The action for civil recovery ... is problematic in using the form of a civil action, in which the standard of proof is the balance of probabilities, to allow a state agency with extensive investigatory powers to seek a punitive order for forfeiture of assets. There is the risk that, in practice, this mechanism could undermine the safeguards of the criminal law, through the use of the more flexible civil procedures. These civil procedures are designed to regulate relations between private individuals rather than to enforce the criminal law: a state body such as the Criminal Assets Recovery Agency should not be considered as approximating to a private party in a tort action. It is questionable whether the low standard of proof that applies under Part 5 [of the Act] is adequate to protect defendants from the excessive, arbitrary or discriminatory use of these powers.[44]

6.056 The obvious concern which is articulated in this passage is that proceedings for a recovery order in the High Court may come to be seen as an attractive and much easier alternative to the pursuit of criminal proceedings in the Crown Court: fraud is notoriously difficult to prove to the requisite criminal standard of proof. The fact that the civil standard of proof and the Civil Procedure Rules apply with respect to High Court proceedings for a recovery order reinforce this position.

6.057 Some of the concerns about the use of civil recovery proceedings as a means to circumvent the rigour of the criminal law may be assuaged by the criteria published by the ARA itself[45] to determine the threshold for a decision to pursue a civil recovery order:

---

[42] Proceeds of Crime Act 2002, s 241(1)-(2).
[43] Proceeds of Crime Act 2002, s 242(1).
[44] *Justice* briefing for the Second Reading of the Bill in the House of Lords, March 2002, para 16, cited in S Biggs, S Farrell and N Padfield, *The Proceeds of Crime Act 2002* (2002), para 6.1.
[45] In a 2004 report.

- the case must normally be referred by a Law Enforcement Agency or a prosecuting authority;

- a criminal prosecution should ordinarily have been considered and either have failed or proved impossible to complete;

- recoverable property should have been identified and have an estimated value of at least £10,000;

- the recoverable property must include property other than cash or negotiable instruments;

- there must be evidence of criminal conduct supported to the criminal standard of proof.

6.058 The connection between criminal proceedings and the "*unlawful conduct*" that can be relied on to bring proceedings for a civil recovery order was considered by Sullivan J in *R (Director of Assets Recovery Agency)* v *Green & Others*.[46] It was held that, in the context of civil recovery order proceedings, the Director of the ARA did not need to allege the commission of a specific criminal offence, but was required to set out the matters alleged to constitute the "*unlawful conduct*" (within the meaning of 241 of the 2002 Act) by which the subject property was obtained. Sullivan J went on to find that a claim for civil recovery could not be sustained simply on the basis that a respondent had no identifiable lawful income on which to sustain his lifestyle.

---

[46] [2006] *The Times*, February 27 (QBD).

Chapter 7

PRACTICE: PLEADING AND CASE MANAGEMENT

1. INTRODUCTION

7.001 This chapter considers a variety of practical matters. It is biased towards personal injury practice,[1] although a number of the issues discussed are capable of wider application to more general pleas and defences of fraud. In circumstances where the Claimant bases his action on an allegation of fraudulent misrepresentation (referred to elsewhere in this book as the tort of deceit) it is clear enough what needs to be pleaded and this is considered below. However, this book is also concerned with more general allegations of dishonest conduct and a key problem in this context lies in identifying what precisely is meant by the Civil Procedure Rules when they refer to fraud in connection with statements of case. Does this mean fraud in the sense of the tort of deceit?[2] Does it simply mean conscious dishonesty and, if so, how does one test dishonesty for these purposes: is the test subjective, objective or both?[3] In at least one unreported case in the county court the judge took the view that fraud, in the present context, simply meant that a party (usually the Defendant) had said to the Claimant, "*You are a liar*".[4] *Bullen, Leake & Jacob*[5] suggest that an action in fraud will usually consist of one or other of the following causes of action: deceit, conspiracy, inducing breach of

---

[1] Where there has, in recent years, been a good deal of judicial commentary and intervention.
[2] It seems most unlikely that there is, in the context of a general plea of dishonest conduct or fraudulent exaggeration, any need for all of the elements of the tort of deceit to be present and the case law does not support such an approach. This issue was directly confronted in *Lawrenson & Lawrenson* v *Lawrenson and Equity Red Star* (2005) 30 June (Liverpool CC *per* HHJ Stewart QC) (unreported) where it was held that the references in the CPR to "*fraud*" refer to the tort of deceit, rather than to more general allegations of lying or dishonesty. Cf. *Cooper* v *P & O Stena Line Limited* [1999] 1 Ll Rep 734 (QBD) and *Humphries* v *Matthews* (2006) 16 June (Liverpool CC *per* Recorder Moran QC) (unreported, but available on Lawtel).
[3] Is there a requirement for dishonesty in the *R* v *Ghosh* [1982] QB 1053 sense?
[4] See *Rooney* v *Graves* [2004] (Liverpool CC, *per* HHJ Stewart QC), as referred to by Brooke LJ in *Kearsley* v *Klarfeld* [2005] EWCA Civ 1510, para 47.
[5] Lord Brennan QC and W Blair QC, *Bullen, Leake & Jacob's Precedents of Pleadings* (15th ed, 2004), para 48-01.

contract, bribery and/or claims in equity to trace assets. However, they do not suggest that their list is exhaustive. Questions relating to what fraud means (as it is referred to in the Rules) may seem rather abstract, but they can have considerable practical significance.

7.002 In *Cooper* v *P & O Stena Line Limited*,[6] a personal injury claim, the Defendant alleged that the Claimant was malingering, but had not expressly pleaded fraud[7] because, as counsel boldly submitted to the trial judge, "*it was not the usual practice to plead malingering*" (in express terms) in a Defence. The trial judge disagreed. It is tolerably clear that some judges regard exaggeration and, perhaps, a touch of malingering as being very far from synonymous with fraud. In a recent (and unreported) first instance decision by a county court district judge the following appeared in the course of judgment:

> This court deals day in and day out with road traffic claims where personal injury is alleged and I have no doubt that in a significant number of those cases the degree of personal injury suffered is exaggerated, not nearly so much, I might say, as the claims for legal costs are exaggerated. It is a fact of life that the court deals with every day and does not necessarily imply that the person guilty of the exaggeration is acting fraudulently.[8]

7.003 The district judge was not prepared to find that the Claimant had acted fraudulently, notwithstanding that the court could not necessarily accept all of her evidence as "*being entirely frank and honest, let alone accurate.*" Some of the dilemmas confronting the pleader of a statement of case in this situation have now been resolved, or largely resolved, by recent Court of Appeal intervention. However, the Court of Appeal, while setting out what needs to be pleaded where a party alleges that another is lying,[9] has not described with any degree of precision what is meant by use of the word "*fraud*" in the context of an allegation of dishonesty about the circumstances of an accident or the consequences of the same. The Civil Procedure Rules direct, in rather less stringent terms than the Rules of the Supreme Court, that fraud and illegality need to be spelt out in Particulars of Claim where the same are alleged and the Queen's Bench Guide requires a Defence to provide full particulars of any allegation of dishonesty or fraud. In the circumstances, it seems likely that definitional problems – identifying what is

---

[6] [1999] 1 Ll Rep 734 (QBD).
[7] There was an obligation under the Rules of the Supreme Court expressly to plead fraud where it was alleged: RSC Ord 18, r 8(1)(a).
[8] *Bernice McCauliffe* v *Arriva Bus Company Limited* [2004] (Claim No BI300550) (Birkenhead CC, *per* DJ Travers) (unreported).
[9] E.g. lying about the symptoms with which he alleges he is suffering as a result of an injury.

and is not, for the purposes of the Rules, an allegation of fraud – will continue to crop up.[10]

2. PLEADING FRAUD

Civil Procedure Rules and Code of Conduct

7.004 The basic rule is that an allegation of fraud, and the basis on which the same is alleged, needs to be pleaded expressly in the course of a statement of case:

- *"The Claimant must specifically set out the following matters in his particulars of claim where he wishes to rely on them in support of his claim: (1) any allegation of fraud, (2) the fact of any illegality, (3) details of any misrepresentation … "[11]*

- *"(1) In his defence, the defendant must state – (a) which of the allegations in the particulars of claim he denies; (b) which allegations he is unable to admit or deny, but which he requires the claimant to prove; (c) which allegations he admits. (2) Where the defendant denies an allegation – (a) he must state his reasons for doing so; and (b) if he intends to put forward a different version of events from that given by the claimant, he must state his own version. (3) A defendant who – (a) fails to deal with an allegation; but (b) has set out in his defence the nature of his case in relation to the issue to which that allegation is relevant; shall be taken to require that allegation to be proved. (4) Where the claim includes a money claim, a defendant shall be taken to require that any allegation relating to the amount of money claimed be proved unless he expressly admits the allegation. (5) Subject to paragraphs (3) and (4), a defendant*

---

[10] As indicated above, this chapter is biased towards personal injury practice, but it is intriguing to note that problems in identifying what is meant by fraud are as apt to arise in a commercial context as elsewhere: see, Steven Gee QC, *Commercial Injunctions* (5th ed, 2004), para 7.014.
[11] CPR 16, PD para 8.2. See *Wallingford* v *Mutual Society* (1880) 5 App Cas 685 (HL(E)) where Lord Hatherly emphasised, at p 701, that generalised averments of fraud were not sufficient; what was needed was particularisation of the alleged fraud and the evidence to support this. More recently see also *Three Rivers DC* v *Bank of England (No 3)* [2001] 2 All ER 513, 530d *per* Lord Hope (HL(E)), "*A party is not entitled to a finding of fraud if the pleader does not allege fraud directly and the facts on which he relies are equivocal.*"

> *who fails to deal with an allegation shall be taken to admit that allegation.*[12]

- Whilst Part 16 of the Rules, and the Practice Direction to the same, do not expressly state that a Defence, by contrast to a Particulars of Claim, should plead fraud, this omission is remedied by the Queen's Bench Guide which states,

> In addition to the matters listed ... [in the Practice Direction to Part 16],[13] full particulars of any allegation of dishonesty or malice and, where any inference of fraud or dishonesty is alleged, the basis on which the inference is alleged should also be included.[14]

7.005 Accompanying the CPR obligation to plead fraud where this is alleged are the codes of conduct of the professional bodies. The Bar Code of Conduct provides:

> A barrister must not devise facts which will assist in advancing the lay client's case and must not draft any statement of case, witness statement, affidavit, notice of appeal or other document containing: (a) any statement of fact or contention which is not supported by the lay client or by his instructions; (b) any contention which he does not consider to be properly arguable; (c) any allegation of fraud unless he has clear instructions to make such allegation and has before him reasonably credible material which as it stands establishes a prima facie case of fraud; ... provided that nothing in this paragraph shall prevent a barrister drafting a document containing specific factual statements or contentions included by the barrister subject to confirmation of their accuracy by the lay client or witness.[15]

7.006 It has long been recognised by the courts, whether by reference to the Bar Code of Conduct or otherwise, that a plea of fraud should not be made by counsel *"unless he has clear and sufficient evidence to support it."*[16] The

---

[12] CPR 16.5.

[13] CPR 16, PD para 10 which simply refers back to CPR 16.5.

[14] Queen's Bench Guide, para 5.6.3. Reference should also be made to paras 2.6 and 2.7 of the Chancery Guide which provides as follows, "2.6 ... *a party must set out in any statement of case: (1) full particulars of any allegation of fraud, dishonesty, malice or illegality; (2) where any inference of fraud or dishonesty is alleged, the facts on the basis of which the inference is alleged. 2.7 A party should not set out allegations of fraud or dishonesty unless there is material admissible in evidence to support the contentions made. Setting out such matters without such material being available may result in particular allegations being stuck out and may result in wasted costs orders being made against the legal advisers responsible."*

[15] Bar Code of Conduct, para 704. See also, Law Society's Code for Advocacy, paras 6.6(c) and 7.1(h).

[16] *Associated Leisure Limited* v *Associated Newspapers Limited* [1970] 2 QB 450, 456E *per* Lord Denning MR (CA).

Code of Conduct refers, however, not to *evidence*, but to reasonably credible *material*: is this different to a requirement that counsel be able to rely on admissible evidence to support the fraud alleged? This section of the Code of Conduct, or an earlier version drafted in the same terms, was considered by the House of Lords in *Medcalf* v *Mardell*.[17] It is unnecessary to set out the detailed facts of this case, save that it concerned an appeal by Defendants against a decision in the High Court. In the course of the appeal, and acting on instructions, experienced and competent leading and junior counsel made allegations of fraud against the Claimant in a notice of appeal and a supplementary skeleton argument. The appeal was dismissed. The Claimant applied for a wasted costs order against counsel for the Defendant on the basis that they had contravened the provisions of the Bar Code of Conduct requiring them to have "*reasonably credible material*" with which to support the allegations of fraud. The Defendant declined to waive privilege and, therefore, counsel were in the invidious position of being unable to place before the court the documentary material on which they would rely in resisting the application for wasted costs; there was no allegation that counsel had acted in bad faith. The Court of Appeal held that counsel had acted improperly and made a wasted costs order. Counsel appealed to the House of Lords. Lord Bingham delivered the leading speech. He observed that the receipt of instructions to plead an allegation of fraud will not be sufficient for counsel to comply with his duty under the Bar Code of Conduct. It was also necessary that counsel,

> ... *exercise an objective professional judgment whether it is in all the circumstances proper to lend his name to the allegation ... [and] counsel could not properly judge it proper to make such an allegation unless he had material before him which he judged to be reasonably credible and which appeared to justify the allegation.*[18]

7.007 In a concurring speech Lord Steyn recognised the "*difficult problems for practitioners*" which were generated by the Code:[19] the fact that the relevant section of the Code required counsel to tread carefully between his duty to his client on the one hand and the avoidance of improper or over-zealous conduct on the other. Some latitude is given to counsel in this regard as the slightly earlier case of *Brown* v *Bennett (No 2)*,[20] also decided by reference to the Bar Code of Conduct, makes clear. In this case Neuberger J held that the competing (and, to some extent, irreconcilable) duties of counsel were such that it was only if the decision taken by counsel to plead

---

[17] [2003] 1 AC 120 (HL(E)).
[18] At p 134D-E.
[19] At p 138H.
[20] [2002] 1 WLR 713 (ChD).

dishonesty was "*unreasonable and reckless*" or, to put the matter another way, a decision that "*no reasonable lawyer, properly considering matters, could have reached*" that it could be considered improper.[21]

7.008 Lord Bingham dealt with the difference between reasonably credible material and admissible evidence in the following way:

- At the preparatory stage, counsel could plead fraud without falling into breach of the Code if he had before him

    ... material of such a character as to lead responsible counsel to conclude that serious allegations could properly be based on it.[22]

    Accordingly, at this stage it was not necessary that such material should be in the form of admissible evidence;[23]

- By contrast, at the hearing stage,

    ... counsel cannot properly make or persist in an allegation which is unsupported by admissible evidence, since if there is not admissible evidence to support the allegation the court cannot be invited to find it has been proved, and if the court cannot be invited to find that the allegation has been proved the allegation should not be made or should be withdrawn.

The House of Lords allowed the appeal in *Medcalf* because, in the absence of disclosure of the evidential material before counsel, it was not possible to conclude that they had acted improperly in breach of the Bar Code of Conduct.

The tort of deceit

7.009 It is clearly necessary that the Particulars of Claim plead all of the elements of the tort. Accordingly, the following should be clearly pleaded in Particulars of Claim where the Claimant relies on an allegation of fraudulent misrepresentation:

---

[21] At p 750F-G.
[22] [2003] 1 AC 120, 134E-G.
[23] It has been recognised at the highest level that, in appropriate cases, counsel is entitled to plead fraud at an early stage on the basis that evidence might emerge before trial or even in cross-examination at trial which will justify the pleading: see *Three Rivers DC* v *Bank of England (No 3)* [2001] 3 All ER 513, 562-563 *per* Lord Hutton (HL(E)).

- the (mis)representation – setting out (a) whether the same was made orally or in writing (using the words which constituted the same and, where contained in a document, identifying the document); (b) the date on which made; (c) identifying the misrepresentor and misrepresentee;[24]

- the basis on which it is alleged that the representation was false;

- the Defendant's dishonest knowledge of the falsity of his representation[25] and his intention that the Claimant should act on it;

- the Claimant's reliance on the representation;

- the loss suffered as a result.

7.010 It is not necessary for a statement of case to refer, in terms, to fraud or deceit, provided that the elements of the tort are spelt out and that the allegations relied on in respect of the same are particularised.[26] It is clearly insufficient simply to allege that a false statement has been made without going further and particularising the other elements of the tort because to do so fails to identify for the Defendant the case that he has to meet. Equally, there is little point in pleading the facts relied on in support of an allegation of fraud where such facts are as consistent with an allegation of innocent misrepresentation as fraudulent misrepresentation; the Claimant who files an equivocal statement of case in these circumstances will likely be met with a striking out application.[27]

---

[24] See *Seligmann* v *Young* [1884] WN 93.

[25] The basis on which it is alleged that the Defendant had knowledge of the falsity of what is represented should be pleaded where there is an allegation of dishonesty: see, *Belmont Finance Corporation Limited* v *Willams Furniture Limited* [1979] 1 Ch 250, 268C-D *per* Buckley LJ (CA) "*The facts alleged may sufficiently demonstrate that dishonesty is allegedly involved, but where the facts are complicated this may not be so clear, and in such a case it is incumbent upon the pleader to make it clear when dishonesty is alleged. If he uses language which is equivocal, rendering it doubtful whether he is in fact relying on the alleged dishonesty of the transaction, this will be fatal; the allegation of its dishonest nature will not have been pleaded with sufficient clarity.*"

[26] In *Davy* v *Garrett* (1878) 7 ChD 473 (CA) Thesiger LJ observed, at p 489, that in most ordinary cases it was not necessary to make use of the word "*fraud*" in a statement of case (where there was no room for doubt that this was what was being alleged and where the facts and matters relied on in support of the same were properly set out). See also *Belmont Finance Corporation Limited* v *Willams Furniture Limited* [1979] 1 Ch 250, 268B-C *per* Buckley LJ (CA).

[27] Although cf. *Garden Neptune Shipping Limited* v *Occidental Worldwide Investment Corporation* [1989] 1 Ll Rep 305, 308 *per* Tudor Evans J (QBD) which might be regarded as supportive of the contrary proposition.

7.011 There was judicial consideration of the question whether it is necessary for the Claimant expressly to plead the Defendant's knowledge of the falsity of the representation made in the unreported decision of the Court of Appeal in *Rigby* v *Decorating Den Systems Limited & another*.[28] After a survey of the case law which is considered above, Peter Gibson LJ stated that general and imprecise allegations of fraud were to be avoided and that, what he described as, "*rolled-up*" pleas that a Defendant knew or ought to have known the falsity of his representation should, where dishonesty is alleged, be properly particularised. However, Peter Gibson LJ went on to state,

> It does not seem to me a necessary requirement for a pleading of this nature, where it is quite clear that fraud is being alleged and where the pleading expressly states that the defendants had the relevant knowledge that particulars of knowledge should be given.

It was pointed out that if there were any room for uncertainty or ambiguity about the particulars in this regard then it was open to the Defendant to seek further information (in accordance with what is now Part 18 of the Rules).

7.012 The decision in *Rigby* simply emphasises that what is important is that the Defendant is alerted, in clear and unambiguous terms, to the case which he has to meet. In cases where the allegation of fraud is clearly made and where the Defendant's knowledge of the falsity of the representation is pleaded, it may be unnecessary to go as far as pleading particulars of the Defendant's knowledge. However, it is suggested that where such particulars are available at the pleading stage it would generally be sensible to set them out. It is conventional to provide particulars of knowledge after the pleaded allegation that the Defendant made the representation fraudulently, knowing that it was false.

7.013 As a bare minimum one would expect a Defence in a case where fraudulent misrepresentation is alleged against the Defendant to contain the following:

- an averment that the representation was true (a bare denial that it was false may be regarded as insufficient to comply with CPR 16.5(2) where the allegation made by the Claimant is as serious as an allegation of fraud);

- a denial of knowledge that the representation was false/a denial of dishonesty or, where appropriate, a denial of conscious indifference

---

[28] (1999) 15 March (CA). The transcript is available on Lawtel.

to the truth. Again, if it is possible to plead a positive case (conventionally expressed in the statement of case as "*an honest belief in the truth*" of the representation) then it would be sensible to do so.

7.014 There may, of course, be a number of other bases on which to resist the claim (of a sort common to other species of misrepresentation); for example, it may be denied that the representation was made or, if made, that it was addressed to the Claimant or was intended to be acted on or, alternatively, it may be denied that the Claimant relied on the representation or that he suffered any loss as a result.

General allegations of dishonesty: the road to Kearsley v Klarfeld

7.015 This section takes us back to the discussion in the introduction above. It covers those cases where there is an allegation of dishonesty based on the contention in a Defence, rather than Particulars of Claim, that the Claimant has lied about some aspect of his case. In the context of personal injury claims this is most often located in an allegation that the Claimant has lied about the circumstances of the accident and/or that he has lied and is lying about the effects of the injury.

7.016 A number of the cases which have already been considered above suggest, in trenchant terms, that general allegations of dishonesty of this kind – as distinct from cases where a cause of action in fraudulent misrepresentation is relied upon – also need spelling out in any statement of case together with full particulars. In *Three Rivers DC v Bank of England (No 3)*[29] Lord Hope said that allegations of "*fraud, dishonesty and bad faith*" needed to be specifically alleged and particularised and it is tolerably clear that he did not intend his remarks to be confined to cases involving the tort of deceit in the strict sense.[30] Similarly, in *Belmont Finance Corporation Limited v Willams Furniture Limited*[31] Buckley LJ saw no need to confine his directions about what should be pleaded to "*fraud*" in the strict sense; indeed, he stated in terms that the same approach should be adopted for allegations of "*dishonesty*".[32]

7.017 The high water mark for the strict approach to the pleading of allegations of dishonesty which do not amount to fraudulent misrepresentation is, at least in a personal injury context, *Cooper v P& O*

---

[29] [2001] 2 All ER 513, 530 (HL(E)).
[30] Cited by Neuberger J in *Brown v Bennett (No 2)* [2002] 1 WLR 713, 749 (ChD).
[31] [1979] 1 Ch 250 (CA).
[32] At p 268B.

Stena Line Limited.[33] *Cooper*, an employer's liability claim, arose out of an accident which was alleged by the Claimant to have occurred when he slipped over in very wet conditions caused by a flood in the plate room of the ship on which he worked. The vessel was at sea at the time. Liability, causation and quantum were all in issue at trial. The Defendant's defence to primary liability was that the Claimant was lying about the circumstances of the accident and, in particular, that the plate room floor was flooded (the Defendant relied on evidence that it was either impossible or, at least, very unlikely that the plate room floor could have flooded in the manner alleged by the Claimant). The defence in respect of causation and quantum was based on the contention that the Claimant should have recovered within, at most, three months of his alleged accident and that, accordingly, he was fabricating his (back) symptoms and distorting the physical signs for his own ends. The trial judge regarded these allegations made by the Defendant (and, in particular, the allegation made in respect of causation and quantum which was maintained to the conclusion of the trial) as synonymous with allegations of fraud. She made it clear that the Rules of the Supreme Court required this to be pleaded in specific terms and that it was "*surprising*" that the Defendant had failed to plead its case as to causation and quantum in the body of the Defence. While the Defendant had made reference in the Defence to a medico-legal report which expressed the view that the Claimant was fabricating his symptoms, this was not sufficient, the trial judge held, to satisfy the Defendant's obligation to plead a defence of fraud, as required by the Rules of the Supreme Court. She rejected the submission that it was "*not the usual practice to plead malingering*" and asked for the allegation (regarded by her as an allegation of fraud) to be pleaded by amendment of the Defence. Permission was, however, given to the Defendant in this regard.[34] It should, of course, be remembered that *Cooper* was decided by reference to the Rules of the Supreme Court which are, as the discussion above points out, drafted differently to the Civil Procedure Rules (at least in respect of Defences).

7.018 *Lawrenson & Lawrenson v Lawrenson and Equity Red Star*[35] concerned an appeal from the decision of a county court district judge dismissing the Claimant's claims in a fast track road traffic accident case where it was alleged that the Claimants had sustained personal injury. In this appeal the Defendant was criticised by the Claimants for failing to plead "*fraud*" in the context of a contention that the Claimants had suffered no injury at all. The facts of the case permitted no explanation that the

[33] [1999] 1 Ll Rep 734 (QBD). This case is also discussed in other chapters of this book.
[34] The amendment made no difference to the outcome. The trial judge accepted the Claimant's evidence in its entirety.
[35] (2005) 30 June (Liverpool CC *per* HHJ Stewart QC) (unreported).

Claimants were innocently mistaken about having suffered injury and, therefore, the Defendant insurer's denial that the Claimants had suffered no injury must mean that it was being alleged that they were lying. On appeal, it was held that the insurer was not alleging "*fraud*" which, where referred to in the Rules, meant only the tort of deceit and was, therefore, subject to special pleading rules.[36] However, the appellate judge was critical that the Defendant's Defence simply put the Claimants to proof as to the circumstances of their accident and contained non-admissions as to the circumstances of the accident and the causation of injury; he described the Defence as consisting of "*a denial in non admission clothing*". It was held that it was necessary, in order for the Defendant insurer to comply with CPR 16.5, to plead a denial as to the Claimants' allegations and a positive case that they were lying (with particulars where relied on):

> This does not necessarily require a specific pleading of dishonesty. It depends on the circumstances. If a Claimant is on notice that a Defendant denies that an accident occurred or that injury was suffered based on … a … [medical] record, then it may well be sufficient to state this. If it becomes clear in evidence that dishonesty can be properly alleged so be it. The crux is that what is in effect a denial must be pleaded as such and reasons given under Rule 16.5(2)(a).

7.019 The judge recognised that it may be that evidence as to dishonesty emerged, for the first time, during cross-examination at trial. He indicated that such cases would be rare and would need to be dealt with on a case by case basis in accordance with the overriding objective.

7.020 The Court of Appeal took hold of these issues in *Kearsley* v *Klarfeld*.[37] This appeal also arose out of a relatively low (fast track) value road traffic personal injury claim. Most of the issues discussed in the Court of Appeal concern case management and this is separately discussed below. There was, however, a pleading point. Among other matters, the Defence pleaded: (a) that the accident occurred when the Defendant's vehicle was travelling at only a few miles per hour (a low velocity collision); (b) a reference to a liability expert's report that the accident took place at three miles per hour which would have caused minimal force; (c) the contents of a medico-legal report in which the opinion was expressed that it was very unlikely that the Claimant had suffered any injury and that, therefore, the likelihood was that he was fabricating his symptoms. The Court of Appeal was quite satisfied that this was sufficient to comply with CPR 16.5 and the material provisions of the Queen's Bench Guide (referred to above). The contents of the Defence,

---

[36] Cf. the approach by the trial judge in the *Cooper* case discussed above.
[37] [2005] EWCA Civ 1510.

coupled with "*a general traverse of the assertion that injuries were suffered*" did not need to be accompanied by a specific reference to "*fraud*" or "*fabrication*" in order to comply with the Rules. The Court qualified this slightly by indicating that where a positive case could be asserted in this regard – perhaps by reference to medical evidence from an expert instructed by the Defendant – then this might be pleaded in the Defence.

7.021 The Court of Appeal commented on *Cooper* in the following terms:

> We were puzzled, however, by the practice that has started to emerge in low velocity impact litigation of requiring the defence to include a substantive allegation of fraud or fabrication. We were told that this practice probably flowed from a judgment given by Belinda Bucknall QC, sitting as a deputy High Court Judge in the Admiralty Court, in Cooper ... [38]

7.022 While deprecating the practice for which *Cooper* was being used as justification, the Court of Appeal did not go as far as deciding that the approach taken in that case was wrong; it was observed that if the Defendant in *Cooper* had made its pleaded position as clear as the Defendant in *Kearsley* then it might have been unnecessary for the Defendant to be given permission to amend. In *Kearsley*, by contrast to the appellate county court decision in *Lawrenson*, the Court of Appeal clearly did not regard the references to "*fraud*" in the Rules and the Guides as synonymous with the tort of deceit.[39] It should be noted that, in more recent Court of Appeal authority in the field of low velocity impact road traffic accident claims, it has been directed that a Defendant should, in its Defence, (a) expressly identify the claim as a low velocity impact claim and, (b) expressly raise the issue of causation (that is, the Defendant should state, in terms, that a collision at the low velocity involved could not have caused the Claimant to suffer any or the alleged injury.[40] In the event that these matters are not raised in the Defence then the Defendant may be refused permission to rely on expert evidence to support its case on causation.

7.023 A pleading point was also taken in *Newman* v *Laver*.[41] The Claimant complained on appeal (in a personal injury claim) that there was no allegation of fabrication of symptoms in the Defence. The Court of Appeal held, following *Kearsley*, that,

---

[38] At para 41 *per* Brooke LJ.
[39] Although this was not the subject of any separate discussion and *Lawrenson* is not referred to in the Court of Appeal judgment.
[40] See *Casey* v *Cartwright* [2006] *The Times*, October 10 (CA); [2006] EWCA Civ 1280.
[41] [2006] EWCA Civ 1135.

> ...there was no need of any blanket allegation of fraud, fakery or fabrication in the pleaded defence;

it was held that the Defence, the counter schedule, the expert's reports and the video relied on at trial

> ...sufficiently put in issue the defendant's lack of acceptance that Mr Newman had suffered the injuries and sequelae of which he complained.[42]

Arguably, *Newman* goes rather further than *Kearsley* in suggesting that the totality of the evidential and other ammunition deployed by the Defendant at trial, beyond the narrow confines of the Defendant's pleaded case, can be relied on to demonstrate compliance with the Rules. This decision indicates that *Cooper* was wrongly decided and sits a little uncomfortably alongside CPR 16.5(2).

Illegality

7.024 This plea is available in contract, as we have seen from the discussion above, where a party alleges that a contract is illegal and so should be treated as void and not enforced. Some rather anomalous pleading rules have arisen in respect of allegations of this sort and these justify separate consideration.

7.025 First, and conventionally enough, the party intending to rely on an allegation of illegality is required to particularise the facts and matters which he relies on to prove the illegality. The Civil Procedure Rules make this expressly clear in respect of Particulars of Claim,[43] although this proposition is also recognised by well-established authority.[44]

7.026 There is, however, an exception to this which is articulated in the speech of Viscount Haldane LC in *North Western Salt Company Limited* v *Electrolytic Alkali Company Limited*:[45]

> ... it is no doubt true that where on the plaintiff's case it appears to the Court that the claim is illegal, and that it would be contrary to public policy to entertain it, the Court may and ought to refuse to do so. But this must only be when either the agreement sued on is on the face of it illegal, or where, if facts relating to such an agreement are relied on, the plaintiff's case has been completely presented. If the point has not been raised on the

---

[42] At para 81 *per* Rix LJ.
[43] CPR 16, PD para 8.2(2).
[44] See, e.g. *Bullivant* v *Attorney-general for Victoria* [1901] AC 196, 204 *per* Lord Davey (HL(E)) and *Lipton v Powell* [1921] 2 KB 51, 60 *per* Lush J (KBD).
[45] [1914] AC 461 (HL(E)).

pleadings so as to warn the plaintiff to produce evidence which he may be able to bring forward rebutting any presumption of illegality which might be based on some isolated fact, then the Court ought not to take a course which may easily lead to a miscarriage of justice. On the other hand, if the action really rests on a contract which on the face of it ought not to be enforced then ... the Court ought to dismiss the claim, irrespective of whether the pleadings of the defendant raise the question of illegality.[46]

7.027 This approach was picked up by the Court of Appeal in *Bank of India v Trans Continental Commodity Merchants Limited*[47] and, more recently, in *Birkett* v *Acorn Business Machines Limited*.[48] In *Birkett* Colman J summarised the position as follows:[49]

- if a transaction is on its face (that is, merely by looking at its terms and without the need for any additional evidence) manifestly illegal then the court will refuse to enforce it even if the illegality has not been pleaded (in an appropriate case, illegality may *"override" "all questions of pleading"* – including any admissions);[50]

- if the transaction is not manifestly illegal, but there is compelling (*"persuasive and comprehensive"*) evidence of illegality before the court, then the court may refuse to enforce the transaction even if the illegality has not been pleaded.

7.028 The justification for the court's intervention *"of its own notion"* was

> ...to ensure that its process is not being abused by inviting it to enforce sub silentio a contract whose enforcement is contrary to public policy.

Colman J went on to direct that particular care should be taken where evidence or allegations of illegality emerged for the first time (regardless of any omission or oversight in the statement of case) at trial. In these circumstances the court should not exercise its discretion to refuse to enforce a contract (notwithstanding the absence of any pleading to this effect) unless satisfied (a) that the whole of the relevant circumstances were before it and (b) that there was no material risk of injustice. Sedley LJ agreed, albeit with some reluctance, with the approach taken by Colman J. He commented on

---

[46] At p 469.
[47] [1982] 1 Ll Rep 427, 433 *per* Sir David Cairns (CA).
[48] [1999] 2 All ER (Comm) 429 (CA).
[49] At p 433.
[50] *Obiter* observation of Donaldson J in *Belvoir Finance Company Limited* v *Harold Cole & Company Limited* [1969] 2 All ER 904, 908B (QBD).

the manner in which the issue of illegality had arisen at trial in the following terms,

> ... the defendant, in full possession of all the material facts ... failed to plead the illegality as part of its case. Instead its counsel insinuated the issue into the evidence with his first few questions in cross-examination of the plaintiff and then left it to the judge to act as investigator, prosecutor and jury.[51]

7.029 In *Pickering v Deacon, trading as J A McConville*[52] the first instance judge had concluded that there was a conspiracy to defraud a local authority in obtaining a disabled facilities grant to construct an extension to the Claimant's house. The intention was to inflate the costs of the extension and then to split the excess between the Claimants, Defendant and a go-between. In the context of a contractual claim the trial judge refused the Claimants permission to call evidence from the go-between and asked the parties to address him on the issue of illegality. He concluded that there was an illegal contract and, notwithstanding the fact that this issue emerged in evidence at trial, rather than in the statements of case, he declined to enforce the contract. On appeal it was held, allowing the same, that where unpleaded allegations of illegality came before the court as evidence the court should not act on them of its own initiative unless satisfied that the whole of the relevant circumstances were before it; the court could not be so satisfied where such evidence appeared at a late stage in the proceedings.

3. INTERIM REMEDIES

7.030 It is likely, in respect of claims which involve a central allegation of fraud or, indeed, where fraud provides some of the necessary background, that a party will seek to utilise one or other of the interim remedies which are now listed in Part 25 of the Civil Procedure Rules. The best known of these are, perhaps, the freezing injunction and search order, although some readers may still be more familiar with the pre-CPR nomenclature: *Mareva* injunction and *Anton Piller* Order (named after the cases in which these forms of relief were first granted).

7.031 Detailed consideration of the procedural law in this area lies beyond the scope of this book and readers interested in pursuing further research will

---

[51] [1999] 2 All ER (Comm) 429, 434f (CA).
[52] [2003] *The Times*, April 19 (CA).

wish to consult the excellent summary which appears in the *White Book*[53] or in one of the specialist works.[54]

7.032 The relief sought in the context of a fraud claim may involve:

- an order restraining a party from removing assets from the jurisdiction or restraining a party from dealing with assets whether or not located within the jurisdiction – a freezing injunction[55] (perhaps preceded by an order requiring a party to provide information about the location of any relevant property or assets);[56]

- an order requiring a party to admit another party to premises for the purposes of preserving evidence located there – a search order;[57]

- an order for the detention, custody or preservation of relevant property or for the inspection of the same;[58]

- an order for disclosure of documents or inspection of property before a claim has been made;[59]

- an order for disclosure of documents or inspection of property against a person who is not a party to the proceedings.[60]

7.033 Unless the court has ordered otherwise, applications for interim relief must be supported by evidence[61] and, where made without notice, should state the reasons why notice was not given.[62] Applications for freezing injunctions or search orders are usually sought without notice. It should be noted that injunctive relief is an equitable remedy and that the court has a discretion whether to grant or refuse such relief. In cases where the conduct of the applicant is such that public policy militates against the grant of the relief sought then the court is likely to exercise its discretion against the applicant. A well-founded allegation of fraud or illegality or a culpable

---

[53] Vol I, 25.1.1ff in the present (2006) edition.
[54] See eg. Steven Gee QC, *Commercial Injunctions* (5th ed, 2004).
[55] CPR 25.1(f).
[56] CPR 25.1(g).
[57] CPR 25.1(h).
[58] CPR 25.1(c).
[59] CPR 25.1(i) and Supreme Court Act 1981, s 33; County Courts Act 1984, s 52.
[60] CPR 25.1(j) and Supreme Court Act 1981, s 34; County Courts Act 1984, s 53.
[61] CPR 25.3(2).
[62] CPR 25.3(3).

failure, in the context of an application made without notice, to give full and frank disclosure may well lead to the refusal of the relief.[63]

7.034 Proving fraud or dishonesty may be an expensive business and there may be some anxiety about incurring costs where it is suspected that the fraudulent party, even if found liable and required to pay costs, will evade any liability. In such cases it may be appropriate, in the event that the conditions listed in CPR 25.13 can be met, to make an application for security for costs under CPR 25.12.

4. CASE MANAGEMENT

7.035 In cases where fraud or, in the more general sense, dishonesty is alleged, the following may well be applied to the commencement and management of the claim:

- it will usually be wholly inappropriate to commence proceedings by use of the Part 8 alternative procedure[64] and, if commenced in this way, such claims will usually be *"converted"* into a Part 7 claim;[65]

- where an allegation of fraud or dishonesty is made it may well be sensible to allocate the claim to the multi track even where the value of the sum at stake would ordinarily lead to fast track allocation (see, CPR 26, PD paragraph 9.1 which permits allocation to the multi track where the case cannot be justly dealt with on the fast track and directs the procedural judge's attention to,

  > ...the limits likely to be placed on disclosure, the extent to which expert evidence may be necessary, and whether the trial is likely to last more than a day")[66]

- parties should ensure, both at allocation stage and thereafter, that the court is given accurate information about the issues involved and the number of factual and expert witnesses;

---

[63] See the useful discussion in Steven Gee QC, *Commercial Injunctions* (5th ed, 2004), paras 2.035-2.036.
[64] CPR 8, PD para 1.1, *"A claimant may use the Part 8 procedure where he seeks the court's decision on a question which is unlikely to involve a substantial dispute of fact."* See also, *re Deadman (deceased)* [1971] 2 All ER 101 (ChD).
[65] CPR 8, PD para 1.6.
[66] See the commentary in *Kearsley* v *Klarfeld* [2005] EWCA Civ 1510, paras 28-36 *per* Brooke LJ.

- it is important that the trial is given an accurate time estimate and that any amendment of the time estimate for trial is brought to the court's attention as soon as possible;

- it will usually be sensible, where an allegation of fraud or dishonesty is made, for the parties to attend a pre-trial review hearing, as opposed to this being handled on paper and on the basis of pre-trial checklists.

5. LOW VELOCITY COLLISION CLAIMS

7.036 These claims were defined by Brooke LJ in *Kearsley* v *Klarfeld*[67] in the following terms:

> In this type of case ... the driver or front seat passenger in a motor vehicle claims damages for personal injury (usually in the form of soft tissue injuries to some part of the spine) after their vehicle has been hit by another vehicle. The insurers of the other vehicle then assert that the impact was so insignificant that they cannot have suffered the injuries of which they have made complaint. They rely on principles of bio-mechanics in support of their contention that the claimants cannot be telling the truth.

7.037 These claims often have the following additional features:

- they are of low value in respect of any damages claimed;

- they involve expert witness evidence, particularly as to issues of causation (on which, see below);

- they are fact-sensitive and the trial judge's assessment of witness credibility will be of considerable importance (in respect of both lay and expert witnesses);

- the cost of litigating them substantially exceeds the value of any damages claimed.

7.038 As I have indicated, the causation issue generally looms large in these cases. There is a body of expert opinion that, at very low speeds (say, for example, impact velocities of five to ten miles per hour), injury to the

---

[67] [2005] EWCA Civ 1510, para 23.

occupants of the vehicle which is struck is very unlikely to occur and, as an extension to this, in the event that any injury does occur, it is unlikely to result in any symptoms which last longer than a day or so. The reason for this (which has an intuitive appeal) is that the forces which can be attributed directly to the impact velocity are modified by the absorption of energy from the two vehicles impacting. The resultant change in the velocity of the struck vehicle following collision is referred to as the delta velocity or "Delta V". On a very simplistic analysis, albeit one to which the Court of Appeal has referred,[68] the Delta V is half the impact velocity (i.e. impact velocity of ten miles per hour might, all things being equal, result in Delta V of 5 miles per hour). Some experts take the view that if the Delta V is below a certain speed (e.g. 5 miles per hour) then injury is unlikely to have occurred.

7.039 It is in the context of applications for expert evidence as to causation – Delta V and so forth – (in claims of very low relative value) that particular case management problems have arisen.[69]

7.040 In *Kearsley* v *Klarfeld* Brooke LJ observed that he had been informed by counsel for the parties that there was a *"vast difference of approach amongst different members of the judiciary"* with respect to the case management of these claims. He suggested that it would be useful if a number of test cases could be dealt with by a High Court Judge with experience in personal injuries litigation.[70] Accordingly, in March 2006 McCombe J met the four designated civil judges on the Northern Circuit with a view to organising the trial of a test case or cases.[71] At that time, however, a syndicate of insurers indicated that the trial of a test case should be deferred because they were unable to identify any case or cases that might prove suitable. It is understood that this remains the position at the time of writing (at least, the decision in any test case has not yet been reported) and this has recently prompted expressions of disappointment in the Court of

---

[68] *Casey* v *Cartwright* [2006] *The Times*, October 10 (CA). [2006] EWCA Civ 1280, para per Dyson LJ.

[69] Although it is right to say, as Brooke LJ pointed out in *Kearsley* v *Klarfeld*, that these claims and the knotty case management problems to which they give rise are just the latest arrival in a succession of satellite litigation issues with which the courts, and ultimately the Court of Appeal, have had to grapple in recent years (following, appeals in the context of credit hire litigation, time limits for service of Claim Forms/Particulars of Claim, CFA litigation and resiling from admissions of liability).

[70] [2005] EWCA Civ 1510, para 35.

[71] McCombe J issued a Practice Direction, with the consent of Dyson LJ, that all applications to adduce expert evidence as to causation in the context of low velocity road traffic claims on the Northern Circuit should be transferred to the relevant designated civil judge. It was hoped that, by so directing, some consistency of approach to case management might be achieved.

Appeal (which, pending the resolution of a test case, is still having to deal with these claims on a piecemeal basis).[72]

7.041 The Court of Appeal most recently visited the case management problems to which low velocity impact claims give rise in *Casey* v *Cartwright*.[73] The factual background concerned a collision between two cars: a rear end collision. Breach of duty was admitted, but causation was put in issue and the Defendant's insurers made this clear at an early stage. The Defence pleaded that the collision was a gentle one and that the speed of the Defendant's vehicle at the relevant time was just two miles per hour. It was the Defendant's case that the force generated by the collision at such a low speed was insufficient to cause any personal injury to the Claimant. The claim was allocated to the multi track. The district judge gave the Claimant permission to rely on a medico-legal report from an expert who stated that the Claimant had sustained a whiplash injury causing symptoms of nine months' duration. The parties were given permission to rely on expert evidence from a single joint expert in the field of orthopaedics. This permission was revoked by Judge Holman and the Defendant appealed against this decision (permission to appeal having been granted by Judge Holman). On appeal the Court of Appeal expressed disappointment that the attempt in *Kearsley* v *Klarfeld* to give guidance on case management with a view to achieving consistency had proved unsuccessful. The Court concluded, somewhat reluctantly, that the guidance previously given needed to be amplified. The following markers were laid:

- Most ordinary road traffic whiplash cases would require no expert medical evidence on the issue of causation.

  > The question of whether such evidence should be permitted only arises where the defendant contends that the nature of the impact was such that it was impossible or very unlikely that the claimant suffered any injury or any more than trivial injury as a result of the collision and that accordingly the claimant has fabricated the claim.[74]

- In the event that the Defendant wished to raise causation as an issue then it was incumbent on him to satisfy certain formalities so as to avoid later confusion and delay. Accordingly, the Defendant should,

[72] See *Casey* v *Cartwright* [2006] *The Times*, October 10 (CA); [2006] EWCA Civ 1280, at paras 13 and 23 *per* Dyson LJ. At the time that judgment was given in *Casey*, on 5 October 2006, no test case trial was in prospect.
[73] [2006] *The Times* October 10 (CA); [2006] EWCA Civ 1280.
[74] At para 29 *per* Dyson LJ.

within three months of receipt of the letter of claim, notify the other parties in writing that he considers the index case to be "a *low impact case*" and that he wishes to raise causation. In addition, the Defendant should expressly raise this issue in the Defence which should be accompanied by a Part 22 statement of truth. Within 21 days of filing and serving a Defence the Defendant should file and serve a witness statement setting out the basis on which causation is put in issue and dealing with the Defendant's evidence on the same.

- Upon receipt of the witness statement the court will, if satisfied that the issue has been properly identified by the Defendant, give permission for the Claimant to be examined by a medical expert nominated by the Defendant.

- If, upon receipt of medical evidence served by the Defendant after an examination, the court is satisfied (on the entirety of the evidence served by the Defendant) that he has properly identified a case on causation which has a real prospect of success then it will generally give the Defendant permission to rely on such evidence at trial.

- While single joint experts had an invaluable role to play, procedural judges should be slow to order that the parties should make use of single joint experts where causation is in issue in a low velocity claim (at least until the test case has been decided).

- There may, however, be cases where, although the Defendant has identified a case on causation with a real prospect of success, the overriding objective nevertheless militates against the grant of permission to the Defendant to rely on expert evidence. The Court of Appeal was reluctant to list all of the circumstances in which this may be the case. However, it would usually be appropriate to refuse the Defendant permission to rely on expert evidence where he had failed to comply with the three month time limit for raising the causation issue. Second, it would usually be appropriate to refuse the Defendant permission to rely on expert evidence where there is a factual dispute, the resolution of which is likely to be determinative of causation. Third, where the injury alleged and the value of the claim is very modest, the grant of permission to rely on expert evidence may be refused – a matter that the Court of Appeal was content to leave to "*the good sense of the Judge*".

7.042 The final bullet point may be regarded as a little self-defeating; the reported authorities in this area invariably involve claims of very modest value. Indeed, as I have indicated, low value may be regarded as a defining characteristic of low velocity impact claims.

7.043 The Defendant's appeal against the revocation of permission to rely on a single joint expert in orthopaedics in *Casey* v *Cartwright* was dismissed. The reason that the circuit judge had revoked permission was because the expert had demonstrated, by his dogmatic approach to claims of this kind, his unsuitability to provide expert evidence;[75] this basis for revoking permission was unappealable.

7.044 One might be forgiven for thinking that case management skirmishing in respect of low velocity claims is prompted by the anxiety that the evidence of one or other expert witness will dispose of the causation issue and, therefore, dispose of liability. However, in spite of the importance of expert evidence to the causation issues in claims of this kind, the courts have made it clear that expert evidence – even from a single joint expert whose analysis is found to have "*stood up* to ... *questioning*" – will not necessarily be treated as determinative.

7.045 *Armstrong* v *First York*[76] concerned a low velocity collision in York City Centre. The Claimants, a couple, were respectively the driver and front seat passenger in a Ford Fiesta. Their vehicle was dealt a glancing blow to its rear nearside corner by a bus; the bus driver had erroneously judged that he could squeeze his vehicle down the nearside of the Fiesta. The damage to the Ford Fiesta was very minor and the evidence was that the bus was probably travelling at ten to 15 miles per hour. The Claimants alleged that they had both sustained hyper-extension soft tissue injuries to their spines; in other words, whiplash. Their claims were of very modest value: a little over £1,000 and a little over £2,000 in respect of each Claimant (as agreed between the parties, subject to liability). The Defendant's case, put to the Claimants "*fairly and squarely*" at trial was that they were dishonestly alleging injury. In support of this contention, the Defendant relied on the evidence of a jointly-instructed forensic motor vehicle engineer.[77] The engineer did not – at least insofar as one can tell from the transcript of judgment – rely on Delta V analysis. Instead, it was his evidence, on analysis of the damage to the Fiesta,

---

[75] At para 20 *per* Dyson LJ, "*The judge's concern as to the suitability of Mr Williams was heightened by the answers he gave to claimant's solicitor's questions. His answer 'Whiplash injuries are uncommon in Singapore, New Zealand, Quebec, Greece, Russia and Lithuania. These countries either have no or restricted mechanisms of compensation'. The judge said that this answer clearly demonstrated a lack of objectivity.*"
[76] [2005] *The Times*, January 19 (CA); [2005] EWCA Civ 277.
[77] The Claimants had not sought to rely on any expert evidence to challenge that of the single joint expert.

that the vehicle had no distortion of its panels and had not moved on its springs and that, therefore, it had not moved in the collision. In the absence of evidence of movement of the vehicle there was no evidence that there was any movement of the occupants of the vehicle, still less any evidence of movement which could possibly injure their spines. The trial judge in this case (Judge Stewart QC in the Liverpool County Court) faced a dilemma. On the one hand, he had found the Claimants to be of blameless character and to have given their evidence in a truthful, honest and guileless manner. On the other, he found that the engineer's evidence which had – exceptionally – been given live at trial, stood up to questioning and was logical. In the light of his conclusions as to the veracity and plausibility of the Claimants' evidence, the judge held that there was no rule of law that compelled him to reject their case and to accept the expert evidence. He decided to prefer the evidence of the Claimants as to causation. The corollary of this was that he rejected the evidence of the single joint expert; Judge Stewart QC held that there must be some mistake in the expert's analysis, although he conceded that he had not been able to identify what this was. There was an appeal with permission of the judge. The appeal was dismissed and the principal judgment was given by Brooke LJ:

> In my judgment there is no principle of law that an expert's evidence in an unusual field – doing his best, with his great experience, to reconstruct what happened to the parties based on the second hand material he received in this case – must be dispositive of liability in such a case and that a Judge must be compelled to find that, in his view, two palpably honest witnesses have come to court to deceive him in order to obtain damages, in this case a small amount of damages, for a case they know to be a false one … we are not opening the door to a whole lot of dishonest claimants to recover just because there may be cases in which the honesty and force of a claimant's evidence impresses a trial judge in the way the evidence of these claimants did on this particular occasion. In very many cases the evidence of a witness like … [the expert] may very well be sufficient to tip the balance strongly in the defendant's favour.[78]

7.046 In a short concurring judgment Arden LJ stated that the credibility of the Claimants' evidence could provide a perfectly justifiable reason for the rejection of expert evidence and Longmore LJ observed that judges, rather than experts, were responsible for trying cases.

7.047 It is worth noting that *Armstrong* was decided between *Cooper* v *P & O Stena Line Limited* and *Kearsley* v *Klarfeld* at a time when Defendants

---

[78] At paras 27 and 29. In *Hindmarch* v *Hasford* (2005) 16 May (Newcastle CC *per* HHJ Moir) (unreported, but available on Lawtel) the decision in *Armstrong* was relied on to refuse the Defendant permission to adduce evidence from a forensic engineer.

took the view that if their case was that the Claimants could not have suffered injury then they were constrained to plead fraud (in terms) and to allege the same (giving the Claimants the opportunity to comment on this allegation at trial). One cannot help thinking that if the trial judge had been given the alternative option of finding that the Claimants were honestly mistaken in attributing their very modest symptoms to the index minor collision then a different result might have been achieved.[79]

---

[79] A finding that a witness has lied is, as observed above, nearly always an unpalatable finding for a judge to make.

Chapter 8

PRACTICE: DETECTING AND PROVING FRAUD

1. INDICATORS OF FRAUD/EXAGGERATION

8.001 This chapter concentrates on dishonest or exaggerated personal injury claims and the procedural and tactical techniques that can be deployed in order to expose them. A useful starting point is to analyse the manner in which the claim is presented with a view to identifying whether it justifies suspicion.

Claims farmers

8.002 These organisations solicit business (on the high street and elsewhere) and are responsible for a large volume of work. The bulk nature of their business means that corners are often cut in the preparation and presentation of the claim. While this does not, of course, mean that a claim from this source is either fraudulent or exaggerated, it is probably right to say that such claims have not been subjected to the same process of investigation and analysis that one would expect from a competent solicitor devoting attention to a smaller case load. For this reason, claims from this source should be treated with particular care and investigated with particular thoroughness at the earliest stage.

Claimants

8.003 A claim presented by a Claimant involved in criminal activity at the time that he sustains injury should, obviously, be regarded with scepticism. Equally, a Claimant who was, or is likely to have been, intoxicated at the time of injury should be thoroughly investigated. Some Claimants have a long history of presenting claims and a number of insurers now share information about repeat Claimants.[1] A Claimant who alleges that he has

---

[1] See, e.g. *Humphries* v *Matthews* (2006) 16 June (Liverpool CC *per* Recorder Moran QC) (unreported, but available on Lawtel). Insurers share such information with each other and with

sustained a major injury as a result of a relatively trivial accident should be looked at critically; the exaggerated nature of the injury will often justify suspicion about the circumstances of the accident itself.[2]

Accidents

8.004 Some accidents are more improbable than others. In cases involving spinal injuries sustained after slipping and falling into standing water it is not unusual for there to be at least a suspicion that the Claimant dived, rather than slipping, into the water.[3] The more improbable the accident the less likely it is to happen and such accidents require enhanced scrutiny at the investigation stage.

8.005 Insurers and those advising them should also be suspicious where:

- a large number of passengers on a bus or coach involved in an accident all claim to have been injured;

- a Claimant claims to have been injured by a pavement defect or other feature which has not been the subject of any previous complaint or accident;

- a Claimant fails to make any contemporaneous complaint to the person or organisation that he holds liable for the accident;

- a Claimant alleges that he has suffered injury, but fails to seek medical attention at an early stage;

- a Claimant fails to provide, at any early stage in the proceedings, details of any witnesses;

- a Claimant has a patchy or incomplete employment record;

- a Claimant pursues a claim for continuing loss of earnings without any benefits recorded as paid on a Compensation Recovery Unit certificate.

---

the police: see, with respect to the data protection issues raised by this, Data Protection Act 1998, s 29.
[2] See the section on low velocity impact claims above.
[3] See, e.g. *Healy* v *Cosmosair Plc* [2005] EWHC 1657 (QB).

Injuries

8.006 The injuries which the Claimant claims that he has sustained as a result of an accident may also justify scepticism about the genuineness of the claim. In those cases where the Claimant's injuries and the consequences of the same appear to be out of all proportion to the seriousness of the accident, it is not uncommon for a medical expert to conclude that the Claimant's physical symptoms cannot be explained or have no "organic" cause. In the past Claimants commonly responded to opinion in these terms by instructing a Consultant Psychiatrist to assess whether there might be some psychiatric or psychological component to the Claimant's injuries. In recent years, however, a new category of injury has started to feature in cases where there is no obvious or readily identifiable physical cause for the Claimant's symptoms. It is now common to find the following referred to in medico-legal reports as explanation for symptoms which do not have an obvious physical or even psychiatric[4] cause:

- chronic pain syndrome;
- fibromyalgia;
- chronic fatigue syndrome;
- reflex sympathetic dystrophy;
- somatoform disorder.

8.007 These categories of injury are now officially recognised; there are Judicial Studies Board guidelines which apply to these injuries.[5] The result of this is that symptoms (sometimes highly incapacitating symptoms) for which there is no obvious physical cause will not necessarily mean that there is no claim. It is increasingly common for pain management clinicians to make a diagnosis of chronic pain syndrome, or some variant of the same, which will ordinarily justify making an award. In these circumstances, the focus for the Defendant insurer has to be upon investigating the genuineness of the Claimant's evidence about the extent of his symptoms. This requires a multi-faceted approach which makes the best use of all of the available evidence.

---

[4] E.g. post-traumatic stress disorder, adjustment disorder, specific phobia or other psychiatric condition classifiable using the World Health Organisation, ICD-10 Chapter V criteria.
[5] See the current edition of the Judicial Studies Board, *Guidelines for the Assessment of General Damages in Personal Injury Cases* where these injuries are gathered under the heading, "*Chronic Pain*". This new category was first introduced in the 7th edition of the Guidelines (published in 2006).

2. DISCLOSURE AND INSPECTION

Civil Procedure Rules

8.008 Parts 31, 32 and 33 of the Civil Procedure Rules contain a tight web of rules to govern the disclosure and inspection of documents. The judicious use of the Rules can assist in the exposure of the fraudulent Claimant. Unless the court directs otherwise (on the application of a party under CPR 31.12 and Part 23 of the Rules) a party is under a duty to provide only standard disclosure.[6] Standard disclosure requires a party to disclose not only the documents on which he relies, but also the documents

> ...which aversely affect his own case; ... adversely affect another party's case; or ... support another party's case.[7]

It should, of course, be noted that the duty of disclosure continues during the proceedings;[8] it is not limited to the time at which the first search takes place.[9] It should be noted that standard disclosure will follow pre-action disclosure in accordance with any relevant protocol or order for pre-action disclosure.[10] There is, of course, nothing to prevent a party from requesting, in advance of the commencement of proceedings, all of the documentation which it might hope to obtain on standard disclosure. To this extent standard disclosure can be viewed as a mopping up exercise; indicating the existence and identity of documents which are already known to exist and providing fruitful lines of enquiry for targeted applications for specific disclosure or inspection.

8.009 The Rules enforce the requirement to provide accurate and truthful disclosure:

---

[6] CPR 31.5(1).
[7] CPR 31.6(b)(i)-(iii).
[8] CPR 31.11.
[9] Generally the first step after allocation to track.
[10] CPR 31.16.

- A party is not entitled to rely on a document which he has not disclosed or for which he has not given permission to inspect, unless the court grants permission.[11]

- A party who makes or causes to be made a false disclosure statement ("*without an honest belief in its truth*") runs the risk of proceedings for contempt of court.[12]

- The same arsenal of costs sanctions are available for misdemeanours in this context as in others.[13]

8.010 It is, of course, unlikely that the Claimant who is prepared to present a fraudulent or exaggerated claim will be overcome by a fit of conscience in the context of disclosure. There are a number of caveats and qualifications to the duty to disclose which are set out in the Rules and these will be exploited by the fraudulent Claimant. The Rules make detailed provision for the withholding (from inspection) of certain documents or categories of document on a variety of grounds; for example, where it would be disproportionate to permit inspection of the documentation in issue[14] and where the documentation is privileged, injurious to the public interest or might tend to incriminate the party giving disclosure or expose him to a penalty (see section 14 of the Civil Evidence Act 1968).[15] In a more general sense the duty to disclose is limited to disclosing only:

- such documentation as is necessary in each case;

- such documentation as is, in appropriate cases, ordered by the court (it is increasingly common for courts to order split trials or trials of a preliminary issue and, in these circumstances, it is likely that directions given for disclosure will be similarly limited);[16]

---

[11] CPR 31.21.

[12] CPR 31.23. Such proceedings may only be brought by the Attorney-General or with the permission of the court. See also the equivalent provision in CPR 32.14 which contains the same provision with respect to documents, e.g. witness statements/affidavits, which contain a false statement of truth. This is considered in more detail in Chapter 5 above.

[13] See Chapter 9 below.

[14] CPR 31.3(2).

[15] The Rules refer collectively to these categories, somewhat opaquely, as where, "*the party disclosing the document has a right or duty to withhold inspection of it*": CPR 31.3(1)(b).

[16] CPR 31.13 contains rules to deal with disclosure in stages. It should be noted that disclosure in stages is not limited to those cases where the court has ordered that disclosure should take place in this way. The Rules also make provision for the parties to agree, in writing, to disclose and/or inspect documents in stages.

- the documents which are in the control of the disclosing party;[17]

- documents which can be located after a reasonable search (reasonable is assessed by reference to the number of documents involved, the nature/complexity of the proceedings, the ease and expense of retrieving the relevant documents and the significance of any document which might be located during the search).[18]

8.011 The limitations on and qualifications to the duty to disclose are, however, balanced by provisions which can be used to test a party's claim to withhold a document from disclosure or inspection. First, an application can be made to the court for specific disclosure or inspection of a particular document or class of document.[19] Such applications (made under Part 23) have to be carefully prepared and supported by evidence. An application of this kind should be focused and specific (a court will be resistant to an application which is speculative or unfounded or which does too little to identify the issues in the case to which the application relates). A party who suspects fraud, but is not yet in a position to prove it, will, of course, have to be astute to avoid alerting the other party to its suspicion in an application of this kind (particularly in cases where covert video surveillance is planned, but has not yet taken place).

8.012 In addition to the right to seek specific disclosure, disclosure can be requested of any document referred to in: (a) a statement of case; (b) a witness statement; (c) a witness summary; (d) an affidavit.[20] Accordingly, if a party has, whether intentionally or inadvertently, included some stray references in a statement of case or witness statement to documentation which it would rather keep from the eyes of the other party then it is at risk of being ordered to produce the same.

8.013 As a useful, and comparatively under-used supplement to the provisions for seeking further information (set out in CPR Part 18[21]), the Rules also contain provision requiring a party, on notice, to admit facts or to admit/produce documents (the latter is, in effect, a notice requiring proof of

---

[17] CPR 31.3(1)(a) and 31.8.
[18] CPR 31.7.
[19] CPR 31.12.
[20] CPR 31.14.
[21] In the context of allegations of fraud Part 18 questions (focused on issues of credibility and carefully/precisely worded) should usually be made after all the relevant available evidence has been obtained (perhaps by use of applications for specific disclosure). The party seeking further information will want to avoid the possibility that evidence useful to a suspected fraudster might be obtained/manufactured after the Part 18 questions have been put.

the authenticity of the document).[22] These provisions are subject to time limits (a notice to admit facts must be served no later than 21 days before trial and a notice to admit/produce documents by the latest date for serving witness statements or within seven days of disclosure of the relevant document, whichever is the later). The sanction for failing to admit facts which ought to have been admitted lies in an appropriate costs order.

8.014 Part 33 of the Rules (derived in large part from the Civil Evidence Act 1995) contains provisions dealing with the rather loose arrangements for admission of hearsay evidence in the civil courts. In circumstances where a party provides notice of intention to rely on hearsay evidence from the maker of a statement it is open to the other party to make an application for an order from the court that the witness be called to give oral evidence and be cross-examined;[23] this power of the court is unlikely to be effective in circumstances where a hearsay notice has been served because a witness is overseas. It should also be noted that where a hearsay notice has been served in respect of a witness and the other party wishes to adduce evidence to attack the credibility of the witness, then the party wishing to attack credibility must give notice of his intention to the other party (and must give notice not more than 14 days after the date of service of the hearsay notice).[24] A relatively little known and little used provision in the Rules relates to real evidence (plans, photographs and models) which are not referred to in a witness statement or expert's report and/or which are hearsay evidence of which notice should be given under the Rules. Notice of intention to rely on such evidence should be given to the other party and, in the absence of such notice, the evidence will not be admissible at trial unless the court so orders.[25] This rule sits uneasily alongside CPR 32.19 (considered above) which has been relied on by appellate courts in their approach to the admission of video surveillance.

8.015 In a personal injury case where fraud or exaggeration is suspected or has already been alleged, disclosure (obtained by provision of forms of consent) should ordinarily include the following: medical records (GP, hospital, physiotherapist, occupational health, alternative therapies); social security records (including applications for benefit); Inland Revenue tax returns and accounts; personnel records (including those from former employers); school records (in appropriate cases).

---

[22] CPR 32.18 (notice to admit facts) and CPR 32.19 (notice to admit or produce documents). It should be noted that a disclosing party is entitled, absent service of a notice to admit/produce documents, to assume that the authenticity of the disclosed document is admitted.
[23] CPR 33.4.
[24] CPR 33.5.
[25] CPR 33.6.

8.016 As an important, and sometimes neglected, caveat to the discussion above it is worth noting that a court is likely to expect a Defendant who pursues a fraud or dishonest conduct allegation against a Claimant to exhibit a scrupulously "clean hands" approach to its own disclosure. The Admiralty decision case, *Cooper* v *P & O Stena Line Limited*,[26] provides a neat example of what can go wrong. In this personal injury case the Claimant alleged that he had, while in the course of his employment by the Defendant as a steward, suffered serious injury after a slipping accident on board a ship which was at sea. The Claimant's case was that he had slipped over while wading through the plate room of the vessel which was awash with water that had flooded onto the floor as a result of poor maintenance. He alleged that he had suffered serious and debilitating back injury as a result. The Defendant contested liability and quantum at trial and a contributory negligence allegation was also raised. The essence of the Defendant's case as to liability and quantum was that the Claimant had (1) lied about the volume of water on the floor of the plate room at the material time and (2) had also lied about the effect of the accident on the Claimant. The Defendant supported its defence as to primary liability by means of oral evidence from an engineer and safety officer who were serving on board at the same time as the accident. Their evidence was to the effect that the drainage system in the plate room was such that flooding of the floor was either impossible or, at least, very improbable. The Defendant's difficulty in pursuing this line (which was the subject of specific criticism by the trial judge) was that the Defendant's disclosure was inadequate. On the second day of the trial it produced, for the first time, the log book of the ship's carpenter and this contained a number of references to flooding in the plate rooms on board at and around the relevant time. Equally, the Defendant did not, at any stage, disclose a book recording problems which had been reported to the on board safety team nor records relating to day to day safety issues which, it emerged at trial, had existed, but had not been disclosed. Ultimately, the deficiencies in the Defendant's disclosure – in the context of vigorously pursued cross-examination along the lines that the Claimant and his witnesses were lying about the accident circumstances – eventually led counsel for the Defendant to seek an adjournment. When he returned after the adjournment he signalled that the defence to primary liability and the allegation of contributory negligence were no longer pursued. This did not stop the trial judge from going on to find, in terms, that the Claimant and his witnesses were telling the truth about the circumstances of the accident.[27]

---

[26] [1999] 1 Ll Rep 734 (QBD).

[27] Notwithstanding the fact that counsel for the Defendant had also, in the circumstances, stated that he did not invite the court to draw any inferences (with respect to the residual quantum issues) from the evidence given about the accident circumstances.

Privilege

8.017 It has long been the case that a claim of privilege[28] will usually be defeated by a strong *prima facie* case of fraud; where, for example, communications passing between solicitor and client are with a view to the furtherance of a fraud or the commission of a crime.[29] It does not matter, in this context, whether the fraud is by the party, the legal adviser or a third party[30] and privilege can be set aside as between solicitor and client on the application of the solicitor where he suspects fraud by his client.[31] In *Derby & Company Limited* v *Weldon (No 7)*[32] it was emphasised that an application for disclosure in such circumstances required a balancing of the public policy on which legal professional privilege is based and the gravity of the charge of fraud or dishonesty which a party seeks to advance:

> There is a continuous spectrum and it is impossible to, as it were, calibrate or express in any simple formula the strength of the case that the plaintiff must show in each of these categories. An order to disclose documents for which legal professional privilege is claimed lies at the extreme end of the spectrum. Such an order will only be made in very exceptional circumstances but it is, I think, too restrictive to say that the plaintiff's case must always be founded on an admission or supported by affidavit evidence or that the court must carry out the preliminary exercise of deciding on the material before it whether the plaintiff's case will probably succeed, a task which may well present insurmountable difficulties in a case where fraud is alleged and the court has no more than affidavit evidence.[33]

8.018 Ultimately, the court suggested that a strong *prima facie* case of fraud would be sufficient to override the claim of privilege.[34] It is clear that "*fraud*" is to be widely construed for these purposes and is capable of embracing criminal conduct, general dishonesty and other forms of "*iniquity*".[35] It has been held that the fraud alleged need not be the foundation of the claim (for the purposes of defeating a claim of privilege)

---

[28] Whether legal advice privilege or litigation privilege: see *Kuwait Airways Corporation* v *Iraqi Airways Company (No 6)* (2005) *The Times*, April 25 (CA).
[29] See, e.g. *R* v *Cox & Railton* (1884) 14 QBD 153 (CCR).
[30] See *R* v *Central Criminal Court, ex parte Francis & Francis* [1989] 1 AC 346 (HL(E)).
[31] See *Finers (a Firm)* v *Miro* [1991] 1 All ER 182 (CA).
[32] [1990] 1 WLR 1156 (Ch).
[33] At p 1173E-F *per* Vinelott J.
[34] See also, *Kuwait Airways Corporation* v *Iraqi Airways Company (No 6)* [2005] *The Times*, April 25 (CA) where the requirement was expressed as a "*very strong*" *prima facie* case of fraud.
[35] See *Barclay's Bank Plc* v *Eustice* [1995] 4 All ER 511, 521f-j *per* Schiemann LJ (CA).

provided that the communications for which disclosure is sought are relevant to an issue in the action.[36]

3. VIDEO SURVEILLANCE

Procedural framework

8.019 A video film or recording falls clearly within the extended definition of "*document*" which appears in CPR 31.4. As such, evidence of this kind is subject to the "*rules about the disclosure and inspection of documents*"[37] which appear in Part 31 of the Rules. Where video evidence is disclosed (whether by citation on a list in standard disclosure[38] or subsequently[39]), the consequence of this, as explained by the Court of Appeal in *Rall* v *Hume* is that,

> ... the claimant will be deemed to admit the authenticity of the film unless notice is served that the claimant wishes the document to be proved at trial. If the claimant does so, the defendant will be obliged to serve a witness statement by the person who took the film in order to prove its authenticity. If the claimant does not challenge the authenticity of the film, however, it is, in the absence of any ruling by the court to the contrary, available to the defendant for the purposes of cross-examining the claimant and/or the claimant's expert.[40]

8.020 The Court of Appeal clearly based this assessment on CPR 32.19 (a notice requiring a document to be proved must be served by the latest date for serving witness statements or within seven days of disclosure of the document whichever is later). Accordingly, video evidence which is admissible and properly disclosed in time can be relied on without the need for a statement from the enquiry agent responsible for obtaining it, unless the Claimant serves the notice required by CPR 32.19.

8.021 In case management terms, the court clearly has a wide-ranging power to control the admission of video evidence by, first, directing the issues on

---

[36] See *Dubai Bank Limited* v *Galadari* [1991] *The Times*, April 22 (ChD).
[37] CPR 31.1(1).
[38] CPR 31.6.
[39] In accordance with the duty of continuing disclosure: CPR 31.11.
[40] [2001] EWCA Civ 146, para 16 *per* Potter LJ.

which such evidence is required and the way in which the evidence is to be placed before the court and, second, by ordering the exclusion of video evidence that might otherwise be admissible (CPR 32.1). It has been emphasised that this power is to be exercised in accordance with the overriding objective so as to ensure, among other things, that the parties are on an equal footing and that any applications for the admission or exclusion of video evidence are dealt with fairly and expeditiously. In *Rall* v *Hume* it was clearly indicated that the Defendant which had decided to rely on video surveillance evidence should disclose the evidence at an appropriate stage in the proceedings (in order to avoid trial by ambush)[41] and should seek to ventilate with the procedural judge, at the earliest opportunity, its intention to adduce such evidence (in order that appropriate technical arrangements could be made for the viewing of such evidence at trial and that an adequate time estimate could be given). It was further held that Part 23 of the Rules (and its Practice Direction) indicated the procedural route by which the Defendant might bring the management of video surveillance evidence before the managing court (whether at a scheduled hearing or, where necessary, by separate application). By contrast, in *Uttley* v *Uttley*[42] it was held that the Defendant was justified in withholding disclosure of covert video surveillance evidence until after the Claimant had complied with an order to serve a full, updated witness statement and a schedule of losses. The Defendant's decision was reasonable because it wished to use the video surveillance as material for cross-examination; it was held that if the Claimant had complied with the orders for an updated statement and schedule then he would have received disclosure of the video surveillance at an earlier stage. The effect of disclosure of the video evidence, when it took place, was that the Claimant accepted a payment into court.

8.022 It is not uncommon for Human Rights Act issues (primarily, the balancing of the Article 6 right to a fair trial against the Article 8 right to respect for private and family life) to be canvassed in the context of case management hearings concerning the admissibility of video surveillance evidence. This was the position in *Jones* v *University of Warwick*.[43] The Claimant in this case dropped a cash box on her wrist while at work. She brought a claim against her employer alleging a significant continuing disability and seeking special damages which exceeded £135,000. The Defendant employer conceded liability, but relied on medical evidence to the

---

[41] And to give the Claimant and the medical experts an opportunity to see and to comment upon it.
[42] [2002] PIQR P 123 (QBD).
[43] [2003] EWCA Civ 151. In *Rall* v *Hume* some of the evidence on video (that taken through the window of the Claimant's home and through the window of a nursery attended by the Claimant's child) was inadmissible because it constituted a breach of the right to privacy.

effect that the Claimant had, effectively, made a full recovery from the tenosynovitis injury which she had sustained as a result of its admitted breach of duty. The Defendant relies on two tranches of video evidence obtained on its behalf by an enquiry agent. The agent had obtained the footage inside the Claimant's home to which she had gained access by pretending to be a market researcher. Unsurprisingly, the Defendant accepted that its enquiry agent was guilty of trespass and would not have obtained any permission to enter if her true identity had been revealed.[44] It was alleged, although not accepted, that the video film showed the Claimant with a satisfactory function in the index wrist/hand. The Defendant applied for directions for the admission of the surveillance evidence. This application was opposed; the Claimant relied on CPR 32.1(2) and Article 8(1). At first instance the district judge excluded the evidence. This decision was reversed by the Deputy High Court Judge on appeal. In the course of a further appeal hearing the Court of Appeal gave the following guidance:

- Where the Defendant had infringed the Claimant's Article 8(1) right to privacy this was an important consideration in the exercise of the court's discretion in the management of the proceedings.

- Article 8(1) of the Convention could not be relied on directly by the Claimant because the Defendant's insurer (which had commissioned the video evidence) was not a public authority, although the court (a public authority) could not exercise its discretion in a manner incompatible with the Claimant's Convention rights.

- The Convention did not itself direct what the consequence of obtaining evidence in breach of Article 8(1) should be – this remained an issue to be determined by the domestic courts.

- The Court should seek to reconcile the public's interest that, in litigation, the truth should be revealed against the public interest in not permitting a party to rely on video evidence which had been obtained unlawfully.

- The starting point was, as Potter LJ directed in *Rall* v *Hume*, that where, according to the Defendant, the video evidence undermined the Claimant's case to an extent which would substantially reduce the award of damages to which she would otherwise be entitled, then the interests of justice would normally require that the

---

[44] It is, of course, unlikely that the agent would have obtained any footage worth using if the Claimant had been made aware of her true identity.

Defendant be permitted to cross-examine the Claimant and her medico-legal expert(s) on the evidence.

- However, it was important that the admission of such video evidence should not amount to trial by ambush – this would require examination of the conduct of the Defendant.

8.023 Ultimately, the Court of Appeal decided the issue in *Jones* as follows:

> This is not a case where the conduct of the defendant's insurers is so outrageous that the defence should be struck out. The case, therefore, has to be tried. It would be artificial and undesirable for the actual evidence, which is relevant and admissible, not to be placed before the judge who has the task of trying the case. We accept Mr Owen's submission that to exclude the use of the evidence would create a wholly undesirable situation. Fresh medical experts would have to be instructed on both sides.[45] Evidence which is relevant would have to be concealed from them, perhaps resulting in a misdiagnosis; and it would not be possible to cross-examine the claimant appropriately. For these reasons we do not consider it would be right to interfere with the Judge's decision not to exclude the evidence.[46]

8.024 The sanction which the Court of Appeal imposed to penalise the Defendant's insurers for obtaining the evidence unlawfully was to order the Defendant to pay the costs of resolving the issue of the admissibility of the evidence before the district judge and during the two tiers of appeal (together with a direction to the trial judge to consider the Defendant's conduct in the context of the exercise of his discretion as to the costs of the action). In a case decided under the pre-CPR rules (albeit, after the Rules had come into force) the Court of Appeal held, where a Claimant whose symptoms were suggested by video evidence to be exaggerated and who failed to beat a payment in, that the Claimant should not pay the Defendant's costs after the date of the payment in.[47] A key reason for the departure from the usual rule as to costs was that the video evidence on which the Defendant relied was served excessively late. The Court of Appeal held that the position might have been different if, contrary to the trial judge's finding, the Claimant's exaggeration had been deliberate and dishonest, rather than innocent.[48]

---

[45] Because the Defendant's expert had seen and commented on the video surveillance.
[46] Para 28 of the judgment *per* Lord Woolf CJ.
[47] See *Ford* v *GKR Construction Limited* [2000] 1 WLR 1397 (CA).
[48] See also, *Booth* v *Britannia Hotels Limited* [2002] EWCA Civ 579 where it was held that the exaggeration was deliberate. *Ford* and *Booth* are considered in more detail in Chapter 9 below.

8.025 *Jones* was applied in the decision of the Employment Appeal Tribunal in *XXX* v *(1) YYYY and (2) ZZZ.*[49] In this case the Applicant, in Employment Tribunal proceedings concerning a claim of sex discrimination and victimisation, sought to rely on covert video evidence which was alleged to show the Respondent, her employer, making sexual advances to her in front of his child (whom the Applicant was employed by the Respondent to look after). The Tribunal held that the admission of the evidence at a public hearing might infringe the Article 8(1) rights of the child (and, conceivably, of his father, the Respondent), but this had to be weighed against the Article 6 rights of the Applicant. The Tribunal determined that these competing rights could be reconciled by the Tribunal members viewing the video evidence in private – rather than in public hearing – and then assessing its relevance in the light of all of the other evidence.

8.026 It is clear that the courts are concerned to safeguard the admissibility of relevant video surveillance evidence and are usually prepared, at least for the purposes of initial case management, to rely on the Defendant's assurances about the relevance of such evidence.[50] However, it is also right to say that the balancing exercise referred to in recent judgments of the Court of Appeal is less likely to result in a decision for admission where the Defendant has:

- delayed obtaining or disclosing such evidence in a manner which might be said to have materially prejudiced the Claimant or the medical experts – the "*trial by ambush*" issue – in *Cooper* v *P & O Stena Line Limited*[51] the trial judge was, among a series of criticisms of the Defendant's conduct, critical of the Defendant's failure to disclose video surveillance which, the Claimant was aware, they had obtained;[52]
- failed to ensure that the court is given a timely opportunity to provide directions for the admission of such evidence at trial (by arranging for video equipment to be available at trial and for an adequate trial timetable to be provided);

---

[49] (2004) IRLR 137.
[50] See also the first instance decisions in *Taylor* v *Ashwood Residential Developments Limited* [2003] CLY 279 (Leeds CC, HHJ Grenfell) and *Martin* v *McGuinness* [2003] CLY 5272 (OH) which support this proposition.
[51] [1999] 1 Ll Rep 734 (QBD).
[52] In this case the Claimant made an application at trial for the disclosure of the video evidence. The Defendant conceded the application, but did not seek to rely on the disclosed evidence to make out the allegations of fraud which it pursued at trial (no doubt because it contained nothing that would support the Defendant's allegations).

- obtained the evidence unlawfully or in such a manner that infringes the right to privacy of the person filmed (whether the Claimant or some other person).

8.027 It should be remembered that even where the video surveillance evidence is admitted, the court has an arsenal of sanctions (particularly adverse costs orders) which it can deploy with a view to penalising the Defendant's conduct.[53] The use of such sanctions may, in some cases, eliminate any advantage gained by the admission of the video evidence.

Practice

8.028 This section will concentrate, like the case law discussed above, on the video surveillance evidence necessary to challenge and defeat the Claimant's claim for damages in a personal injury action. An appropriate starting point is the medical evidence assessed in the context of the schedule of losses and expenses. It is clearly important to identify precisely which physical or other tasks the Claimant complains that he is prevented from carrying out as a result of the index injury. Second, it is necessary to tie the injury to the items for which claim is made on the schedule. It may, as indicated above, be useful to ask questions of the medical expert witnesses with a view to identifying, as precisely as possible, what exactly the Claimant is and is not capable of doing (a witness statement in which the Claimant describes, in detail and at length, the tasks he cannot manage can be a useful prompt for the medical experts in this regard).

8.029 Only when this task has been completed should an enquiry agent be instructed. It probably goes without saying that the enquiry agent should, of course, be furnished with statements of case, witness statements, medical reports and schedules and counter-schedules of loss and expense. However, the agent will also need to be instructed on the basis of the exercise which has just been described; namely, the identification, with as much precision as can be managed, of the tasks which the Claimant says he cannot, by reason of his injury, manage. In order to ensure that video surveillance evidence is relevant (and, therefore, useful and admissible) it needs to be targeted. The Claimant's home address should be checked prior to the commencement of surveillance and a Land Registry copy plan might also usefully be obtained. The video surveillance operation needs to be carefully planned in order to make the best use of resources and to increase the prospects of obtaining

---

[53] If the court admits contested video evidence on the basis of the Defendant's assertion that it is relevant in circumstances where the trial judge takes the view that it is irrelevant, then it is likely that costs consequences will flow from this.

useful covert footage (perhaps the most important aspect of this is to ensure that the enquiry agent can identify the Claimant).[54]

8.030 A common response by a Claimant confronted with video surveillance evidence which appears to show them performing a variety of tasks which they claim they cannot manage is to allege either that the footage caught them on "*a good day*"[55] and/or that they had just taken pain relieving or other medication which enabled them to do far more than they would normally be able to manage.[56] The easiest way to ensure that the Defendant can respond to this sort of explanation is to ensure that (a) the footage is taken over more than one day; (b) the footage is taken at different times of day; and, (c) the footage is taken of the Claimant performing a variety of tasks relevant to the injury or injuries in issue.

4. EXPERTS

Know your expert

8.031 The Protocol provides guidance on the appointment of expert witnesses for a good reason: namely, to ensure that both parties are content with the person appointed and, therefore, to minimise any challenge to the contents of the report on the basis that an inappropriate expert has been appointed or, more unusually, that the expert has failed to comply with his duty to help the court with the matters within his expertise (which duty overrides any obligation to the person calling him).[57] Accordingly, the Protocol directs advance nomination of expert witnesses (with an accompanying time limit of 14 days during which the other party can raise objections to the instruction of the expert).[58]

8.032 There are cases in which a party wishes to object to the instruction of an expert either on the basis that the expert is known to them and is,

---

[54] This can perhaps be done most safely by ensuring that the enquiry agent knows when the Claimant is scheduled to attend a medical examination.

[55] This obviously requires the Claimant to allege, as did the Claimant in *Jones* v *University of Warwick* [2003] EWCA Civ 151, that he has good and bad days.

[56] This explanation, accepted by the trial judge without demur, was proffered by the Claimant in *Cooper* v *P & O Stena Line Limited* [1999] 1 Ll Rep 734 (QBD) in order to explain some inconsistencies as to a straight leg raising examination that were found by the Defendant's medical expert.

[57] CPR 35.3.

[58] Pre-action Protocol for Personal Injury Claims, paras 3.15-3.21. There are similar provisions in the Pre-action Protocol for Disease and Illness Claims, paras 9.1-9.12.

therefore, unsuitable or is otherwise inappropriate (perhaps on the basis that evidence he has given in the past has been judicially criticised). In most cases, however, the raising of objections requires the provision of information. There are some advance indicators that might give rise to suspicion. For example, if an expert is nominated to give expert evidence in an area outside his obvious area of specialism (for example, the use of a hand surgeon to provide a report in spinal injury case). Alternatively, an advance nomination of an expert may contain only one name (rather than the conventional two or three names). Finally, and not uncommonly, there may be a breach of the Protocol (for example, the first notice that an expert has been instructed may arrive at the same time that the Particulars of Claim are served with an accompanying report). Judges tend to be critical of the selection of the treating physician to provide a medico-legal report (and nomination/selection of the treating physician should ordinarily be challenged). These circumstances might, where appropriate, justify an enquiry into the expert's credentials. There are, of course, a large number of sources from which to investigate the qualifications, expertise and experience of an expert. First, the General Medical Council website can be consulted; all consultants with a National Health Service appointment are required to register with the GMC. The online GMC site contains a list of registered medical practitioners (the list can be searched under a variety of headings – including an alphabetic search). The Register contains, among other pieces of information, the medical qualifications of the expert, their membership of a specialist or GP register, their registration date and GMC number. Once the expert has been identified the website of the hospital where he or she is employed can be consulted as a further source of information (the Medical Directory which is published annually will assist in identifying the home hospital/clinic of the expert if the GMC website does not provide an answer). It probably goes without saying that an expert who cannot be identified either from the GMC List or in the Medical Directory and who appears to lack any hospital/clinic appointment may well be an inappropriate choice of expert witness.

8.033 If there is doubt about the suitability of an expert then questions can be asked. This can clearly be done in advance of the issue of proceedings. The Protocol provides, at paragraph 3.20, that,

> Either party may send to an agreed expert written questions on the report, relevant to the issues, via the first party's solicitors. The expert should send answers to the questions separately and directly to each party.

Duties of an expert

8.034 Rule 51 of the GMC Guide to Good Medical Practice[59] provides,

Writing reports, giving evidence and signing documents

> You must be honest and trustworthy when writing reports, completing or signing forms, or providing evidence in litigation or other formal inquiries. This means that you must take reasonable steps to verify any statement before you sign a document. You must not write or sign documents which are false or misleading because they omit relevant information. If you have agreed to prepare a report, complete or sign a document or provide evidence, you must do so without unreasonable delay.

8.035 Similar obligations, designed to ensure the probity of documentation relied on in court, appear in the Civil Procedure Rules. As indicated above, CPR 35.3 provides that the expert's overriding duty is to the court, rather than the party instructing or paying him. This provision is reinforced by the CPR Protocol for the instruction of experts which, while emphasising the duty of experts to *"exercise reasonable skill and care to those instructing them"*, also reminds expert witnesses (and those instructing them) of the overriding principle set out in CPR 35.3.[60] The Protocol states that opinions should be independent and sets out a means by which an expert might assess whether his opinion is independently given; namely that he would be giving the same opinion if given the same instructions by an opposing party.[61]

8.036 In the event that a party instructs an expert to provide advice, rather than for the purpose of court proceedings, the Protocol makes it clear that the advice obtained remains confidential and its provisions do not apply.[62] The Protocol will apply, however, in the event that an expert – originally instructed for advisory purposes – is subsequently instructed as an expert witness in the proceedings.

8.037 The expert is required to attach a statement of truth to his report (a special form of words appears at paragraph 2.4 of CPR 35, PD). In addition, the report must contain a declaration that,

> ...the expert understands his duty to the Court; and ... has complied with that duty.
> (CPR 35.10(2)).

---

[59] (3rd ed, 2001).
[60] See also CPR 35, PD, paras 1.1-1.6.
[61] Protocol for the instruction of experts to give evidence in civil proceedings.
[62] Protocol, paras 5.1-5.3.

8.038 The Rules emphasise the importance attached to the expert's coverage of the relevant subject-matter in a manner which reflects the fact that the overriding duty is owed to the court, rather than the parties: where there is a range of opinion on the material in the report the expert is required to summarise the range of opinion and to give reasons for his own opinion.[63] In the same vein, the courts have emphasised that an expert's duty is to cover in their report and to give opinions upon the whole of the relevant subject-matter and not to select only the evidence which is supportive of the position of the party instructing them (see, among other cases, *Royal & Sun Alliance Trust Co Ltd* v *Healey & Baker* [2000] (unreported)).

8.039 A number of sanctions are available for those cases where the expert has failed to provide evidence and conduct himself in compliance with the Rules. First, the Court can simply refuse the party permission to rely on the expert evidence or, alternatively, can disregard the evidence in whole or in part. In addition, and in more serious cases, the court can refer the conduct of the expert to his governing body.[64] In appropriate cases an expert who, by flagrant and reckless disregard of his duties to the court, causes significant expense to be incurred, can be ordered to pay costs.[65]

Practice

8.040 Increasingly, in fast track value (and even moderate multi track value) claims the trend is to appoint a single joint expert (see *Daniels* v *Walker* [2000] 1 WLR 1382 (CA) and subsequent case law). The result of this is that one party may be stuck at an early stage with the other party's expert and find that there is little that they can later do about this. It is important, therefore, to ensure that there is proper compliance with the Protocol and that proper objection is taken to any nominated expert at the appropriate (early) stage in the proceedings. A better tactic for those acting for Defendants is to seek to influence the appointment of expert – perhaps by nominating their own choice of experts to the Claimant before the latter has had an opportunity to make the first nomination.

8.041 In the event that an unsuitable expert is instructed prior to an application that he be the single joint expert, an appropriate challenge should be made to this at the earliest opportunity – perhaps at an allocation

---

[63] CPR 35, PD, para 2.2(6) and Protocol, paras 13.12-13.13.
[64] See *Hussein* v *William Hill Group* [2004] EWHC 208 (QBD).
[65] See *Phillips* v *Symes* [2004] EWHC 2330 (ChD) where Peter Smith J sets out the relevant principles in the course of an extended commentary on section 51 of the Supreme Court Act 1981.

directions hearing or early case management conference. I have sketched out above some of the bases on which challenge may be made to the expert's appointment/instruction; namely, that he is the treating physician or an expert in an inappropriate discipline or field of specialism. In the event that such challenge is successful then the initiative should immediately be grasped with nomination of a new expert so that the same can be named in the court order. In the event that the court orders the parties to agree the identity of a new joint expert, the Defendant should ensure that a list of nominees is immediately available. It goes without saying that a careful watch should be kept over the terms of instruction of any single joint expert.

8.042 It is essential that an expert is properly instructed. In the event that fraud or exaggeration is suspected or alleged, it is essential that any expert is provided with sufficient material to be able to comment appropriately on this issue. This will mean, as a minimum, that forms of consent are obtained so as to ensure that the medico-legal expert is furnished with General Practitioner, hospital, occupational health, ambulance and physiotherapist records and any pertaining to alternative remedies.[66] It is usually worth ensuring that the records are carefully reviewed prior to their receipt by the expert; if there are, therefore, any specific entries that need to be considered then they can be brought to the expert's attention prior to the compiling of the report. I have dealt above with video surveillance evidence (the key to reliance on this evidence is timing, providing that the timing of disclosure of this evidence is not so late as to jeopardise its admission by the court).

8.043 Questions can be asked of the expert witnesses and the Rules make provision for this at CPR 35.6.[67] Subject to an order of the court or the agreement of the other party, written questions can only be put once; must be put within 28 days of receipt of the report; and, must be put for the purposes of clarification of the report. Any questions in a case where fraud or exaggeration is suspected or alleged should ordinarily be asked after the evidence is complete (to ensure that a party or his expert has limited opportunity to have recourse to additional evidence to evade difficult or uncomfortable questions). Where a party has obtained its own expert evidence, then that expert may be asked to assist in the drafting of written questions. Any questions which are put should be focused and clear. It should, of course, be remembered that it is not necessary in every case to ask questions of the expert; there may be cases in which the only questions that can be put are likely to yield answers that support the opinions that are set out in a report. Absent a clear, knock-out blow of the sort that is

---

[66] E.g. osteopath, chiropractor, acupuncturist, reflexologist and aromatherapist.
[67] See also, CPR 35, PD, paras 5.1-5.3 and Protocol, paras 16.1-16.4.

occasionally obtained from video surveillance evidence, a question which baldly asks an expert to consider whether a Claimant is, for example, malingering is unlikely to produce a helpful response.

8.044 In cases where more than one expert has been appointed, it is important to ensure that a party's expert is properly instructed to attend a joint meeting with the other side's expert and to fight his corner in an appropriately robust way.[68] Some direction of the manner in which the joint discussion proceeds can be achieved by means of drafting the correct agenda. The Protocol for the instruction of experts contains the following provisions with respect to expert evidence,

> The parties, their lawyers and experts should co-operate to produce the agenda for any discussion between experts, although primary responsibility for preparation of the agenda should normally lie with the parties' solicitors. ... The agenda should indicate what matters have been agreed and summarise concisely those which are in issue. It is often helpful for it to include questions to be answered by the experts. If agreement cannot be reached promptly or a party is unrepresented, the court may give directions for the drawing up of the agenda. The agenda should be circulated to the experts and those instructing them to allow sufficient time for the experts to prepare for the discussion.[69]

8.045 Should there be any doubt about the matter the Protocol emphasises that it is not permissible for the parties to instruct their respective experts to avoid reaching agreement (or to defer doing so); the experts are, correspondingly, prohibited from accepting such instructions.[70]

8.046 It is, of course important that the expert witness's opinion on which the Defendant relies is expressed in robust and clear terms in the event that an allegation of fraud – conscious exaggeration for financial gain – is pursued. However, an overbearing or dogmatic approach should be avoided. In *Cooper* v *P & O Stena Line Limited*[71] the trial judge was highly critical of the expert evidence given by the Consultant Orthopaedic Surgeon instructed by the Defendant. She described him as an unsatisfactory witness. His contention was that the Claimant was malingering with respect to the serious and debilitating back injury which he claimed to have suffered. The Claimant's expert evidence was to the effect that he had a fibromyalgia condition (or, at the very least, some form of chronic pain condition

---

[68] It is invariable for the court to order joint statements by experts of like discipline, using the power contained in CPR 35.12.
[69] Protocol, paras 18.5 – 18.6.
[70] Protocol, para 18.7.
[71] [1999] 1 Ll Rep 734 (QBD).

attributable to the accident for which the Defendant was liable). The trial judge's criticism of the Defendant's expert was based on the following:

- the expert categorically refused to acknowledge that fibromyalgia existed as a pathology and expressed this opinion in the witness box in a manner described by the trial judge as "*discourteous and intemperate*" – he indicated, among other things, that the World Health Organisation had, in recognising this condition, had the "*wool pulled over its eyes*";

- the examination of the Claimant had been very fast ("*very much less than 35 minutes*" – the expert's evidence was that his examinations usually lasted for 35 minutes);

- the expert's reliance on discrepancies in the Claimant's ability to perform straight leg raising was explicable on the basis that the Claimant had good days and bad days and that he tended to perform better when relaxed (the evidence suggested that the relationship between the Claimant and the Defendant's expert witness was best described as antagonistic).

8.047 The problems with the expert orthopaedic evidence adduced by the Defendant compelled counsel for the Defendant to disavow reliance on the expert witness in the course of his closing submissions. A measured approach from an expert witness (albeit expressed in clear and robust terms) is, perhaps obviously, going to play better with a judge than an approach which is – or appears to be – over-zealous or coloured by pre-formed opinions or prejudices.[72]

5. HANDLING THE DISHONEST WITNESS

8.048 The keys to this are as follows:

- the availability of objective and, preferably, incontrovertible evidence with which to advance an allegation of dishonesty

---

[72] See also, in the context of a low velocity RTA case, the criticism made of the Defendant's expert in *Casey* v *Cartwright* [2006] *The Times*, October 10 (CA); [2006] EWCA Civ 1280, para 20 *per* Dyson LJ.

(photographs, video evidence or some other form of real evidence is usually needed);[73]

- surprise – this will usually be difficult to achieve with the "*cards on the table*" approach which the Civil Procedure Rules require;

- putting any allegation fairly and clearly so that the witness has an opportunity to comment on it;

- ensuring that there is weight behind and a proper foundation for any attack on the credibility of a witness.[74]

8.049 The Bar Code of Conduct emphasises the duties of an advocate with respect to conduct in court:[75]

> A barrister when conducting proceedings in Court: ... (g) must not make statements or ask questions which are merely scandalous or intended or calculated only to vilify, insult or annoy either a witness or some other person; (h) must if possible avoid the naming in open Court of third parties whose character would thereby be impugned; (i) must not by assertion in a speech impugn a witness whom he has had an opportunity to cross-examine unless in cross-examination he has given the witness an opportunity to answer the allegation; (j) must not suggest that a victim, witness or other person is guilty of crime, fraud or misconduct or make any defamatory aspersion on the conduct of any other person or attribute to another person the crime or conduct of which his lay client is accused unless such allegations go to a matter in issue (including the credibility of the witness) which is material to the lay client's case and appear to him to be supported by reasonable grounds.

8.050 The Code concentrates upon ensuring that allegations of fraud or dishonesty are not made frivolously[76] (which is to say without a sound basis for putting such allegations) and upon giving the witness an opportunity to

---

[73] In *Cooper* v *P & O Stena Line Limited* [1999] 1 Ll Rep 734 (QBD), discussed above, the Defendant's cross-examination of the Claimant and his witnesses was fatally undermined by documents which the Defendant itself disclosed (late) during the course of the trial.

[74] In *Cooper* v *P & O Stena Line Limited* [1999] 1 Ll Rep 734 (QBD) the Defendant suggested, among other things, that the Claimant's credibility as to the extent of back symptoms was undermined by the fact that, during one short adjournment in the course of the trial, one of the Defendant's witnesses had seen the Claimant in the Cock Tavern on the Strand reaching across the bar to place a drink on the bar. The evidence was that the Defendant's witness had caught only a fleeting glimpse of the Claimant across a crowded bar and the trial judge had little difficulty in disregarding his evidence.

[75] Bar Code of Conduct, para 708.

[76] Putting a frivolous allegation may well have unpleasant costs consequences either for the party represented or for the advocate himself (in addition to alienating the trial judge).

respond. The second of these considerations featured in the judgment of Eady J in *Healy* v *Cosmosair Plc*[77] This case concerned an injury sustained in a swimming pool during the course of a package holiday to Portugal in which the Claimant suffered catastrophic spinal injuries. The Claimant's case, supported by the evidence of a number of members of his family with whom he was on holiday, was that he had slipped on tiling around the edge of the swimming pool and entered the pool head first before striking his head on the bottom of the pool; it was the Claimant's case that the tiling was dangerously slippery when wet. The Defendant's case was that the Claimant had dived into the swimming pool (in breach of pool rules) and sustained injury in that way. Accordingly, the first issue for the judge to determine was whether the Claimant had dived or slipped. This issue was resolved in the Claimant's favour, although, for other reasons, the Claimant's claim was dismissed. In the course of his judgment, Eady J, considering the dive/slip issue and the evidence in respect of the same, made the following observations:

> It is important for me to record that the inevitable inference from the way the Defendant's case was put at trial is that … [KG – a member of the Claimant's family and a witness giving evidence on his behalf] perjured herself. I am invited to conclude that (a) she saw the Claimant dive, (b) told … [the Defendant's local representative] this was so, and (c) her denials in court were dishonest. Yet these serious allegations were not put to her fairly and squarely. I wish to make it plain that I regarded her as an honest witness. Moreover, wherever her evidence conflicted with that of [the Defendant's local representative] I preferred that of … [KG]. A telling point made by Mr Wilson Smith QC, for the Claimant, was that if this was indeed a fraudulent claim, and the Claimant's family were prepared to lie for him, it would have been easy for …[KG] and … [TG] to say that they had seen him slip on the wet tiles and that he lost his balance and fell into the pool.

8.051 The Defendant had comprehensively put its case to KG at trial and it was a necessary implication of doing so that KG was lying to the court. The judge was critical however, that this allegation was not put to the witness in terms.[78]

---

[77] [2005]EWHC 1657 (QBD).
[78] Notwithstanding the overwhelming likelihood that if it had been put (baldly) to the witness that she was lying, she would simply have responded by stating that she was not.

Chapter 9

PRACTICE: COSTS

1. INTRODUCTION

9.001 The costs powers of the court provide a useful means by which to police, penalise and, therefore, discourage conduct of which the court disapproves. While,

> ...the general rule is that the unsuccessful party will be ordered to pay the costs of the successful party...

the court retains a discretion to "*make a different order*"[1] and, where allegations of fraud or dishonesty are made, there are many examples where the court has departed from the general rule in order to express its views about the conduct of a party.

9.002 The court's broad discretion in this area must be exercised judicially and in accordance with the overriding objective. The Civil Procedure Rules also contain specific, if generally expressed, guidance:

> In deciding what order (if any) to make about costs, the court must have regard to all the circumstances, including – (a) the conduct of all the parties; (b) whether a party has succeeded on part of his case, even if he has not been wholly successful; and (c) any payment into court or admissible offer to settle made by a party which is drawn to the court's attention (whether or not made in accordance with Part 36).[2]

9.003 It may be significant that, in this recital of the matters to which the court is required to have regard, the "*conduct of all the parties*" is listed first. The Rules go on to provide a non-exhaustive definition of what the conduct of the parties means in this context:

---

[1] CPR 44.3(2)(a)-(b).
[2] CPR 44.3(4).

(a) conduct before, as well as during, the proceedings, and in particular the extent to which the parties followed any relevant pre-action protocol; (b) whether it was reasonable for a party to raise, pursue or contest a particular allegation or issue; (c) the manner in which a party has pursued or defended his case or a particular allegation or issue; and (d) whether a claimant who has succeeded in his claim, in whole or in part, exaggerated his claim.[3]

9.004 This list is supplemented by CPR 44.5 which sets out the factors to be considered in deciding the amount of the costs awarded. Again, conduct is a matter to which the court's specific attention is directed, in addition to several factors which might have a particular relevance to an action where there is an allegation of dishonesty or fraud:

> ...the importance of the matter to all the parties ... the particular complexity of the matter or the difficulty or novelty of the questions raised ... the time spent on the case.

In *Lownds* v *Home Office*[4] the Court of Appeal emphasised that an essential element in considering whether an item of cost was reasonably incurred is the conduct of the other (paying) party. This case seeks to encourage co-operation between the parties by making it clear that unco-operative conduct will increase the costs which may well be paid by the obstructive party.

9.005 The court has the power to make a wide variety of costs orders which include, among other things, an order that a party must pay:

- a proportion of another party's costs;
- a stated amount in respect of those costs;
- costs from or until a specific date;
- costs incurred prior to the commencement of proceedings or in respect of a specific step in the proceedings;
- interest on costs.[5]

---

[3] CPR 44.3(5).
[4] [2002] 1 WLR 2450, 2457G-H *per* Lord Woolf CJ (CA).
[5] The list appears at CPR 44.3(6). Again, the list is non-exhaustive. The court has the additional power (a) to order that costs be paid on account (CPR 44.3(8)) and (b) to order that the costs which a party is liable to pay to another party be set off against any amount that the latter is entitled to be paid (CPR 44.3(9)(a)).

9.006 The court's power to make indemnity costs orders[6] and wasted costs orders are important elements of its costs arsenal and have been regularly deployed in the context of allegations of dishonesty and fraud. Allegations of fraud are likely to be expensive and time consuming to prosecute and defend; they will almost always add to the complexity of an action and this will impact on the costs. It may be that this feature of these actions – coupled with the dim view that the court takes of allegations of dishonesty or fraud which do not succeed – is as effective a deterrent to the pleading of allegations of this kind as the professional conduct rules which are considered above.

2. SUCCESSFUL ALLEGATIONS OF DISHONESTY/FRAUD

9.007 In this category of case the general rule contained in CPR 44.3(2)(a) (viz that costs follow the event) will usually be observed. However, the conduct of a party against whom an allegation of dishonesty or fraud is successfully pursued will often face an additional penalty in the form of an application for the costs of the successful party to be assessed on the indemnity basis. Equally, the court may decide to depart from the usual winner takes all approach to costs where a party who is ultimately held liable has nevertheless succeeded in establishing that the claimant has been dishonest. Particular difficulties have arisen where the dishonesty is located in the deliberate exaggeration of a claim and/or where there has been a Part 36 offer or payment.

9.008 The cases considered below do not invariably involve a finding of dishonesty or fraud, but the approach of the courts to more innocent forms of exaggeration assists to illuminate the approach that is likely to be taken where the exaggeration is calculated and intentional. It will become apparent that the focus in recent case law on answering the question "*Who is the real winner?*" will inevitably be a fact-sensitive exercise. It is not always easy to

---

[6] See CPR 44.4 for rules on the basis of assessment. The general distinction between costs on the standard and indemnity basis is that (a) on a standard basis assessment, the burden of proving that costs were reasonably incurred falls on the receiving party, whereas on the indemnity basis the court will resolve any doubts about the reasonableness of the costs sought in the receiving party's favour and (b) on the standard basis the costs allowed must be proportionate to the matters in issue, whereas this requirement does not apply where the costs are assessed on the indemnity basis. The effect of the indemnity basis of assessment is, therefore, as Lord Woolf CJ observed in *Lownds* v *Home Office* [2002] 1 WLR 2450, 2452C, "*considerably more favourable to the receiving party than the standard basis of costs*".

extract any consistent principles beyond those which are already listed as relevant factors in the Civil Procedure Rules.

9.009 *Molloy* v *Shell UK Limited*[7] concerned a claim for personal injury that was brought by the Claimant against the Defendant. There was no issue as to liability and the Defendant paid £20,000 into court. The Claimant pursued a claim for loss of earnings and his case was that he had, by reason of the Defendant's breach of duty, been rendered unfit for any form of work for a period in excess of two years and then unfit for employment as a scaffolder on oil rigs for a further extended period. His claim for past and future loss of earnings, as set out in a schedule of loss, exceeded £300,000. The Defendant disclosed evidence that this claim was grossly and deliberately exaggerated. Evidence had come to light that the Claimant had, in fact, returned to work as a scaffolder on oil platforms within 15 months of his accident and had continued to work fairly regularly in this field ever since. The Claimant was awarded £18,897. At first instance the judge held that the Claimant should pay the entirety of the Defendant's costs prior to the payment in. In respect of the period after the payment into court became effective the judge held that the Defendant had, effectively, won the case. However, the Claimant had been successful to a limited extent and, taking account of his "*gross deceit*" in the prosecution of a claim held to be fraudulent, it was decided that the Claimant should pay 75% of the Defendant's costs after the payment in. The Defendant appealed on the basis that the judge had fallen into error in not awarding it the whole of its costs of the action. An issue arose at first instance and on appeal as to whether or not the Claimant had "beaten" the Defendant's payment into court. This issue turned on the proper calculation of the payment in and the effect of deduction of recoupable social security benefits. These matters are dealt with in Part 36 of the Rules and lie outside the ambit of this book; the Court of Appeal held that, on a proper application of Part 36, the Claimant had failed to beat the payment into court and should, therefore, pay the whole of the costs of the action. However, the court went on to hold that, even if the Claimant's award had exceeded the Defendant's payment in, the dishonest nature of his claim meant that he should pay the whole of the Defendant's costs:

> The judge was obliged by Part 44.3(5) ... to consider the whole of the party's conduct. It does appear that he may have considered the respondent's conduct only after the date of the Part 36 payment. If that is so, he fell into error. At least since the particulars of claim were filed ... and until he was found out the respondent's approach to this action has been nothing short of a cynical and dishonest abuse of the court's process. For my part I entertain considerable qualms as to whether, faced with manipulation

---

[7] [2002] PIQR P56 (CA).

of the civil justice system on so grand a scale, the court should once it knows the facts entertain the case at all save to make the dishonest claimant pay the defendant's costs. However, all that is sought here is an order for 100 per cent of the appellant's costs instead of 75 per cent, the costs in question being only those incurred after the date of the Part 36 payment. The appeal certainly cannot be resisted on that basis.[8]

9.010 *Painting* v *University of Oxford*[9] also involved an exaggerated claim for personal injury. Again, liability had been conceded with an agreed deduction of 20% for contributory negligence. At the assessment of damages hearing the Claimant sought £400,000 (that is, £500,000, less the contributory negligence); it was her case that she had sustained a long term debilitating back injury as a result of the Defendant's breach of duty and would not work again. She was awarded around £25,000 (after contributory negligence was deducted). At that time the payment into court was £10,000. The trial judge awarded the Claimant the entirety of her costs of the action and the Defendant appealed this Order. The background to the appeal was that the Defendant had originally paid £184,000 into court. It had then obtained video surveillance evidence which showed the Claimant performing physical tasks that she alleged she was, by reason of her relevant symptoms, incapable of managing. The video evidence was obtained in the period September 2003 to November 2003 and had been in the Defendant's solicitors' possession since December 2003. In February 2004, and on application by the Defendant, permission was granted to withdraw all but £10,000 of the monies in court. A trial date for the same month was vacated. The Claimant had never sought to accept the monies in court (either before or after the Defendant's application). It remained her case that she was, by reason of the seriousness of her injury, incapable of work. The judge rejected this contention and held that the Claimant had exaggerated her symptoms and had misled a jointly instructed medico-legal expert. It was common ground that the Claimant had been deliberately exaggerating the extent and duration of her symptoms; the Court of Appeal described her conduct as fraudulent. Nevertheless, the trial judge awarded the Claimant the entirety of her costs of the action on the basis that the exaggerated nature of the Claimant's evidence was, as a factor in the exercise of the costs discretion, outweighed by the inadequacy of the payment into court; the judge held that the payment into court was, after it was reduced to £10,000, obviously

---

[8] At P60 *per* Laws LJ. See also *Bajwa* v *British Airways PLC* [1999] PIQR Q 152 (CA) where one of three conjoined appeals involved a claim for damages for personal injury damages where the method of assessment adopted by the Claimant was described by the Court of Appeal as "*extravagantly wrong*". There was no finding that the Claimant had been dishonest, but her lack of success in persuading a court to adopt her method of assessment nevertheless justified an award of costs to the Defendant, even though the Claimant had beaten a payment into court.
[9] [2005] PIQR Q5; [2005] EWCA Civ 161.

inadequate even when the Claimant's exaggeration was taken into account. The Court of Appeal disagreed. It was held that the trial judge had, in concentrating too narrowly on the payment into court, failed to see the bigger picture which required him to consider which party could be said, in reality, to have won the claim. The real winner was, so the Court of Appeal held, the Defendant and the Defendant was entitled to its costs of the action and the appeal. In addition to the " *Who is the real winner?*" factor,[10] the Court's decision was influenced by the following additional factors:

- the fact that the Claimant's exaggeration of her claim was deliberate – it was " *fraudulent*";[11]

- the fact that the Claimant had steadfastly failed to consider negotiating a settlement of her claim and had made no offers to settle.

9.011 The importance to be attached to these factors can be traced back to some of the pre-CPR case law in which Defendants have sought to rely on video surveillance evidence, suggestive of exaggeration, which was served late.[12] In *Ford* v *GKR Construction Limited*[13] the Defendant had, in the context of a road traffic accident personal injury claim where liability was conceded, made a payment into court well in advance of the trial date and, in the event, the payment in exceeded the damages that were awarded to the Claimant. The trial judge nevertheless ordered that the Defendant should pay the Claimant's costs. There were two reasons for this. First, the assessment of damages hearing took place over a number of days and was adjourned, part-heard, on more than one occasion. The Defendant obtained video surveillance evidence which suggested that there was exaggeration by the Claimant (the judge held that there was exaggeration and that this impacted on the proper award to make, but also held that such exaggeration was unintentional and innocent). However, this video evidence was obtained and disclosed very late (during one of the adjournments of the assessment of damages hearing); it nevertheless prompted the Claimant to offer to accept the monies in court, provided that the Defendant paid her costs (this offer was rejected by the Defendant). Second, the Defendant raised issues as to the appropriateness of a pleaded life multiplier for future care, but had left it

---

[10] For an example of the real-winner approach in a non-personal injury context: see *Islam* v *Ali* [2003] EWCA Civ 612.
[11] It might, however, be borne in mind that CPR 44.3(5)(d) requires the court to have regard to whether a Claimant has exaggerated his claim whether such exaggeration is fraudulent or not.
[12] With due deference to Lord Woolf and *Biguzzi* v *Rank Leisure* [1999] 4 All ER 934 (CA) these cases still have relevance in the post-CPR period.
[13] [2000] 1 WLR 1397 (CA).

until very late to raise such issues and had also made very late disclosure of expert evidence as to the Claimant's life expectancy. The Defendant appealed the judge's order as to costs and argued that the normal rule should be followed; namely, that the Claimant should pay the Defendant's costs in the period following the payment into court. The Court of Appeal rejected this contention and declined to interfere with the exercise of the trial judge's discretion (adopting, largely, the same reasons that he gave for ordering the Defendant to pay the Claimant's costs):

> Sometimes claimants do lie, embellish or fantasise, but if that is to be the defendant's case fairness demands that the claimant should have a reasonable opportunity to deal with these allegations. Sometimes sensible grounds for maintaining surveillance on a claimant may arise after the trial has begun. If they do, the defendants cannot be criticised for taking advantage of the opportunity given by an adjournment to do so. Every case, and every consequential costs order, depends on the individual facts of the case. In the present case, it is sufficient to say that I can find nothing in the evidence to explain why the defendants found it necessary to maintain surveillance on the claimant after the trial had begun when they had not done so before it. It would be flattering to describe this decision as a last-minute idea. It did not occur until after the trial had begun and for no apparent reason, save that the defendants hoped to use the adjournment to improve their prospects in the litigation by taking steps that they could and should have taken much earlier.[14]

9.012 The Court went on to state that the Defendant's appeal might have been looked on more kindly if one of three factors had been present:

- if the Claimant's exaggeration had been deliberate and dishonest, rather than, as the trial judge held, a manifestation of the mental state to which her injuries had reduced her;

- if the Claimant had when confronted with the video, attempted to brazen it out, rather than making an effort to settle the claim;

- if the Defendant had, by advancing an appropriate offer to settle, acknowledged the problems created by its late service of the video evidence.

9.013 The impact on the costs order of a finding that the Claimant has deliberately exaggerated symptoms is demonstrated by a similar appeal, also involving late disclosure of video surveillance evidence and also decided by

---

[14] At p 1401B-C *per* Judge LJ.

reference to the pre-CPR rules: *Booth* v *Britannia Hotels Limited.*[15] In this case liability was conceded and video evidence served late (albeit, not quite as late as in the *Ford* case) meant that the Claimant, who had originally presented a claim for £617,000, accepted the Defendant's payment into court in the sum of £2,500 (on the agreed basis that the Defendant would pay the Claimant's costs to be taxed on the standard basis). The Claimant submitted a costs bill for £82,000. The Defendant invited the judge, at taxation, to adopt a percentage approach to the overall bill and the judge, in recognition of the fact that the video evidence was served late, ordered the Defendant to pay 60% of the Claimant's bill. The Defendant appealed on the basis that the percentage was too high. The appeal was unsuccessful. There was a further appeal. The Court of Appeal held that the application of a percentage (before consideration of the reasonableness of the individual items sought) had resulted in a costs order of £57,000 for a claim with a value of £2,500: a result which it described as a "*nonsense*". The lateness of the video evidence did not materially alter the position in circumstances where the Claimant had pursued

> ... a claim for personal injuries which she knows or must be taken to know have not been suffered.

Accordingly, it was concluded that there was no reason why the Defendant should bear any of the costs that she expended in that "*unreasonable pursuit*", even though the video evidence was served late.[16] The case was remitted for taxation to the district judge.

9.014 In more recent, post-CPR, case law, the "real winner" approach evident in *Painting* has continued to be adopted. In *Hooper* v *Biddle & Company,*[17] a professional negligence action, the Claimant's claim was originally presented as having a value of £3.75 million. It then dropped to £350,000 plus interest. In the event the Claimant accepted an open offer of £38,000 just prior to trial. The trial judge held that the claim was, as originally presented and then pursued to just prior to trial, "*grossly exaggerated*"[18] and she accepted the submission made by the Defendant that

---

[15] [2002] EWCA Civ 579.
[16] At para 28 *per* Kennedy LJ. See also para 32 *per* Jonathan Parker LJ, "*... a Claimant who pursues an exaggerated and inflated claim for damages must expect to bear the consequences when his costs come to be assessed. Moreover in the absence of special circumstances a claimant who knows, or who must be taken to know, that his claim for damages is unsustainable in whole or in part cannot, in my judgment, be heard to assert that a defendant who has disclosed evidence which establishes the unsustainability of the claim ought to have disclosed that evidence at an earlier stage in the proceedings.*"
[17] [2006] EWHC 2995 (ChD).
[18] It was not found that such exaggeration was intentional.

there should be no order as to costs. The trial judge made reference to *Painting* in the course of her judgment; it is not wholly clear why the Defendant made the unambitious submission that there should be no order as to costs, rather than seeking its costs of the action.[19] By contrast, in *E Ivor Hughes Education Foundation* v *Leach*[20] the Claimant registered charity (which owned three independent schools) sought damages of £610,000 against the Defendant (a member of its Board of Governors) for dishonesty and breach of fiduciary duty (the claim for damages included a claim of £60,000 for alleged false claims for expenses). The Defendant denied the allegations and made a counter-claim. The Defendant made a payment into court in the sum of £5,000 which related only to the expenses claim. The Claimant elected to accept the payment into court and to abandon the remainder of the claim. The Claimant sought its costs of the action. By the time that the payment into court was accepted the Claimant's costs stood at £170,000 whereas the Defendant's costs were £140,000. The settlement figure was within the small claims track limit. The Defendant accepted that he was liable to pay the Claimant's costs of the claim for expenses. However, the Court accepted that he was the real winner when it came to considering the remainder of the claim. It was ordered that the Claimant should pay the Defendant's costs of the remainder of the action.[21]

9.015 Where a Claimant in a personal injury action has, by reason of the exaggeration of symptoms, ensured that a claim is allocated to the fast track which ought to have been dealt with on the small claims track then, in the event that damages within the small claims track limit are awarded, he may find that the court permits only fixed costs.[22]

---

[19] The open offer which the Claimant accepted was for £38,000 to be paid and for the trial judge to determine the issue of costs.

[20] [2005] EWHC 1317 (ChD).

[21] In *Jackson* v *Ministry of Defence* [2006] EWCA Civ 46 the Claimant initially made a claim for £1,000,000, but abandoned all but £240,000 of this after receipt of medical evidence which did not support his claim for residual disability. The Defendant made a payment into court of £150,000 and the Claimant was awarded £155,000 at trial. The Court of Appeal held that the trial judge had acted within the ambit of his proper discretion in reducing the Claimant's costs by just 25% (to recognise the fact that he had only just beaten the payment into court and had exaggerated his claim). The Court of Appeal took the view that the Claimant had beaten the payment into court and had, notwithstanding his exaggeration, been awarded a substantial sum. The Claimant's conduct was recognised by the judge's 25% deduction and by the fact that the Claimant's costs could be challenged on detailed assessment.

[22] See *Devine* v *Franklin* [2002] EWHC 1846 (QBD). On appeal, the court largely confined the Claimant to fixed small claims track costs, even though the Defendant had sought allocation of the claim to the multi track because it wished to raise a defence of fraud (some modest additional costs were allowed to recognise a degree of unreasonable conduct by the Defendant).

9.016 It was made clear in *Ultraframe (UK) Limited (No 2) and Others* v *Fielding and Others,*[23] an appeal arising out of actions to recover intellectual property rights and company shares, that where a party wishes to raise the dishonest conduct of a party as a relevant consideration in respect of any costs order then he should raise that issue before the judge making the costs order (usually, the trial judge). While a party should not be prevented from subsequently raising the issue of conduct before the costs judge, it was important that the dishonest party was not penalised twice for the same misconduct. Accordingly, trial judges should make it clear, when making a costs order reflecting a party's dishonesty, whether misconduct could still be raised before the costs judge.

3. UNSUCCESSFUL ALLEGATIONS OF DISHONESTY/FRAUD

9.017 It has long been the position that the court will penalise a party who unnecessarily or unsuccessfully raises an allegation of fraud. In some of the early case law the party relying on the tort of deceit in circumstances where innocent misrepresentation could be established has been penalised. In *Bellotti* v *Chequers Developments Limited,*[24] for example, the Claimant was successful in his action for innocent misrepresentation and was awarded damages. However, he also made an allegation that the misrepresentation was fraudulent and this allegation failed. The court held that the Claimant should be awarded his general costs of the action

> ...except in so far as the Master finds the costs have been increased by the addition of the allegation of fraud.[25]

9.018 More recently it has become clear that an allegation of fraud which fails may lead to an adverse costs order in which the assessment is on the indemnity basis.

9.019 In *Cooper v P & O Stena Line Limited,*[26] a personal injury claim, the Defendant initially denied liability on the basis that it denied that the Claimant had been involved in an accident at all. This contention was abandoned on the fifth, penultimate, day of trial. However, the Defendant

---

[23] [2007] *The Times,* January 8 (CA); [2006] EWCA Civ 1660.
[24] [1936] 1 All ER 89 (KBD).
[25] See also *Forester* v *Read* (1870) 6 Ch App 40 (CA).
[26] [1999] 1 Ll Rep 734 (QBD). This case is also the subject of discussion in earlier chapters.

continued to pursue an allegation that the Claimant was fraudulently exaggerating the extent and duration of his symptoms. These arguments were rejected by the trial judge in forthright terms; she was critical of the conduct of the Defendant in a number of respects. The result was an order that the successful Claimant's costs be paid on the indemnity basis. The reasons given for this order were as follows:

- the Defendant had, in respect of liability, conducted the litigation on a basis which was wholly false and would have discovered that its contention that the accident had not occurred at all was false if it had taken the trouble of carrying out a proper investigation;

- in maintaining a false allegation the Defendant had commensurately increased the complexity and, therefore, the costs of the action;

- insofar as the Defendant's stance on quantum was concerned (the allegation of malingering)

> ...the defence was based upon the allegation of fraud which has failed in its entirety, and in my view there was never sufficient material upon which that allegation could properly be based.[27]

4. WASTED COSTS

9.020 This might be regarded as the ultimate sanction where a legal adviser has advanced an unsubstantiated and/or unsustainable allegation of fraud. The jurisdiction to make such orders is found in section 51(6) of the Supreme Court Act 1981(the procedure is prescribed by CPR 48.7 (and section 53 of the accompanying Practice Direction)).[28] The CPR confirms the three-stage

---

[27] At p 746 *per* Miss Belinda Bucknall QC (Dep Judge). See also, for an example of a commercial case where a similar approach was taken, *The Griparion (No 2)* [1994] 1 Ll Rep 533 (QB (Comm Ct)).

[28] The procedural position is not set out in this book, although it is right to say that the general position will be that the legal representative should be told in the clearest terms what he is alleged to have done wrong. He should be given a reasonable opportunity to be heard and to show cause why the wasted costs should not be borne by him. However, the requirement to show cause does not place a burden of proof on the respondent to an application; the persuasive burden remains with the applicant for a wasted costs order (although it has been acknowledged that there might be an evidential burden for the respondent to discharge: see *Ridehalgh* v *Horsefield* [1994] Ch 205, 239C *per* Sir Thomas Bingham MR (CA)).

process with respect to the making of these orders which can be found in the pre-CPR case law:[29]

- Has the legal representative of whom complaint is made acted improperly, unreasonably or negligently?

- If so, did such conduct cause the applicant to incur unnecessary costs?

- If so, was it in all the circumstances just to order the legal representative to compensate the applicant for the whole or part of the relevant costs?

9.021 The requirement for improper, unreasonable or negligent conduct has been the subject of further judicial commentary:

> 'Improper' means what it has been understood to mean in this context for at least half a century. The adjective covers, but is not confined to, conduct which would ordinarily be held to justify disbarment, striking off, suspension from practice or other serious professional penalty. It covers any significant breach of a substantial duty imposed by a relevant code of professional conduct. But it is not in our judgment limited to that. Conduct which would be regarded as improper according to the consensus of professional (including judicial) opinion can be fairly stigmatised whether or not it violates the letter of a professional code. 'Unreasonable' also means what it has been understood to mean in this context for at least half a century. The expression aptly describes conduct which is vexatious, designed to harass the other side rather than advance the resolution of the case, and it makes no difference that the conduct is the product of excessive zeal and not improper motive. But conduct cannot be described as unreasonable simply because it leads in the event to an unsuccessful result or because other more cautious legal representatives would have acted differently. The acid test is whether the conduct permits of a reasonable explanation. If so, the course adopted may be regarded as optimistic and as reflecting on a practitioner's judgment, but it is not unreasonable. The term 'negligent' was the most controversial of the three ... it was said, conduct cannot be regarded as negligent unless it involves an actionable breach of the legal representative's duty to his own client, to whom alone a duty is owed. We reject this approach ... Since the applicant's right to a wasted costs order against a legal representative depends on showing that the latter is in breach of his duty to the court it makes no sense to superimpose a requirement under this head (but not in the case of impropriety or unreasonableness) that he is also in breach of his duty to his client ... 'negligent' should be understood in an

---

[29] See *In re A Barrister (Wasted Costs)* [1993] QB 293 (CA) and *Ridehalgh* v *Horsefield* [1994] Ch 205 (CA).

untechnical way to denote failure to act with the competence reasonably to be expected of ordinary members of the profession. In adopting an untechnical approach to the meaning of negligence in this context, we would however wish firmly to discountenance any suggestion that an applicant for a wasted costs order under this head need prove anything less than he would have to prove in an action for negligence.[30]

9.022 The advancement by a legal representative of an allegation of fraud in circumstances where there is no evidential material (or insufficient material) to satisfy responsible counsel exercising a professional judgment that such a case can properly be advanced may be held to constitute improper conduct and:[31]

- the Order can be made in favour of the legal representative's own client or in favour of the opposing party;

- the Order can be made in respect of conduct when exercising a right of audience in open court as well as in respect of conduct preparatory to the exercise of that right (for example, settling statements of case or skeleton arguments).

9.023 There is, of course, no reason why the advancement of a baseless allegation of fraud should not also be regarded, in appropriate circumstances, as negligent: the Court of Appeal has recognised that there may be considerable overlap between the three headings under which wasted costs are made.[32]

---

[30] *Ridehalgh* v *Horsefield* [1994] Ch 205, 232-233 *per* Sir Thomas Bingham MR (CA)
[31] See *Medcalf* v *Mardell* [2003] 1 AC 120 (HL(E)). In this case (which is also discussed in an earlier chapter of this book) it was held that, in the preparatory stages of action, it was not necessary, for the proper advancement of an allegation of fraud, that the evidence relied on by counsel be admissible and/or reasonably credible, provided that responsible Counsel, exercising an objective judgment, would be satisfied that the available material supported the advancement of a serious allegation like fraud. On appeal the wasted costs orders made against counsel were quashed because a refusal by lay clients to waive legal professional privilege deprived counsel of the opportunity to present an answer to the application by showing cause why they should not pay the wasted costs.
[32] *Ridehalgh* v *Horsefield* [1994] Ch 205, 233E *per* Sir Thomas Bingham MR (CA).

5. MISCONDUCT IN CONNECTION WITH A DETAILED OR SUMMARY ASSESSMENT OF COSTS

9.024 The Court's powers in respect of misconduct (that is, unreasonable or improper conduct) in connection with the assessment of costs are prescribed by CPR 44.14 which provides:

> (1) The Court may make an order under this rule where – (a) a party or his legal representative, in connection with a summary or detailed assessment, fails to comply with a rule, practice direction or court order; or (b) it appears to the court that the conduct of a party or his legal representative, before or during the proceedings which gave rise to the assessment proceedings was unreasonable or improper.

9.025 These powers are likely to be exercised by costs judges and an investigation into misconduct may be initiated by the court or by the parties. Where a party's legal representative submits a fraudulent or dishonest bill of costs, it appears that an order may be made under CPR 44.14. It appears likely that "*unreasonable or improper*" will be defined, at least where the legal representative's conduct is at stake, in a manner consistent with the approach taken where a wasted costs order application is made.[33] Again, where a legal representative's conduct is at stake, the respondent to any application for an order under CPR 44.14 must be given an opportunity at a hearing to show cause why such an order should not be made.[34]

9.026 Where an order is made under CPR 44.14 the court may,

> (a) disallow all or part of the costs which are being assessed; or (b) order the party at fault or his legal representative to pay costs which he has caused any other party to incur.[35]

Where such an order is made against a legal representative in the absence of his lay client, the Rules require that the solicitor inform the lay client of the order within seven days of the solicitor receiving notice of the order.[36]

---

[33] See, however, *Sinclair-Jones* v *Kay* [1988] 2 All ER 611 (CA) and *Mainwaring* v *Goldtech Investments Limited* [1991] *The Times*, February 19 (CA).
[34] CPR 44, PD para 18.1.
[35] CPR 44.14(2).
[36] CPR 44.14(3).

SELECTED STATUTORY MATERIALS

Marine Insurance Act 1906

...

Insurance is uberrimae fidei
17. A contract of marine insurance is a contract based upon the utmost good faith, and, if the utmost good faith be not observed by either party, the contract may be avoided by the other party.

Disclosure by assured
18. (1) Subject to the provisions of this section, the assured must disclose to the insurer, before the contract is concluded, every material circumstance which is known to the assured, and the assured is deemed to know every circumstances which, in the ordinary course of business, ought to be known by him. If the assured fails to make such disclosure, the insurer may avoid the contract.

(2) Every circumstance is material which would influence the judgment of a prudent insurer in fixing the premium, or determining whether he will take the risk.

(3) In the absence of inquiry the following circumstances need not be disclosed, namely:

(a) Any circumstance which diminishes the risk;

(b) Any circumstance which is known or presumed to be known to the insurer. The insurer is presumed to know matters of common notoriety or knowledge, and matters which an insurer in the ordinary course of his business, as such, ought to know;

(c) Any circumstance as to which information is waived by the insurer;

(d) Any circumstance which it is superfluous to disclose by reason of any express or implied warranty.

(4) Whether any particular circumstance, which is not disclosed, be material or not is, in each case, a question of fact.

(5)   The term "circumstance" includes any communication made to, or information received by, the assured.

Disclosure by agent effecting insurance

19.   Subject to the provision of the preceding section as to circumstances which need not be disclosed, where an insurance is effected for the assured by an agent, the agent must disclose to the insurer –

(a)   Every material circumstance which is known to himself, and an agent to insure is deemed to know every circumstance which in the ordinary course of business ought to be known by, or to have been communicated to, him; and

(b)   Every material circumstance which the assured is bound to disclose, unless it come to his knowledge too late to communicate it to the agent.

Representations pending negotiation of contract

20.   (1)   Every material representation made by the assured or his agent to the insurer during the negotiations for the contract, and before the contract is concluded, must be true. If it be untrue the insurer may avoid the contract.

(2)   A representation is material which would influence the judgment of a prudent insurer in fixing the premium, or determining whether he will take the risk.

(3)   a representation may be either a representation as to a matter of fact, or as to a matter of expectation or belief.

(4)   A representation as to a matter of fact is true, if it be substantially correct, that is to say, if the difference between what is represented and what is actually correct would not be considered material by a prudent insurer.

(5)   A representation as to a matter of expectation or belief is true if it be made in good faith.

(6)   A representation may be withdrawn or corrected before the contract is concluded.

(7)   Where a particular representation be material or not is, in each case, a question of fact.

When contract is deemed to be concluded

21.   A contract of marine insurance is deemed to be concluded when the proposal of the assured is accepted by the insurer, whether the policy be then issued or not; and, for the purpose of showing when the proposal was accepted, reference may be made to the slip or covering note or other customary memorandum of the contract [...]

Limitation Act 1980

Postponement of limitation period in case of fraud, concealment or mistake

32.   (1)   Subject to subsections (3) and (4A) below, where in the case of any action for which a period of limitation is prescribed by this Act, either –

        (a)   the action is based upon the fraud of the defendant; or

        (b)   any fact relevant to the plaintiff's right of action has been deliberately concealed from him by the defendant; or

        (c)   the action is for relief from the consequences of a mistake;

the period of limitation shall not begin to run until the plaintiff has discovered the fraud, concealment or mistake (as the case may be) or could with reasonable diligence have discovered it.

References in this subsection to the defendant include references to the defendant's agent and to any person through whom the defendant claims and his agent.

(2)   For the purposes of subsection (1)_ above, deliberate commission of a breach of duty in circumstances in which it is unlikely to be discovered for some time amounts to deliberate concealment of the facts involved in that breach of duty.

(3)   Nothing in this section shall enable any action –

        (a)   to recover, or recover the value of, any property; or

        (b)   to enforce any charge against, or set aside any transaction affecting, any property;

to be brought against the purchaser of the property or any person claiming through him in any case where the property has been purchased for valuable consideration by an innocent third party since the fraud or concealment or (as the case may be) the transaction in which the mistake was made took place.

(4)   a purchaser is an innocent third party for the purposes of this section –

        (a)   in the case of fraud or concealment of any fact relevant to the plaintiff's right of action, if he was not a party to the fraud or (as the case may be) to the concealment of that fact and did not at the time of the purchase know or have reason to believe that the fraud or concealment had taken place; and

       (b)   in the case of mistake, if he did not at the time of the purchase know or have reason to believe that the mistake had been made.

(4A)   Subsection (1) above shall not apply in relation to the time limit prescribed by section 11A(3) of this Act or in relation to that time limit as applied by virtue of section 12(1) of this Act.

(5)   Sections 14A and 14B of this Act shall not apply to any action to which subsection (1)(b) above applies (and accordingly the period of limitation referred to in that subsection, in any case to which either of those sections would otherwise apply, is the period applicable under section 2 of this Act)...

Perjury Act 1911

...

1   **Perjury**

(1)   If any person lawfully sworn as a witness or as an interpreter in a judicial proceeding wilfully makes a statement material in that proceeding, which he knows to be false or does not believe to be true, he shall be guilty of perjury, and shall, on conviction thereof on indictment, be liable to penal servitude for a term not exceeding seven years, or to imprisonment with or without hard labour for a term not exceeding two years, or to a fine or to both such penal servitude or imprisonment and fine.

(2)   The expression "judicial proceeding" includes a proceeding before any court, tribunal, or person having by law power to hear, receive, and examine evidence on oath.

(3)   Where a statement made for the purposes of a judicial proceeding is not made before the tribunal itself, but is made on oath before a person authorised by law to administer an oath to the person who makes the statement, and to record or authenticate the statement, it shall, for the purposes of this section, be treated as having been made in a judicial proceeding.

(4)   A statement made by a person lawfully sworn in England for the purposes of a judicial proceeding –

  (a)   in another part of His Majesty's dominions; or

  (b)   in a British tribunal lawfully constituted in any place by sea or land outside His Majesty's dominions; or

  (c)   in a tribunal of any foreign state;

shall, for the purposes of this section, be treated as a statement made in a judicial proceeding in England.

(5)   Where, for the purposes of a judicial proceeding in England, a person is lawfully sworn under the authority of an Act of Parliament –

  (a)   in any other part of His Majesty's dominions; or

  (b)   before a British tribunal or a British officer in a foreign country, or within the jurisdiction of the Admiralty of England;

a statement made by such person so sworn as aforesaid (unless the Act of Parliament under which it was made otherwise specifically provides) shall be treated for the purposes of this section as having been made in the judicial proceeding in England for the purposes whereof it was made.

(6)   The question whether a statement on which perjury is assigned was material is a question of law to be determined by the court of trial.

1A   False unsworn statement under Evidence (Proceedings in Other Jurisdictions) Act 1975

If any person, in giving any testimony (either orally or in writing) otherwise than on oath, where required to do so by an order under section 2 of the Evidence (Proceedings in Other Jurisdictions) Act 1975, makes a statement –

(a)   which he knows to be false in a material particular, or

(b)   which is false in a material particular and which he does not believe to be true,

he shall be guilty of an offence and shall be liable on conviction on indictment to imprisonment for a term not exceeding two years or a fine or both.

2   False statements on oath made otherwise than in a judicial proceeding

If any person –

(1)   being required or authorised by law to make any statement on oath for any purpose, and being lawfully sworn (otherwise than in a judicial proceeding) wilfully makes a statement which is material for that purpose and which he knows to be false or does not believe to be true; or

(2)   wilfully uses any false affidavit for the purposes of the Bills of Sale Act 1878, as amended by any subsequent enactment,

he shall be guilty of a misdemeanour, and, on conviction thereof on indictment, shall be liable to penal servitude for a term not exceeding seven years or to imprisonment, with or without hard labour, for a term not exceeding two years or to a fine or to both such penal servitude or imprisonment and fine.

3   False statements, etc., with reference to marriage

(1)   If any person –

(a)   for the purpose of procuring a marriage, or a certificate or licence for marriage, knowingly and wilfully makes a false oath, or makes or signs a false declaration, notice or certificate required under any Act of Parliament for the time being in force relating to marriage; or

(b)   knowingly and wilfully makes, or knowingly and wilfully causes to be made, for the purpose of being inserted in any register of marriage, a false statement as to any particular required by law to be known and registered relating to any marriage; or

(c)   forbids the issue of any certificate or licence for marriage by falsely representing himself to be a person whose consent to the marriage is required by law knowing such representation to be false, [or

(d)   with respect to a declaration made under section 16(1A) or 27B(2) of the Marriage Act 1949 –

    (i)   enters a caveat under subsection (2) of the said section 16, or

    (ii)   makes a statement mentioned in subsection (4) of the said section 27B,

which he knows to be false in a material particular,] he shall be guilty of a misdemeanour, and, on conviction thereof on indictment, shall be liable to penal servitude for a term not exceeding seven years or to imprisonment, with or without hard labour, for a term not exceeding two years, or to a fine or to both such penal servitude or imprisonment and fine [and on summary conviction thereof shall be liable to a penalty not exceeding [the prescribed sum]].

(2)   No prosecution for knowingly and wilfully making a false declaration for the purpose of procuring any marriage out of the district in which the parties or one of them dwell shall take place after the expiration of eighteen months from he solemnization of the marriage to which the declaration refers.

4   False statements, etc., as to births or deaths

(1)   If any person –

(a)   wilfully makes any false answer to any question put to him by any registrar of births or deaths relating to the particulars required to be registered concerning any birth or death, or, wilfully gives to any such registrar any false information concerning any birth or death or the cause of any death; or

(b)   wilfully makes any false certificate or declaration under or for the purposes of any Act relating to the registration of births or deaths, or, knowing any such certificate or declaration to be false, uses the same as true or gives or sends the same as true to any person; or

(c)   wilfully makes, gives or uses any false statement or declaration as to a child born alive as having been still-born, or as to the body of a deceased person or a still-born child in any coffin, or falsely pretends that any child born alive was still-born; or

(d)   makes any false statement with intent to have the same inserted in any register of births or deaths:

he shall be guilty of a misdemeanour and shall be liable –

(i)   on conviction thereof on indictment, to penal servitude for a term not exceeding seven years, or to imprisonment, with or without hard labour, for a term not exceeding two years, or to a fine instead of either of the said punishments; and

(ii)   on summary conviction thereof, to a penalty not exceeding [the prescribed sum].

(2)   A prosecution on indictment for an offence against this section shall not be commenced more than three years after the commission of the offence.

5   False statutory declarations and other false statements without oath

If any person knowingly and wilfully makes (otherwise than on oath) a statement false in a material particular, and the statement is made –

(a)   in a statutory declaration; or

(b)   in an abstract, account, balance sheet, book, certificate, declaration, entry, estimate, inventory, notice, report, return, or other document which he is authorised or required to make, attest, or verify, by any public general Act of Parliament for the time being in force; or

(c)   in any oral declaration or oral answer which he is required to make by, under, or in pursuance of any public general Act of Parliament for the time being in force,

he shall be guilty of a misdemeanour and shall be liable on conviction thereof on indictment to imprisonment, with or without hard labour, for any term not exceeding two years, or to a fine or to both such imprisonment and fine.

6   False declarations, etc., to obtain registration, etc., for carrying on a vocation

If any person –

(a)   procures or attempts to procure himself to be registered on any register or roll kept under or in pursuance of any public general Act of Parliament for the time being in force of persons qualified by law to practise any vocation or calling; or

(b)   procures or attempts to procure a certificate of the registration of any person on any such register or roll as aforesaid,

by wilfully making or producing or causing to be made or produced either verbally or in writing, any declaration, certificate, or representation which he knows to be false or fraudulent, he shall be guilty of a misdemeanour and shall be liable on conviction thereof on indictment to imprisonment for any term not exceeding twelve months, or to a fine, or to both such imprisonment and fine.

7   **Aiders, abetters, suborners, etc.**
(1)   Every person who aids, abets, counsels, procures, or suborns another person to commit an offence against this Act shall be liable to be proceeded against, indicted, tried and punished as if he were a principal offender.
(2)   Every person who incites ... another person to commit an offence against this Act shall be guilty of a misdemeanour, and, on conviction thereof on indictment, shall be liable to imprisonment, or to a fine, or to both such imprisonment and fine.

8   **Venue**
Where an offence against this Act or any offence punishable as perjury or as subornation of perjury under any other Act of Parliament is committed in any place either on sea or land outside the United Kingdom, the offender may be proceeded against, indicted, tried, and punished... in England.

...

12   **Form of indictment**
(1)   In an indictment –
    (a)   for making any false representation punishable under this Act; or
    (b)   for unlawfully, wilfully, falsely, fraudulent, deceitfully, maliciously, or corruptly taking, making, signing or subscribing any oath affirmation, solemn declaration, statutory declaration, affidavit, deposition, notice certificate, or other writing,

it is sufficient to set forth the substance of the offence charged, and before which court or person (if any) the offence was committed without setting forth the proceedings or any part of the proceedings in the course of which the offence was committed, and without

setting forth the authority of any court or person before whom the
offence was committed.

(2)   In   an   indictment   for   aiding,   abetting,   counselling,
suborning, or procuring any other person to commit any offence
herein-before in this section mentioned, or for conspiring with any
other person .... to commit any such offence, it is sufficient –

> (a)   where such offence has been committed, to allege
> that offence, and then to allege that the defendant
> procured the commission of that offence; and
>
> (b)   where such offence has not been committed, to set
> forth the substance of the offence charged against
> the defendant without setting forth any matter or
> thing which it is unnecessary to aver in the case of
> an indictment for a false statement or false
> representation punishable under this Act.

13   Corroboration

A person shall not be liable to be convicted of any offence against
this Act, or of any offence declared by any other Act to be perjury or
subornation of perjury, or to be punishable as perjury or
subornation of perjury, solely upon the evidence of one witness as to
the falsity of any statement alleged to be false.

14   Proof of certain proceedings on which perjury is assigned

On a prosecution –

(a)   for perjury alleged to have been committed on the trial of an
indictment for ... misdemeanour; or

(b)   for procuring or suborning the commission of perjury on
any such trial,

the fact of the former trial shall be sufficiently proved by the
production of a certificate containing the substance and effect
(omitting the formal parts) of the indictment and trial purporting to
be signed by the clerk of the court, or other person having the
custody of the records of the court where the indictment was tried,
or by the deputy of that clerk or other person, without proof of the
signature or official character of the clerk or person appearing to
have signed the certificate.

15   Interpretation, etc.

(1)   For the purposes of this Act, the forms and ceremonies used
in administering an oath are immaterial, if the court or person
before whom the oath is taken has power to administer an oath for
the purpose of verifying the statement in question, and if the oath
has been administered in a form and with ceremonies which the

person taking the oath has accepted without objection, or has
declared to be binding on him.

(2)   In this Act –

The expression "oath" ... includes "affirmation" and
"declaration", and the expression "swear"...includes
"affirm" and "declare"; ...

Contempt of Court Act 1981

...

1   **The strict liability rule**
In this Act "the strict liability rule" means the rule of law whereby conduct may be treated as a contempt of court as tending to interfere with the course of justice in particular legal proceedings regardless of intent to do so.

2   **Limitation of scope of strict liability**
(1)   The strict liability rule applies only in relation to publications, and for this purpose "publication" includes any speech, writing, [programme included in a service] or other communication in whatever form, which is addressed to the public at large or any section of the public.
(2)   The strict liability rule applies only to a publication which creates a substantial risk that the course of justice in the proceedings in question will be seriously impeded or prejudiced.
(3)   The strict liability rule applies to a publication only if the proceedings in question are active within the meaning of this section at the time of the publication.
(4)   Schedule 1 applies for determining the times at which proceedings are to be treated as active within the meaning of this section.
(5)   In this section "programme service" has the same meaning as in the Broadcasting Act 1990.

3   **Defence of innocent publication or distribution**
(1)   A person is not guilty of contempt of court under the strict liability rule as the publisher of any matter to which that rule ap0plies if at the time of publication (having taken all reasonable care) he does not know and has no reason to suspect that relevant proceedings are active.
(2)   A person is not gui8lty of contempt of court under the strict liability rule as the distributor of a publication containing any such matter if at the time of distribution (having taken all reasonable care) he does not know that it contains such matter and has no reason to suspect that it is likely to do so.
(3)   The burden of proof of any fact tending to establish a defence afforded by this section to any person lies upon that person.

4   **Contemporary reports of proceedings**
(1)   Subject to this section a person is not guilty of contempt of
court under the strict liability rule in respect of a fair and accurate
report of legal proceedings held in public, published
contemporaneously and in good faith.
(2)   In any such proceedings the court may where it appears to
be necessary for avoiding a substantial risk of prejudice to the
administration of justice in those proceedings or in any other
proceedings, or any part of the proceedings, be postponed for such
period as the court thinks necessary for that purpose.

5   **Discussion of public affairs**
A publication made as or as part of a discussion in good faith of
public affairs or other matters of general public interest is not to be
treated as a contempt of court under the strict liability rule if the risk
of impediment or prejudice to particular legal proceedings is merely
incidental to the discussion.

...

9   **Use of tape recorders**
(1)   Subject to subsection (4) below, it is a contempt of court –
(a)   to use in court, or bring into court for use, any tape
recorder or other instrument for recording sound,
except with the leave of the court;
(b)   to publish a recording of legal proceedings made by
means of any such instrument, or any recording
derived directly or indirectly from it, by playing it in
the hearing of the public or any section of the
public, or to dispose of it or any recording so
derived, with a view to such publication;
(c)   to use any such recording in contravention of any
conditions of leave granted under paragraph (a).
(2)   Leave under paragraph (a) of subsection (1) may be granted
or refused at the discretion of the court, and if granted may be
granted subject to such conditions as the court thinks proper with
respect to the use of any recording made pursuant to the leave; and
where leave has been granted the court may at the like discretion
withdraw or amend it either generally or in relation to any particular
part of the proceedings.
(3)   Without prejudice to any other power to deal with an act of
contempt under paragraph (a) of subsection (1), the court may order
the instrument, or any recording made with it, or both, to be
forfeited; and any object so forfeited shall (unless the court

otherwise determines on application by a person appearing to be the owner) be sold or otherwise disposed of in such manner as the court may direct.

(4)   This section does not apply to the making or use of sound recordings for purposes of official transcripts of proceedings.

10   Sources of information

No court may require a person to disclose, nor is any person guilty of contempt of court for refusing to disclose, the source of information contained in a publication for which he is responsible, unless it be established to the satisfaction o the court that disclosure is necessary in the interests of justice or national security or for the prevention of disorder or crime.

11   Publication of matters exempted from disclosure in court

In any case where a court (having power to do so) allows a name or other matter to be withheld from the public in proceedings before the court, the court may give such directions prohibiting the publication of that name or matter in connection with the proceedings as appear to the court to be necessary for the purpose for which it was so withheld...

Proceeds of Crime Act 2002

327 **Concealing etc.**
(1)   A person commits an offence if he –
    (a)   conceals criminal property;
    (b)   disguises criminal property;
    (c)   converts criminal property;
    (d)   transfers criminal property;
    (e)   removes criminal property from England and Wales or from Scotland or from Northern Ireland.
(2)   But a person does not commit such an offence if –
    (a)   he makes an authorised disclosure under section 338 and (if the disclosure is made before he does the act mentioned in subsection (1)) he has the appropriate consent;
    (b)   he intended to make such a disclosure but had a reasonable excuse for not doing so;
    (c)   the act he does is done in carrying out a function he has relating to the enforcement of any provision of this Act or of any other enactment relating to criminal conduct or benefit from criminal conduct.
[(2C)   A deposit-taking body that does as an act mentioned in paragraph (c) or (d) of subsection (1) does not commit an offence under that subsection if –
    (a)   it does the act in operating an account maintained with it, and
    (b)   the value of the criminal property concerned is less than the threshold amount determined under section 339A for the act.]
(3)   Concealing or disguising criminal property includes concealing or disguising its nature, source, location, disposition, movement or ownership or any rights with respect to it.

328 **Arrangements**
(1)   A person commits an offence if he enters into or becomes concerned in an arrangement which he knows or suspects facilities (by whatever means) the acquisition, retention, use or control of criminal property by or on behalf of another person.
(2)   But a person does not commit such an offence if –
    (a)   he makes an authorised disclosure under section 338 and (if the disclosure is made before he does

the act mentioned in subsection (1)) he has the appropriate consent;

(b)   he intended to make such a disclosure but had a reasonable excuse for not doing so;

(c)   the act he does is done in carrying out a function he has relating to the enforcement of any provision of this Act or of any other enactment relating to criminal conduct or benefit from criminal conduct.

[(5)   A deposit-taking body that does an act mentioned in subsection (1) does not commit an offence under that subsection if –

(a)   it does the act in operating an account maintained with it, and

(b)   the arrangement facilitates the acquisition, retention, use or control of criminal property of a value that is less than the threshold amount determined under section 339A for the act."]

329   Acquisition, use and possession

(1)   A person commit an offence if he –

(a)   acquires criminal property;

(b)   uses criminal property;

(c)   has possession of criminal property.

(2)   But a person does not commit such an offence if –

(a)   he makes an authorised disclosure under section 338 and (if the disclosure is made before he does the act mentioned in subsection (1)) he has the appropriate consent;

(b)   he intended to make such a disclosure but had a reasonable excuse for not doing so;

(c)   he acquired or use or had possession of the property for adequate consideration;

(d)   the act he does is done in carrying out a function he has relating to the enforcement of any provision of this Act or of any other enactment relating to criminal conduct or benefit from criminal conduct.

[(2C)   A deposit-taking body that does an act mentioned in subsection (1) does not commit an offence under that subsection if –

(a)   it does the act in operating an account maintained with it, and

(b)   the arrangement facilities the acquisition, retention, use or control of criminal property of a value that is less than the threshold amount determined under section 339A for the act.]

(3)   For the purposes of this section –

(a)   a person acquires property for inadequate consideration if the value of the consideration is significantly less than the value of the property;

(b)   a person uses or has possession of property for inadequate consideration if the value of the consideration is significantly less than the value of the use or possession;

(c)   the provision by a person of goods or services which he knows or suspects may help another to carry out criminal conduct is not consideration.

330   Failure to disclose: regulated sector

(1)   A person commits an offence if [the conditions in subsections (2) to (4) are satisfied].

(2)   The first condition is that he –

(a)   knows or suspects, or

(b)   has reasonable grounds for knowing or suspecting,

that another person is engaged in money laundering.

(3)   The second condition is that the information or other matter –

(a)   on which his knowledge or suspicion is based, or

(b)   which gives reasonable grounds for such knowledge or suspicion,

came to him in the course of a business in the regulated sector.

[(3A)   The third condition is –

(a)   that he can identify the other person mentioned in subsection (2) or the whereabouts of any of the laundered property, or

(b)   that he believes, or it is reasonable to expect him to believe, that the information or other matter mentioned in subsection (3) will or may assist in identifying that other person or the whereabouts of any of the laundered property.

(4)   The fourth condition is that he does not make the required disclosure to-

(a)   a nominated officer, or

(b)   a person authorised for the purposes of this Part by the Director General of the Serious Organised Crime Agency,

as soon as is practicable after the information or other matter mentioned in subsection (3) comes to him.

(5)   The required disclosure is a disclosure of-

(a)   the identity of the other person mentioned in subsection (2), if he knows it,

> (b)   the whereabouts of the laundered property, so far as he knows it, and
>
> (c)   the information or other matter mentioned in subsection (3).

(5A)   The laundered property is the property forming the subject-matter of the money laundering that he knows or suspects, or has reasonable grounds for knowing or suspecting, that other person to be engaged in.

(6)   But he does not commit an offence under this section if –

> (a)   he has a reasonable excuse for not making the required disclosure,
>
> (b)   he is a professional legal adviser and –
>
> > (i)   if he knows either of the things mentioned in subsection (5)(a) and (b), he knows the thing because of information or other matter that came to him in privileged circumstances, or
> >
> > (ii)   the information or other matter mentioned in subsection (3) came to him in privileged circumstances, or
>
> (c)   subsection (7) applies to him.]

(7)   This subsection applies to a person if –

> (a)   he does not know or suspect that another person is engaged in money laundering, and
>
> (b)   he has not been provided by his employer with such training as is specified by the Secretary of State by order for the purposes of this section.

(8)   In deciding whether a person committed an offence under this section the court must consider whether he followed any relevant guidance which was at the time concerned –

> (a)   issued by a supervisory authority or any other appropriate body,
>
> (b)   approved by the Treasury, and
>
> (c)   published in a manner it approved as appropriate in its opinion to bring the guidance to the attention of persons likely to be affected by it.

(9)   A disclosure to a nominated officer is a disclosure which –

> (a)   is made to a person nominated by the alleged offender's employer to receive disclosures under this section, and
>
> (b)   is made in the course of the alleged offender's employment...

[(9A)   But a disclosure which satisfies paragraphs (a) and (b) of subsection (9) is not to be taken as a disclosure to a nominated officer if the person making the disclosure –

(a)   is a professional legal adviser,

(b)   makes it for the purpose of obtaining advice about making a disclosure under this section, and

(c)   does not intend it to be a disclosure under this section.]

(10)   Information of other matter comes to a professional legal adviser in privileged circumstances if it is communicated or given to him –

(a)   by (or by a representative of) a client of his in connection with the giving by the adviser of legal advice to the client,

(b)   by (or by a representative of) a person seeking legal advice from the adviser, or

(c)   by a person in connection with legal proceedings or contemplated legal proceedings.

(11)   But subsection (10) does not apply to information or other matter which is communicated or given with the intention of furthering a criminal purpose.

(12)   Schedule 9 has effect for the purpose of determining what is –

(a)   a business in the regulated sector;

(b)   a supervisory authority.

(13)   An appropriate body is any body which regulates or is representative of any trade, profession, business or employment carried on by the alleged offender.

331   Failure to disclose: nominated officers in the regulated sector

(1)   A person nominated to receive disclosures under section 330 commits an offence if the conditions in subsections (2) to (4) are satisfied.

(2)   The first condition is that he –

(a)   knows or suspects, or

(b)   has reasonable grounds for knowing or suspecting,

that another person is engaged in money laundering.

(3)   The second condition is that the information or other matter –

(a)   on which his knowledge or suspicion is based, or

(b)   which gives reasonable grounds for such knowledge or suspicion,

came to him in consequence of a disclosure made under section 330.

[(3A)   The third condition is –

(a)   that he knows the identity of the other person mentioned in subsection (2), or the whereabouts of any of the laundered property, in consequence of a disclosure made under section 330,

(b)   that that other person, or the whereabouts of any of the laundered property, can be identified from the information or other matter mentioned in subsection (3), or

(c)   that he believes, or it is reasonable to expect him to believe, that the information or other matter will or may assist in identifying that other person or the whereabouts of any of the laundered property.

(4)   The fourth condition is that he does not make the required disclosure to a person authorised for the purposes of this Part by the Director General of the Serious Organised Crime Agency as soon as is practicable after the information or other matter mentioned in subsection (3) comes to him.

(5)   The required disclosure is a disclosure of –

(a)   the identity of the other person mentioned in subsection (2), if disclosed to him under section 330, and

(b)   the whereabouts of the laundered property, so far as disclosed to him under section 330, and

(c)   the information or other matter mentioned in subsection (3).

(5A)   The laundered property is the property forming the subject-matter of the money laundering that he knows or suspects, or has reasonable grounds for knowing or suspecting, that other person to be engaged in.

(6)   But he does not commit an offence under this section if he has a reasonable excuse for not making the required disclosure.]

(7)   In deciding whether a person committed an offence under this section the court must consider whether he followed any relevant guidance which was at the time concerned –

(a)   issued by a supervisory authority or any other appropriate body,

(b)   approved by the Treasury, and

(c)   published in a manner it approved as appropriate in its opinion to bring the guidance to the attention of persons likely to be affected by it.

(8)   Schedule 9 has effect for the purpose of determining what is a supervisory authority.

(9)   An appropriate body is a body which regulates or is representative of a trade, profession, business or employment.

332 **Failure to disclose: other nominated officers**

(1)   a person nominated to receive disclosures under section 337 or 338 commits an offence if the conditions in subsections (2) to (4) are satisfied.

(2)   The first condition is that he knows or suspects that another person is engaged in money laundering.

(3)   The second condition is that the information or other matter on which his knowledge or suspicion is based came to him in consequence of a disclosure made under [the applicable section].

[(3A)   The third condition is –

    (a)   that he knows the identity of the other person mentioned in subsection (2), or the whereabouts of any of the laundered property, in consequence of a disclosure made under the applicable section,

    (b)   that that other person, or the whereabouts of any of the laundered property, can be identified from the information or other matter mentioned in subsection (3), or

    (c)   that he believes, or it is reasonable to expect him to believe, that the information or other matter will or may assist in identifying that other person or the whereabouts of any of the laundered property.

(4)   The fourth condition is that he does not make the required disclosure to a person authorised for the purposes of this Part by the Director General of the Serious Organised Crime Agency as soon as is practicable after the information or other matter mentioned in subsection (3) comes to him.

(5)   The required disclosure is a disclosure of –

    (a)   the identity of the other person mentioned in subsection (2), if disclosed to him under the applicable section,

    (b)   the whereabouts of the laundered property, so far as disclosed to him under the applicable section, and

    (c)   the information or other matter mentioned in subsection (3).

(5A)   The laundered property is the property forming the subject-matter of the money laundering that he knows or suspects that other person to be engaged in.

(5B)   The applicable section is section 337 or, as the case may be, section 338.

(6)   But he does not commit an offence under this section if he has a reasonable excuse for not making the required disclosure].

333   Tipping off

(1)   A person commits an offence if –

(a)   he knows or suspects that a disclosure falling within section 337 or 338 has been made, and

(b)   he makes a disclosure which is likely to prejudice any investigation which might be conducted following the disclosure referred to in paragraph (a).

(2)   But a person does not commit an offence under subsection (1) if –

(a)   he did not know or suspect that the disclosure was likely to be prejudicial as mentioned in subsection (1);

(b)   the disclosure is made in carrying out a function he has relating to the enforcement of any provision of this Act or of any other enactment relating to criminal conduct or benefit from criminal conduct;

(c)   he is a professional legal adviser and the disclosure falls within subsection (3).

(3)   a disclosure falls within this subsection if it is a disclosure –

(a)   to (or to a representative of) a client of the professional legal adviser in connection with the giving by the adviser of legal advice to the client, or

(b)   to any person in connection with legal proceedings or contemplated legal proceedings.

(4)   But a disclosure does not fall within subsection (3) if it is made with the intention of furthering a criminal purpose.

...

335   Appropriate consent

(1)   The appropriate consent is –

(a)   the consent of a nominated officer to do a prohibited act if an authorised disclosure is made to the nominated officer;

(b)   the consent of a constable to do a prohibited act if an authorised disclosure is made to a constable;

(c)   the consent of [an officer of Revenue and Customs] to do a prohibited act if an authorised disclosure is made to [an officer of Revenue and Customs].

(2)   A person must be treated as having the appropriate consent if –

(a)   he makes an authorised disclosure to a constable [an officer of Revenue and Customs], and

(b)   the condition in subsection (3) or the condition in subsection (4) is satisfied.

(3)   The condition is that before the end of the notice period he does not receive notice from a constable or [officer of Revenue and Customs] that consent to the doing of the act is refused.

(4)   The condition is that –

(a)   before the end of the notice period he receives notice from a constable or [officer of Revenue and Customs] that consent to the doing of the act is refused, and

(b)   the moratorium period has expired.

(5)   The notice period is the period of seven working days starting with the first working day after the person makes the disclosure.

(6)   The moratorium period is the period of 31 days starting with the day on which the person receives notice that consent to the doing of the act is refused.

(7)   A working day is a day other than a Saturday, a Sunday, Christmas Day, Good Friday or a day which is a bank holiday under the Banking and financial Dealings Act 1971 (c80) in the part of the United Kingdom in which the person is when he makes the disclosure.

(8)   References to a prohibited act are to an act mentioned in section 327(1), 328(1) or 329(1) (as the case may be).

(9)   A nominated officer is a person nominated to receive disclosures under section 338.

(10)   Subsections (10 to (4) apply for the purposes of this Part.

336   Nominated officer: consent

(1)   A nominated officer must not give the appropriate consent to the doing of a prohibited act unless the condition in subsection (2), the condition in subsection (3) or the condition in subsection (4) is satisfied.

(2)   The condition is that –

(a)   he makes a disclosure that property is criminal property to a person authorised for the purposes of this Part by *the Director General of the National Criminal Intelligence Service,* and

(b)   such a person gives consent to the doing of the act.

(3)   The condition is that –

(a)   he makes a disclosure that property is criminal property to a person authorised for the purposes of this Part by *the Director General of the National Criminal Intelligence Service,* and

(b)   before the end of the notice period he does not receive notice from such a person that consent to the doing of the act is refused.

(4)   The condition is that –

(a)   he makes a disclosure that property is criminal property to a person authorised for the purposes of this Part by *the Director General of the National Criminal Intelligence Service,*

(b)   before the end of the notice period he receives notice from such a person that consent to the doing of the act is refused, and

(c)   the moratorium period has expired.

(5)   A person who is a nominated officer commits an offence if –

(a)   he gives consent to a prohibited act in circumstances where none of the conditions in subsections (2), (3) and (4) is satisfied, and

(b)   he knows or suspects that the act is a prohibited act.

(6)   a person guilty of such an offence is liable –

(a)   on summary conviction, to imprisonment for a term not exceeding six months or to a fine not exceeding the statutory maximum or to both, or

(b)   on conviction on indictment, to imprisonment for a term not exceeding five years or to a fine or to both.

(7)   The notice period is the period of seven working days starting with the first working day after the nominated officer makes the disclosure.

(8)   The moratorium period is the period of 31 days starting with the day on which the nominated officer is given notice that consent to the doing of the act is refused.

(9)   a working day is a day other than a Saturday, a Sunday, Christmas Day, Good Friday, or a day which is a bank holiday under the Banking and Financial Dealings Act 1971 (c 80) in the part of the United Kingdom in which the nominated officer is when he gives the appropriate consent.

(10)   references to a prohibited act are to an act mentioned in section 327(1), 328(1) or 329(1) (as the case may be).

(11)   a nominated officer is a person nominated to receive disclosures under section 338.

337   Protected disclosures

(1)   A disclosure which satisfies the following three conditions is not to be taken to breach any restriction on the disclosure of information (however imposed).

(2)   The first condition is that the information or other matter disclosed came to the person making the disclosure (the discloser) in the course of his trade, profession, business or employment.

(3)   The second condition is that the information or other matter –

      (a)   causes the discloser to know or suspect, or

      (b)   gives him reasonable grounds for knowing or

suspecting,

that another person is engaged in money laundering.

(4)   The third condition is that the disclosure is made to a constable, [an officer of Revenue and Customs] or a nominated officer as soon as is practicable after the information or other matter comes to the discloser.

[(4A)   Where a disclosure consists of a disclosure protected under subsection (1) and a disclosure of either or both of –

      (a)   the identity of the other person mentioned in subsection (3), and

      (b)   the whereabouts of property forming the subject-matter of the money laundering that the disclosure knows or suspects, or has reasonable grounds for knowing or suspecting, that other person to be engaged in,

the disclosure of the thing mentioned in paragraph (a) or *b) (as well as the disclosure protected under subsection (1)) is not to be taken to breach any restriction on the disclosure of information (however imposed).]

(5)   A disclosure to a nominated officer is a disclosure which –

      (a)   is made to a person nominated by the discloser's employer to receive disclosures under [section 330 or] this section, and

      (b)   is made in the course of the discloser's employment...

338   Authorised disclosures

(1)   For the purposes of this Part a disclosure is authorised if –

      (a)   it is a disclosure to a constable, [an officer of Revenue and Customs] or a nominated officer by the alleged offender that property is criminal property,

      (b)   ...and

      (c)   the first[, second or third] condition set out below is satisfied.

(2)   The first condition is that the disclosure is made before the alleged offender does the prohibited act.

[(2A)   The second condition is that –
    (a)   the disclosure is made while the alleged offender is doing the prohibited act,
    (b)   he began to do the act at a time when, because he did not then know or suspect that the property constituted or represented a person's benefit from criminal conduct, the act was not a prohibited act, and
    (c)   the disclosure is made on his own initiative and as soon as is practicable after he first knows or suspects that the property constitutes or represents a person's benefit from criminal conduct.]

(3)   The [third] condition is that –
    (a)   the disclosure is made after the alleged offender does the prohibited act,
    (b)   there is a good reason for his failure to make the disclosure before he did the act, and
    (c)   the disclosure is made on his own initiative and as soon as it is practicable for him to make it.

(4)   An authorised disclosure is not to be taken to breach any restriction on the disclosure of information (however imposed).

(5)   A disclosure to a nominated officer is a disclosure which –
    (a)   is made to a person nominated by the alleged offender's employer to receive authorised disclosures, and
    (b)   is made in the course of the alleged offender's employment...

(6)   References to the prohibited act are to an act mentioned in section 327(1), 328(1) or 329(1) (as the case may be).

339   Form and manner of disclosures

(1)   The Secretary of State may by order prescribe the form and manner in which a disclosure under section 330, 331, 332 or 338 must be made.

[(1A)   A person commits an offence if he makes a disclosure under section 330, 331, 332 or 338 otherwise than in the form prescribed under subsection (1) or otherwise than in the manner so prescribed.

(1B)   But a person does not commit an offence under subsection (1A) if he has a reasonable excuse for making the disclosure otherwise than in the form prescribed under subsection (1) or (as the case may be) otherwise than in the manner so prescribed.

(2)   The power under subsection (1) to prescribe the form in which a disclosure must be made includes power to provide for the form to include3 a request to a person making a disclosure that the

person provide information specified or described in the form if he
has not provided it in making the disclosure.
(3)   Where under subsection (2) a request is included in a form
prescribed under subsection (1), the form must –
    (a)   state that there is no obligation to comply with the
request, and
        (b)   explain the protection conferred by subsection (4)
                on a person who complies with the request.]
(4)   a disclosure made in pursuance of a request under
subsection (2) is not to be taken to breach any restriction on the
disclosure of information (however imposed).
(5), (6) ...
(7)   Subsection (2) does not apply to a disclosure made to a
nominated officer.

340   Interpretation
(1)   This section applies for the purposes of this Part.
(2)   Criminal conduct is conduct which –
    (a)   constitutes an offence in any part of the United
Kingdom, or
        (b)   would constitute an offence in any part of the
                United Kingdom if it occurred there.
(3)   Property is criminal property if –
        (a)   it constitutes a person's benefit from criminal
                conduct or it represents such a benefit (in whole or
                part and whether directly or indirectly), and
        (b)   the alleged offender knows or suspects that it
                constitutes or represents such a benefit.
(4)   It is immaterial –
        (a)   who carried out the conduct;
        (b)   who benefited from it;
        (c)   whether the conduct occurred before or after the
                passing of this Act.
(5)   a person benefits from conduct if he obtains property as a
result of or in connection with the conduct.
(6)   If a person obtains a pecuniary advantage as a result of or in
connection with conduct, he is to be taken to obtain as a result of or
in connection with the conduct a sum of money equal to the value of
the pecuniary advantage.
(7)   references to property or a pecuniary advantage obtained in
connection with conduct include references to property or a
pecuniary advantage obtained in both that connection and some
other.

(8)   If a person benefits from conduct his benefit is the property obtained as a result of or in connection with the conduct.

(9)   Property is all property wherever situated and includes –

    (a)   money;

    (b)   all forms of property, real or personal, heritable or moveable;

    (c)   things in action and other intangible or incorporeal property.

(10)   The following rules apply in relation to property –

    (a)   property is obtained by a person if he obtains an interest in it;

    (b)   references to an interest, in relation to land in England and Wales or Northern Ireland, are to any legal estate or equitable interest or power;

    (c)   references to an interest, in relation to land in Scotland, are to any estate, interest, servitude or other heritable right in or over land, including a heritable security;

    (d)   references to an interest, in relation to property other than land include references to a right (including a right to possession).

(11)   money laundering is an act which –

    (a)   constitutes an offence under section 327, 328 or 329,

    (b)   constitutes an attempt, conspiracy or incitement to commit an offence specified in paragraph (1),

    (c)   constitutes aiding, abetting, counselling or procuring the commission of an offence specified in paragraph (1), or

    (d)   would constitute an offence specified in paragraph (a), (b) or (c) if done in the United Kingdom.

(12)   For the purposes of a disclosure to a nominated officer –

    (a)   references to a person's employer include any body, association or organisation (including a voluntary organisation) in connection with whose activities the person exercises a function (whether or not for gain or reward), and

    (b)   references to employment must be construed accordingly.

(13)   References to a constable include references to a person authorised for the purposes of this Part by *the Director of the National Criminal Intelligence Service.*

[(14)   "Deposit-taking body" means –

(a)   a business which engages in the activity of accepting deposits, or

(b)   the National Savings Bank.]

...

342   Offences of prejudicing investigation

(1)   This section applies if a person knows or suspects that an appropriate officer or (in Scotland) a proper person is acting (or proposing to act) in connection with a confiscation investigation, a civil recovery investigation or a money laundering investigation which is being or is about to be conducted.

(2)   The person commits an offence if –

(a)   he makes a disclosure which is likely to prejudice the investigation, or

(b)   he falsifies, conceals, destroys or otherwise disposes of, or causes or permits the falsification, concealment, destruction or disposal of, documents which are relevant to the investigation.

(3)   A person does not commit an offence under subsection (2)(a) if –

(a)   he does not know or suspect that the disclosure is likely to prejudice the investigation,

(b)   the disclosure is made in the exercise of a function under this Act or any other enactment relating to criminal conduct or benefit from criminal conduct or in compliance with a requirement imposed under or by virtue of this Act, or

(c)   he is a professional legal adviser and the disclosure falls within subsection (4).

(4)   a disclosure falls within this subsection if it is a disclosure –

(a)   to (or to a representative of) a client of the professional legal adviser in connection with the giving by the adviser of legal advice to the client, or

(b)   to any person in connection with legal proceedings or contemplated legal proceedings.

(5)   But a disclosure does not fall within subsection (4) if it is made with the intention of furthering a criminal purpose.

(6)   A person does not commit an offence under subsection 2(b) if –

(a)   he does not know or suspect that the documents are relevant to the investigation, or

(b)   he does not intend to conceal any facts disclosed by the documents from any appropriate officer or (in

                Scotland) proper person carrying out the investigation.

(7)   A person guilty of an offence under subsection (2) is liable –

        (a)   on summary conviction, to imprisonment for a term not exceeding six months or to a fine not exceeding the statutory maximum or to both, or

        (b)   on conviction on indictment, to imprisonment for a term not exceeding five years or to a fine or to both.

(8)   For the purposes of this section –

        (a)   "appropriate officer" must be construed in accordance with section 378;

        (b)   "proper person" must be construed in accordance with section 412...

BIBLIOGRAPHY

The list is not, nor is intended to be, exhaustive. I have not included the journal articles that were consulted; these are cited in footnotes to the text.

A History of English Law (Sir William Holdsworth) 3rd ed (1923).
An Analysis of the Economic Torts (Carty) (OUP).
An Introduction to English Legal History (Baker) 4th ed (2002).
Actionable Misrepresentation (Handley) 4th ed (2000).

Birds' Modern Insurance Law (Birds and Hird) 6th ed (2004).
Blackstone's Guide to the Proceeds of Crime Act 2002 (Rees QC and Fisher) 2nd ed, (2005).
Bullen & Leake & Jacob's Precedents of Pleadings (Lord Brennan QC and Blair QC) 15th ed (2004).

Chitty on Contracts, 29th ed (2004).
Clerk & Lindsell on Torts, 19th ed (2006).
Colinvaux's Law of Insurance (Merkin) 8th ed (2006).
Commercial Injunctions (Gee QC) 5th ed (2004).
Contempt of Court (Miller) 3rd ed (2000).
Cook on Costs 2006 (Cook) (2005).

False Witness: the Problem of Perjury (JUSTICE) (1973).
Fraudulent and Exaggerated Claims in Personal Injury (Kevan, Ward, Heath and Gatzouris) 1st ed (XPL Publishing, 2006)

Guide to Good Medical Practice, GMC, 3rd ed (2001).
Guidelines for the Assessment of General Damages in Personal Injury Cases, Judicial Studies Board, 7th ed (2006).

Illegal Transactions: The effect of Illegality on Contracts and Trusts, Law Commission, CP 154 (1999).
Insurance Law: Doctrines and Principles (Lowry and Rawlings) 2nd ed (2005).

Limitation Periods (McGee) 4th ed (2002).

Macgillivray on Insurance Law (Legh-Jones, Birds and Owen) 10th ed (2002).
McGregor on Damages (McGregor) 17th ed (2003).
Misrepresentation, Mistake and Non-disclosure (Cartwright) 2nd ed (2007).

Personal Injury Law, Practice and Procedure (Kemp & Kemp).

Phipson on Evidence, 16th ed (2005).
Policies and Perceptions of Insurance Law in the Twenty-first Century (Clarke) 1st ed (2005).
Proceeds of Crime Act: a Current Law Guide (2003).

Smith & Hogan Criminal Law (Ormerod) 11th ed (2005).
Sources of English Legal History (Private Law to 1750) (Baker & Milsom) (1986). *Textbook on Torts* (Jones) 8th ed (2002).

The Illegality Defence in Tort, Law Commission, CP 160 (2001).
The Law of Torts (Fleming) 9th ed (1998).
The Proceeds of Crime Act 2002 (Biggs, Farrell and Padfield) (2002).

Winfield & Jolowicz on Tort (Rogers) 15th ed (1998).
World Health Organisation, ICD-10.

INDEX